WHERE WE ARE AT

by THOMAS H. BARBER

It is fair to call *Where We Are At* a primer of enlightened conservatism. It is a sometimes violent, but always persuasive, simple and witty analysis of America's besetting sin—that of legislating money into our own pockets. Contrary to general belief, this process did not begin with the New Deal, or the Income Tax Amendment, or with any particular one of the government enactments so often blamed for it. It began when the first pressure group arrogated to itself special privileges, and secured for them the sanction of law.

One of the effects of this process has been the creation of a huge bureaucracy, so large that it numbers about one-eighth of all Americans gainfully employed. Everyone must pay taxes to support these bureaucrats in their work of redistributing the national wealth: the potential production

★

★

WHERE WE ARE AT

★

★

WHERE WE ARE AT

BY
THOMAS H. BARBER

★

★　　　★

★

CHARLES SCRIBNER'S SONS, NEW YORK
CHARLES SCRIBNER'S SONS, LTD., LONDON
1950

This book is dedicated to Carl M. Sharpe, Robert Chism, Fred and Dorothy Beach and Mary Swain, in affectionate memory of the long and pleasant discussions that shaped its thoughts on many a lamplit winter's evening round the hearth, and on many a moonlit summer's one under the wisteria.

CONTENTS

★

FOREWORD

It will be asked: Who is the author? Of what importance is he? Why should he undertake to write such a book? The answers are quite simple. I have written this book because I feel that it should be written for the benefit of the United States, and because I am the only person I have available to write it. It has been a long and wearisome task, having taken me nearly twelve years. I have, however, some qualifications to write it. In fact it sometimes seems as though my whole life had been a sort of unconscious preparation for it, as the following autobiography will show.

I took my A.B. degree at Harvard in 1910. I took no courses on economics there. In 1913 I received my LL.B. at Columbia and also an A.M. degree in Municipal Administrative law. I spent several months in the New York District Attorney's office as an unpaid deputy assistant district attorney. There I saw all the sordidness and filth of city vice and crime, and the petty injustice and squalor of ward politics. I transferred to the job of unpaid assistant secretary to Lawrence B. Dunham, then Third Deputy Police Commissioner under Arthur Woods. Dunham was in charge of traffic problems and some few classes of crime. There I learned the functions of Police Administration under ideal conditions, for the New York Police at that time was as free from graft and as efficient as could be.

Becoming tired of indoor work I went West, first as a guest on a ranch, then as a chore boy, finally as a cowpuncher. The outfit I worked for was a big one, running 28,000 head of cattle. Ordinary cowpunchers drew $30 a month, top hands $40, horse wranglers $50 and the foreman $75. The outfit provided the horses and excellent food. The "hands" were required to furnish their beds ($12), saddles ($60-$90), and clothes; the Stetson hats and Justin or Higher boots, which were a *sine qua non*, were expensive, costing respectively $10 and $8, but they apparently wore forever. Flannel shirts were around $2, overalls

1

$1.50. The first five months' wages were absorbed by the saddle, bed, hat and boots; after that we had nothing to spend our money on except tobacco (Prince Albert 60 cents a pound), Bull Durham (5 cents a bag and the papers thrown in), and Old Crow whiskey at $2 a gallon. Occasionally when we went to the railroad with shipments of cattle which happened two or three times a year, we went on a terrible bust and blew two or three months' pay in a few days. But the owners (who were much older men and, though extraordinarily tough, were exemplary citizens) discouraged this, and constantly urged us to invest our money, take up land and get established. In those days a weaned heifer cost from $5 to $7, and a two-year-old cow $17, so one could acquire one or two head a month. Having bought them from the outfit, the outfit always ran them for us with their herd till we were ready to break away for ourselves. In this way, and by the natural increase, all the cowboys in a few years acquired herds worth $2,000 to $4,000, and such of them as I am still in touch with are now substantially propertied citizens. Our usual day's work (there were no days off, including Sunday) was twelve hours, but we often did sixteen hours and never thought anything about it. In fact we all enjoyed it enormously. Really we had little to do with our money except invest it. Card playing without stakes and telling stories were our chief amusements and cost nothing. We could get no whiskey while we were on the range because of the transportation problem; during the five or six months we were in the ranch house we usually took a whiskey and sugar when we got up and a whiskey and water before we went to bed. Two dollars a month covered this.

Today a cowpuncher draws down $200 a month but whiskey is now $30 a gallon in Wyoming, a grown cow costs $210 and everything else in proportion. Though he draws down nearly seven times as much as we did, the modern cowboy is, from the point of view of establishing himself economically, only about one-half as well off. I believe this would be found to be the case in most lines of endeavor.

After three years mostly devoted to this life I entered the National Guard and went to the Mexican Border, thence to France and Germany. There I found myself a captain on the staff of Colonel I. L. Hunt, Officer in charge of Civil Affairs in the Rhineland. This afforded me an excellent opportunity to study the mentality of the Germans, their government and their politi- co-economic point of view.

At this time a serious attempt was being made to bolshevize Germany by groups of fiends who called themselves Spartacists. I was assigned as judge-advocate to try one of the leaders who had been captured. This put me in close touch with the counter-espionage, and for six weeks I lived in a cloak and dagger atmosphere with murder and kidnapping all about me. Communism and Spartacism were synonymous terms, and I learned a great deal about Communist theories, characters and practices.

I was discharged in March, 1920. I had inherited just enough income to live in a very frugal way without working. The rise in prices made it inadequate. For seven years I had lived practically in camp and my enthusiasm for hardship and adventure had faded. The flesh pots of New York looked very attractive. An ex-officer under whom I had served offered me a job in his father's shop which was an investment bank. So I went from Captain on the General Staff to cleaning ink-wells and filing cards in a very bare and drab office. Another drop like that and I would have been in Hell.

The old gentleman, W. Emlen Roosevelt, was one of the finest citizens I ever saw. He had perfect integrity and was utterly simple. He had never been to college, but was in finance all his life. He regarded economic laws as the most natural common-sense in the world, as indeed they are, and he under- stood them thoroughly. I don't believe he had ever read a book on "Economics" in his life. But when he made a study of a busi- ness with a view to investing, he went into every facet of it from the character of the various directors on down. He learned all about it. I worked for him for five years as office boy, bond- salesman, investment adviser, and on railroad reorganizations. I made a substantial amount of money—what I figured was all I would ever need—and retired to travel.

Within two years I got married and felt that I had better go back to work. I went into A. Iselin & Co., another investment bank. Mr. Iselin was a great friend of Mr. Roosevelt's and his business ethics and methods were very similar, but a great ma- jority of his customers were foreigners. Therefore, during the five years I was there, mostly as a very junior partner, I had ample opportunity to see the workings of foreign exchange.

In both these jobs I had frequently noticed the hampering and irritating effect of legal regulations. Few, if any, of these seemed to me to do any good whatever, and many were doing actual harm. At that time I, along with most of the rest of Wall Street, attributed them to the malevolence of "the politicians," who, I vaguely believed, were an anti-social class of persons deliberately trying to injure the national economy of the United States for their own selfish benefit. In 1932, I became very active in organizing the National Economy League to cut costs of government. At that time the Federal budget was $4,000,000,000, which appeared to us, and was, too much.

During this period I began to feel that there was little sense in being in business. Business is full of risks. As things were set up, if you lost money, you lost it. If you made it, the government took it. The dice were loaded against me. Therefore in May, 1933, I felt it better to retire a second time. My wife had inherited a farm and a vast tract of woodland in a remote and rather primitive part of New England. I had always hoped to have a farm. We moved up there. At first I tried to do full farm work myself, but I was over 45 years old and unused to it. It exhausted me to such a point that I could neither think, read nor successfully manage the farm. After about a year I turned the manual work over to the hired men and myself did only enough to keep in trim.

Having always been used to people, I became very lonely on that remote hill. Occasionally, someone dropped in for the evening. I hit upon the idea of always having some beer and cider in the living room and sufficient good food for an attractive light lunch. This cost practically nothing on a farm. Word of it got around, and I soon had much general company of an evening.

New England is a very democratic place, with few social lines. My guests were farmers, doctors, lumbermen, small storekeepers, school teachers, farm laborers and mill hands. We all talked freely.

One of the first things that struck me when I became a farmer was the preposterous number of laws and regulations and licenses that bound me down. They bore far heavier on the farmers than they had on the bankers. I could scarcely make a move without an inspection or a license, or some hampering restriction. I mentioned this to my guests and to my amazement discovered that all of them—doctors, school teachers, builders, storekeepers, mill hands, farmers—everybody, in fact, but the farm laborers, were suffering from restrictions on their perfectly legitimate economic endeavors. Evening after evening we anathemized this, always ending up, as had the big business boys in Wall Street, by blaming the trouble on the corrupt and venal "politicians."

In the summer of 1938 a young school teacher whom I liked got a political bee in his bonnet and asked me if he could bring around some political lights. To help him I agreed. He brought round flocks of them, town officers, county officers, state legislators, "leaders" of various sorts in the Republican Party. To my utter amazement I found that far from being corrupt, selfish, venal and malevolent, they turned out to be serious, conscientious, hard-working patriots whose principal desire was the good of their fellow citizens and who frequently would risk re-election to do what they believed to be in the public interest. Most of them preferred to discuss the common weal than to do anything else. They did want to keep in office, but I am convinced that in almost every case it was because they felt they could do more good in than out.

When I realized that these politicians were sincere patriots I was so amazed I was almost stupefied. I began twitting them about the iniquitous laws that were passed. That confused them. They could not see any way to improve or lighten the restrictions. I got the non-politician complainers in and started arguments between them and the politicos. I soon found myself running a sort of backwoods salon. I had about five people three or four nights a week. Once I had thirty. Fortunately the living room—the old eighteenth century kitchen—was enormous. The same people did not come continuously, of course, though I did have a few who were pretty nearly regulars. The discussions became widely known. A big-time banker or two came from Hartford. The governor came twice.

Everybody who came, business man or politician, was agreed on two things. First, that we needed some legal restrictions. Second, that there were a great many too many of them.

One night, some of the disputants asked me to draw the line between necessary laws and regulations and harmful ones, and to do it in such a way that it could be used as a principle or dividing-line to which they could refer. In the valor of my ignorance I gladly accepted, believing I could write the definition in a couple of hours. I worked on it for three months and got nowhere. As well as baffling me, the problem intrigued me to such a degree I never have been able to get it out of my mind, and I have thought about it and worked on it ever since.

All along, I was becoming closer friends with the politicians. My ambitions do not lie in that line, yet to be agreeable to them I went as delegate or alternate to all the Republican conventions and was present in many of "the smoke-filled rooms" while the mighty discussed or decided important questions of State policy. I saw the machinery of government working from the inside. I discovered that there is a vast difference in intelligence and capacity between, on the one hand, the party leaders and elected representatives of the people who respectively make and enact the policies, and the bureaucrats on the other, who are for the most part merely the leg men for the others and are rewarded for their work from the public trough by clerkships and salaries.

I happened unexpectedly to be present at the New York Harvard Club when that extraordinary, private, impromptu debate took place between Wendell Willkie and Felix Frankfurter. I decided then that Willkie should be President. I spent the late winter, spring and summer of 1940 going all over the United States organizing the Willkie Clubs. In this way I met many of the prominent Republican leaders. I attended the Republican Convention at Philadelphia and heard a good many private discussions of policy. Always I was trying to solve the old question of that dividing-line between necessary and harmful legislation. The winter, spring and summer of 1941 I spent reorganizing the Willkie Clubs of Connecticut into the Independent Clubs, to work for better government.

Colonel Hunt, my chief in the Rhineland, was dead. He had asked me, in the event of another war occurring in my life time, to try to get into the section charged with the occupation of conquered territory, so that such future administration might profit by the experience I had had with our administration and our mistakes in the past. I applied seven times for a commission in the Army and was turned down every time because of a bad heart. I ended up a civilian professor in the head School of Military Government at Charlottesville, Virginia, which had ten subordinate schools scattered all over the country. The course was twelve weeks. I taught at Charlottesville for six weeks in each course and spent the remaining six doing three-day stands at the subordinate ones. I often went to Washington for conferences.

In this time I met two new classes of people, as an intimate associate. First, the Federal bureaucrats, of whom I was one. They were a pleasant, easy-going folk, not over bright, interested in their jobs and greatly interested in bettering their personal position in their jobs. I asked many of them what effect they thought their jobs and the jobs of their associates had on the welfare of the country as a whole. I never found one who had thought of it. That is natural. Few clerks or hired men, in fact few people in general, think at all of the effect of their own efforts in their jobs on the country as a whole.

The second group were the labor union leaders. It was the policy of Mr. Roosevelt's administration to send many labor leaders over with our forces of civil administration, to look after the interest of labor in the occupied areas. I made a point of getting to know some of these gentlemen well, and delightful companions they were, easy to get along with, witty, convivial, full of good stories. They were the most cynical group I was ever in contact with. They seemed to regard their job as a legalized racket for their own benefit. I never heard one of them seriously discuss the interest of labor from the point of view of the individual interest of a workman. One of them used to revel in anecdotes of his own picaresque economic immoralities which he would tell for hours on end.

After I left Charlottesville I had to devote myself to the education of my sons. This involved my staying in New York during the school months, and traveling about the country to show it to them in vacations. It gave me a great deal of leisure for study. Always that problem of defining the line between necessary laws and hurtful ones was in my mind. I devoted my time in New York to trying to solve it from books, and my time on trips to discussing it with chance acquaintances or friends.

I have talked of it in Fifth Avenue clubs and over in Hell's Kitchen; with bankers in Wall Street and with tailors and boot-blacks on the East Side; with New England college professors and New England farm and mill hands; with Congressmen in Washington, and with drifters in Okie camps; with business and professional men in the Southern and Gulf states; with farmers and traveling men everywhere; with merchants, doctors and lawyers on the broad sunny streets of the Western towns and with cowpunchers, sheep herders and Indians under the cotton-woods in the sagebrush country; with all kinds of people along the West Coast and the fertile gardens of its hinterland.

Always the story is the same—dislike of and discontent with our government; too much taxation; too many laws and restrictions; not enough income.

Often there are specific complaints against particular in-stances of governmental idiocy: the destruction of 30,000,000 bushels of potatoes, or of the 3,000,000 little pigs; or Govern-ment's buying up and returning to the wilderness "submarginal" farms, while at the same time spending hundreds of dollars an acre to bring remote and sterile bits of sagebrush land under cultivation. There are plenty of complaints about the symptoms of this trouble, but I have never seen or heard a diagnosis of the trouble itself. Such a diagnosis is needed, so that the thought-ful people of the country can put their minds on it and effect in time a cure.

This book is an attempt to furnish the necessary diagnosis. I have written it to develop this principle in as simple and read-able a form as I know how. There are probably errors of detail in it. That is almost inevitable in covering so wide a field. But I firmly believe that there are no errors sufficient to affect the general theses developed.

I can offer no panacea nor suggest any method to bring a cure. I doubt if any single man can. But many men, seeing the situation together, might be able to. This book is written in the fervent and prayerful hope that reading it will inspire some men, more intelligent, thoughtful and experienced than the writer, to find some way to save this country from becoming a totalitarian dictatorship, and recreate it once more into the glori-ous Land of the Free.

CHAPTER 1

THE PROBLEM

FROM 1787 TO 1915 America was the Land of Opportunity. History has known nothing like it.

In 1787 a simple, almost rural, civilization existed along the Atlantic Coast. There was a vast unknown wilderness a couple of hundred miles inland. Between the two lay every gradient from prosperous homestead to trapper's camp.

The little nation of about three million people was impoverished by twelve years of war and weak government. There was a shortage of gold and silver for money, a very much depreciated paper currency, practically no manufactures, scarcely anything that was not produced by the unremitting labor on the farms and in the homesteads. Yet almost at once a great tide of prosperity set in. A stream of immigrants poured over from Europe. For a century and a quarter the tide rose and the stream swelled.

By 1915, the United States stood forth a queen among nations with a population of a hundred million, a wealth of nearly three hundred billion dollars, an integrated land 3000 by 1000 miles in extent, linked with roads and railways, telegraph and telephone, humming with factories, teeming with raw materials. The population enjoyed far more leisure than any other in the world, and there were more comforts in the homes of the workmen and farmers than had existed in the homes of the great a century before.

What caused all this? What was the vision that brought the millions of immigrants from the Eastern seaboard and from Europe to build this empire? No one could have foreseen the development that was to come. No one "planned it that way." What was this vision, which animated millions upon millions to sever irrevocably all their home ties, to start out on untrodden ways, to face discomfort, hardship, even death? Men do not voluntarily take these steps unless they believe that they see great ultimate good arising from the immediate and certain hardships.

We have been told of late that the vision was free land. But contrary to the prevalent belief, land was never legally free in this country until 1862. It always had to be bought, either from the King, the Lords Proprietors, the Colonies, the States, or the Federal Government. The price in colonial times varied from four to fourteen shillings an acre; after the Revolution, from one to two dollars an acre. These prices were cheaper than land could be bought for from private people. Yet when one considers the greater purchasing power of money in those days and the work involved in bringing wilderness land into production, it was a substantial price—all the traffic would bear. Negotiable scrip for land was given to war veterans. There was also, of course, a great deal of land acquired illegally by squatters.

On the other hand, one must remember, there was at the end of the eighteenth century, free, or very cheap, unoccupied land almost everywhere, except in Europe, China, Japan and India. A lot of this land was more accessible to Europeans than that of the present United States. The Czar was trying hard to colonize Siberia, a country much of which is on the same latitude as our own, and from all present appearances potentially quite as rich. He failed miserably. Africa, Australia, and a large part of South America had vast tracts of unoccupied white man's country. But none of these areas, even when more accessible to Europe, filled up.

The North American Colonies themselves had had even more land at about the same price and rather easier to reach, since early in the sixteen hundreds. Yet in the hundred and sixty years prior to 1787, though they had made a great development, it was not a very spectacular one. They were not even particularly prosperous as colonies went, nothing like as prosperous as those in the West Indies, or the East Indies, for instance. It does not appear credible that free land was the vision.

Yet the vision was there. And the vision of "The Green Fields of America" spread from Great Britain to Ireland, to Holland, Germany, Scandinavia, Poland, Russia, Italy, Switzerland and the Balkans. Always the peoples came, for a century and a quarter. Always they went to work. Always there was somehow more work than they could do. Many of these migrants left homes of security and comfort for the new country, for trials, discomfort, hardship, uncertainty, danger. What did they think they were going to gain?

Let us try to acquire their point of view. Let us examine the lot of the people in Europe in the late eighteenth century. Perhaps we can then see why they wanted to take the risks and come. At home their lives were constantly hampered by the laws of their little kingdoms and principalities. Almost each and every unit of government on the Continent, every city, town and district, levied tariffs on both imports and exports. Everything was taxed, not only salt, grain, bread, cloth and tools, but also the right to cross a bridge, to sell in a market. This was the case, not only in passing from one principality to another, but at home within one's own ruler's dominion.

Wars were almost continuous. During them all the men of the lower orders were liable to be kidnapped and forced into the armed services. Outside of England this was true even when their own country was not at war, for many princelings, when at peace, made a practice of selling or renting regiments of their own people to other princelings who were at war.

Laws regulated every phase of a man's life, established his status in society, in many places his dress. They prescribed his duties, his responsibilities, what he could work at, his wages, the prices he must pay, even his private conception of Almighty God and his manner of worshipping Him. Man's inhumanity to man had destroyed freedom, had practically closed the door to opportunity.

But here, in these newly United States, there were scarcely any laws or regulations. The King's laws of economic restriction and exploitation had been abolished by the Revolution and the Constitution. The religious laws had collapsed of their own weight. There were no laws at all except those based on the Ten Commandments, a few rules concerning the registration of legal papers, and the simplest form of government that the impoverished, independent, tax-loathing, liberty-loving citizens had found necessary to set up.

Here was freedom—complete and utter freedom. Here a

man was bound down only by the limits of his strength, his will and his ability. No other force constrained him to or from his chosen goal. Incidentally, there appeared to be unbounded opportunity to produce wealth in the forests, the rivers, the fields and the mines. Wealth ripe for the gathering, a gorgeous plenty waiting to be used.

This was the vision that brought forth the migrants. It is a vision that stirs our breasts and galvanizes our energy today. Complete freedom! Boundless opportunity! Think what it meant to those Europeans whose every act was prescribed. The green light was up! Go! Go ahead! Make a fortune, if you want. Be a fool, if you want. Nobody cares. It is up to you. Of course they wanted land and a home. Everybody does. But freedom and opportunity were the vision.

The great human wave formed and swept forward, first for fur, then for minerals, then for timber, finally for farms and homes. Soon the settlers had to organize for self-protection, for trade, for the necessary government; and they did organize for the problem at hand and solved it according to their needs. No central authority could have planned for them. Any group of uneducated pioneers on the spot knew what they wanted and needed better than the brightest group of planners in Washington (had there been any) could possibly have known. Each group took the trouble to solve its problems, where they rose and while they were small, to its own satisfaction. They did not try to pass them back in large complicated bundles to a central authority.

Lots of people made mistakes. Many were killed by their own bad judgment. Fools are always coming to grief, and it makes little difference to the nation. The living swept on, profiting by past errors, striving desperately to do their best for themselves, and incidentally, since all prosper or decay together, for their fellows.

By the middle 1870's the Sioux were crushed, the Apache were being finished off down in the southwestern deserts. The frontier was gone. The good open land had been taken up. There was, of course, still some free land—sagebrush flats, mountain forests and broken bits of good river bottom were left. They still are left, for that matter. But the type of land of which an hundred and sixty acres would yield a decent living to a family, had disappeared. Except for the short rebirth in 1889, when Oklahoma was opened, the physical frontier had ceased to be.

But another kind of frontier had opened some seventy years before, along the Eastern seaboard, and was going, in the middle 1800's, at full blast. It was not a frontier that developed only the wilderness for man's use, but one that sought to conquer all material things and make them useful to mankind. It was the frontier of development, of supplying necessities, comforts and luxuries, cheaply and in plenty.

Immediately after George Washington was inaugurated our shipping started to boom. Within twenty-five years we were trading as great merchants all over the world. Roads and waterways were opened to get the products of our back country to markets. Railways quickly followed. Communications, mails, telegraph and telephones came in time. Articles of utility were produced in quantity: saddles, rifles, stoves, wagons, carriages, breech-loaders, agricultural tools, agricultural machinery, cotton and woolen cloth. Mass production developed, machines with interchangeable parts. There came a demand, which was met, for articles of luxury: plumbing, gas, electricity, central heating, refrigeration, Pullman cars, ice plants, canned goods, water companies, private telephones and automobiles. A greater improvement in human material comfort was achieved in the United States in its first century and a quarter than had been accomplished in the entire previous history of the world. It was achieved, furthermore, by inventions and devices requiring a minimum of labor and cost.

A legion of great empire-builders arose among our people. Eli Whitney, Samuel F. B. Morse, Cyrus McCormick, Andrew Carnegie, and a host of others, reached towering fame and fortune. All of them rose from obscurity, and most from poverty, by their vision, energy and initiative in building up the country. There was hardly a man here in the 1880's who had not at least seen one of these men, risen by their own exertions to incredible wealth and prominence. In their day they were extravagantly admired and their type of success was the ultimate aim of every citizen.

Looking back on them, one sees that some of them were

bad and some were good. Some of them died with stupendous
fortunes and some died broke. But together, and each in his
way, they opened an empire. They gave creative work and opportunity to millions. They left lasting monuments to themselves
in their inventions, the railroads, the factories, and the businesses
they founded. They served the nation well. Whether they went
broke or not was of little moment to the country. Their creations
stood and functioned, whether they owned them or had lost
them, whether the capital invested was watered or whittled
down. The important point is that their creations survived for
the benefit of the nation at large. The losses they occasioned are
of no national importance, for money lost in speculation is not
wealth lost to the nation. It has merely changed hands.

About 1900 this national impetus, this drive for development, this rush to get rich, began to slacken. Far fewer of the
poor boys who started work in the first decade of this century
became millionaires than had done so in the previous decades.
The flow of immigrants from northern Europe dried up. They
still came in shoals from southern Europe where the economic
restrictions were heaviest, but those who came now congregated
in racial groups in our big cities, and bogged down there. Something seemed to have slipped. The Land of Opportunity was
not functioning as effectively as it had done—as it should do.
It never did get going right again.

There were, of course, the four years of war prosperity in
the 1910's. But no great figures rose. No lasting new development
occurred, save perhaps in the motor and airplane industries and
in the further discoveries and the processing of oil. Even where
they appeared, the developments were of a different kind. They
were simply technical improvements in the methods used by
established big companies. Few, if any, new enterprises rose.
The great names of that decade that come to mind are Cosden,
Chrysler, Ford and Sinclair. These men had not the glamor of
the older business leaders, nor did they contribute quite the
same benefits to the nation.

Then came the wild gambling era of the 1920's. There was
some development. Everybody had a motor, instead of just the
well-to-do. Everybody had a radio he hoped to pay for. A lot
of new oil fields were located and developed. Airplanes changed
from dangerous experiments to the product of a new and prom-

ising industry. There were advances made in electrical equipment, motors, chemicals, etc. A lot of existing public utility companies were merged, and a great deal of water was added to their stock, to the lasting benefit of nobody. The names that contributed to the nation's wealth and prosperity, which stand out of that decade after twenty years, are not the names of men at all, but the names of great corporations like General Electric, DuPont and General Motors. It was primarily an era of pure gambling. Practically everyone was in it, from senators, congressmen and the presidents of the big corporations, to the school mistresses and barbers in the cow towns. It was glorious fun while it lasted, but it was sheer insanity, and it left a terrible hangover.

Beginning in 1930, America ceased being the Land of Opportunity and became the Land of Relief. We did it in a big way, to be sure. Administering Relief and being on Relief became the chief American industry. Nothing useful was created, save unnecessary Post Offices, five-ply highways and parkways. Business was stagnant with the stagnation of death. No one made money. Nothing new started. The wise guys made a beeline for the government pay roll.

What had happened? What had wrecked the Land of Opportunity?

We were told by those in authority that the collapse had come because the frontier was gone. The physical frontier was indeed gone, and had been gone in 1930 for nearly fifty-five years. Almost everybody who remembered it open was long dead. Its long-forgotten departure manifestly had nothing to do with the situation. But the odd thing is that the other frontier, the one of opportunity, of freedom in self-advancement, of creating new industries to fulfill human wants, of starting new enterprises, was gone too.

What closed it? Could it be possible that it was not cheap, unoccupied land that had energized the creation of modern America out of a wilderness in a brief, hectic century, but rather that it was the freedom and opportunity which, in the early days, this country offered to all, alien as well as citizen? Had freedom and opportunity gone with the physical frontier? If so, how, and why? Let us study our history from that point of view.

CHAPTER 2

WHY GOVERNMENT?

"The Best Government is the Least Government."
THOMAS JEFFERSON

SINCE THE STUDY OF this question will lead us along the lines of political economy, it is well to review the objectives for which governments are founded, and the basic natural laws underlying economy.

Every man craves freedom—that is, his own exemption from the interference of others. He craves it with a passion that amounts to a natural instinct. His longing for it is as intense as his desire for food, health, and procreation. It is so intense that it is difficult for him to imagine a happy, or even a satisfactory, life without a very large amount of freedom.

Unfortunately, this strong instinct for personal liberty is almost universally accompanied by an equally strong desire to interfere with others. For it very generally appears to a man that his personal freedom and power of enjoyment can be greatly increased by the subservience of other people to his will. This desire to dominate others and so destroy their liberty is really, therefore, an instinctive effort to increase one's own freedom at the cost of the freedom of others. It is selfish, unreasonable and unjust. It is the antithesis of loving one's neighbor as one's self. It is the most vicious and harmful of the natural human instincts. It is also the most universal.

It may be reasonably supposed that it is the instinct for freedom in these two aspects that has made government of some sort a necessity to mankind. The just and reasonable instinct to escape undue interference by others, and the selfish, unjust

16

instinct to increase one's personal freedom by unduly interfering with that of others, are present in everyone, and are completely contradictory in their effect when applied to any form of society. Some compromise must be reached between them, and that compromise—whatever it is—results in, or is, Government.

The first task of a people, therefore, in forming a government, is to decide what the terms of the compromise will be and to reach a clear and enforceable agreement about it. If they are wise they will keep as much as possible of their personal freedom and give up as much as possible of their power to interfere with that of others. But to make such an agreement work each man must relinquish a part of his personal freedom to society at large, or the state, so that the state can enforce the agreement on any man who violates it—be it himself or another.

The people of a new state set up government to preserve their freedom. It is entirely for their convenience. Its officers and clerks are their servants. It always must be set up, because the freedom which every citizen of a state needs for his own safety and convenience can be supplied only by the joint cooperation of all.

The citizens' first requirement is the maintenance of the agreement, and of order generally, within the state. Each must be compelled not to encroach on the rights and freedom of the others. This calls for a police force, and a fair judiciary to administer justice and to keep records and to prevent future quarrels.

Their second need is for the management of the relations of the whole state with other states, so that its citizens can be protected from interference by outsiders. This requires a system of national defense and the auxiliary system of a diplomatic corps to obtain justice from outsiders without resort to the sword, and to maintain pleasant relations on all sides.

These two functions are essential in any state to preserve individual liberty, because of the greed and selfishness inherent in human nature. They can be carried out only by each citizen delegating his individual authority in these matters to a common pool. This pool contains, as it were, the joint authority of all of them. This general delegation of authority is the basis of the "Social Contract" explained in various ways by Locke, Hobbes and Rousseau. It is pure theory and probably never actually occurred at the inception of any state. It is valuable, however, as the only hypothesis on which a logical theory of government can be based.

To carry out these two necessary functions of government, three auxiliary institutions are essential.

First, there must be a deliberative body to decide the specific laws under which the people of the state shall live. These laws should concern only the conduct of the people toward one another, and the reciprocal relations of their conduct and that of their government. They should be designed to give every individual as much freedom as possible in which to work out his own development and life, so long as he does not unduly interfere with others. Therefore they should be subject to as little change as possible, so that each man can confidently and lastingly arrange the life he wishes for himself, under the laws, without even governmental interference. A state governed on this principle—as the United States and some of the European states largely were, around the middle of the nineteenth century —is said to be governed under "The Rule of Law." Its citizens were, as Kipling put it: "Free to live by no man's leave underneath the Law." The deliberative body also should establish the details of the conduct of the state as a whole and of its citizens in relation to other states.

The second auxiliary institution must be an executive group to enforce the conduct prescribed by the deliberative assembly.

Then, third, the cost of the functions described above must be met by an equitable tax on all the people; for it is for the benefit of everyone of them and each should pay his share. Therefore the power and the machinery to levy and collect taxes must be set up.

These five functions, two necessary and three auxiliary, are probably the only ones that can be performed *only* by government. They are necessary to the happiness of the people of the state. They are the minimum essential functions of government.

All other services that are now considered solely governmental functions can be, and have been, successfully performed by private enterprise. For instance, before governments took them over, the mails were satisfactorily carried by individuals. In ancient Rome fire-fighting companies were commercial concerns, operated under contract. Public roads were long adequately maintained by private parties under the toll-gate system, and were paid for, quite justly, by those that used them. In the sixteenth century the Bohemian Count von Schlitz honestly and successfully minted money that circulated all over the western world. His people found a silver mine in his valley, "Joachimstal." He minted a coin stamped with the figure of St. Joachim. It was known from the source of its origin as the "Joachimsthaler," or sometimes as the "Schlitzthaler." In the course of years its name was shortened to "Thaler" and then corrupted to "dollar." As such it was adopted as the monetary unit of the newly United States. The number of present day governmental services that could be, and have been, equally well handled by private enterprise is legion.

It is probable that no government ever limited its functions to the five essential ones. People always find it a convenient luxury to have their governments do other things for them. All luxuries are expensive and corrupting. This one is peculiarly so.

Theoretically, and as a matter of fact, government can vary all the way from one that performs only these five essential functions under the Rule of Law, to one that considers and treats its people as mere economically productive units, owns and distributes all the wealth they create, and regulates their every act and move, in accordance with the will or whim of its leader. Such was the government of the ancient eastern autocracies. Today all the great western powers are reverting to it. It is illogical in the extreme, for under it its creators become the slaves of their creation. It defeats its own reason for existence, for the only logical reason to set up a government is to insure the maximum of freedom possible, and apportion it equally among all its citizens.

CHAPTER 3

WHAT MAKES WEALTH

"By the sweat of thy face shalt thou eat bread."
GEN. 3, 19.

"WEALTH" IS BY DEFINITION "the object of human desire."

It may be spiritual, intellectual or material. Material wealth is the product of labor expended in finding, cultivating or manufacturing objects of human desire. As human desire changes with circumstances, the same object may be wealth at one place or time and not wealth at another place or time. For instance, money, which is generally a form of wealth, was not wealth to Robinson Crusoe on his island. In fact he devoted some space to deploring the effort he had made to bring the ship's treasure chest ashore. Generally, however, objects of wealth remain fairly constant.

"Money" is by definition "the medium of exchange."

Originally it was something valuable in itself which most people desired because of that intrinsic value. Gold and silver came to be generally used for money, because most people desired them for their use and beauty, because they were easily portable, because they were almost indestructible and because, when divided into parts, the sum of the divided parts was (unlike jewels) equal to the value of the undivided whole. The value of the gold and silver in the money was the value of the work involved in finding, refining and transporting the metals, compared to the value of the work involved in producing other objects of wealth. Very early the metals were for convenience made into coins of a standard weight and fineness.

Money is really a tool of merchants for use in their business, and so it is a commodity. It is useful in trade, and also it has become necessary to pay for the expenses of government. It is a form of wealth, but not a very important one, as can be seen by the fact that in 1760 many people living along our eastern seaboard had sumptuous wealth, when there was practically no money in the colonies. When money is needed it can always be readily purchased with other forms of wealth, which are sold in exchange for it.

There is a great deal of confusion of wealth and money in the popular mind. This is partly due to the habit of expressing the value of all kinds of wealth in terms of money—which in ninety-nine cases out of a hundred it is not—and partly because men, for their convenience, are paid in money for the value of the wealth they produce. They therefore get into the habit of thinking that their income is money. This is not the case. Their income is their share of the wealth they help produce. The money given to them for it is simply a convenient tool by which their production may be exchanged for the production of others.

This confusion is easily clarified if we consider the problem with reference to the country as a whole. A country with three billion dollars in currency on the first and the last day of a given year, may produce one-hundred-billion dollars' worth of goods, i.e., wealth, during that year. Its wealth will have increased, but its money not. On the other hand, suppose the government of that nation then said to its people, "We are going to give you all a year's vacation to enjoy yourselves, and will give each man exactly as much money as he received when working last year," and printed and distributed the money. Nothing would be produced, save the money. By the end of the year there would be one-hundred-and-three billion dollars in circulation in the country, but there would be few goods, and many would be starving and in great lack of everything.

It will be seen from the above that the amount of wealth produced by a nation is all-important to its prosperity. The amount of money it has, provided it is paid out equitably in just proportion to the wealth created, is of no great importance. If

the production of wealth should be constant and the amount
of money in existence should be increased tenfold, all wages
and all prices would shortly increase tenfold, and the result
would be practically nil. The same would be true in reverse if
the amount of money should be reduced tenfold. But when the
production of wealth is reduced, or not increased with the needs
of the people, there comes true poverty and suffering.

Today, money is almost universally "token money;" that is,
printed paper without intrinsic value but supposedly exchange-
able under a government guarantee for a certain weight of bullion of a definite intrinsic value. But since all the important governments of the world have in recent years repudiated these
guarantees, modern money has no real value whatever; only a
fictional one, resulting from the force of habit of unthinking
people and from the fact that it still remains the only convenient
medium of exchange or measuring-stick of value. This measuring-stick is a very deceptive one, because modern governments
under financial pressure constantly resort to printing more of
this fiat money, either openly or clandestinely, in order to meet
their increasing costs without obviously increasing taxation. The
result is, of course, that as the amount of fiat money increases
more rapidly than true wealth, its value diminishes in relation
to goods; that is, prices rise and there is a money inflation such
as we are experiencing now. When such an inflation proceeds
too far it destroys the people's habit of regarding the fiat money
as wealth (which indeed it no longer is) and results in the wild
fear-inflations that have occurred so often in Europe in the last
quarter-century.

An aspect of money rarely considered is, that it is one
of the greatest instruments to obtain freedom ever devised. With
sufficient money a man in a free economy can practically do what
he likes, live as he likes, have what he wants. Men will appear
who will be willing to exchange their skills and labors to produce whatever he wants in exchange for his money. In small
quantities money also purchases freedom by supplying leisure;
leisure, perhaps, to seek rest or more congenial employment.
No other form of wealth confers this freedom, for money—the
receipt, so to speak, for some sort of wealth—can be exchanged
almost instantaneously into any form of wealth without any

trouble. It is to obtain such freedom to fulfill their desires that men work so strenuously at the production of wealth and are so eager for money.

God has so bountifully endowed the world that man under natural or free conditions can by work obtain enough wealth to support himself, and also a surplus to use as a reserve. This reserve, that is the wealth he creates beyond what he consumes in creating it, is called his "Capital." Capital is, then, the result of labor. It is of two kinds. The first is unproductive capital, that is the semi-permanent things that man needs for his own and his family's comfort, such as shoes, clothing, furniture, dwellings, reserves against contingencies, etc. The second is productive capital, or tools, with which he can increase his production without increasing his expenditure of time and effort. Man's nature is such that he generally attends to his own and his family's comfort first, and only when all are comfortable does he begin to exercise his ingenuity on tools and labor-saving devices. His wife usually sees to this!

As soon as men congregate in groups, specialization in activities begins. Almost every man likes to do some one particular kind of work more than any other, and gets so he can do it better and faster than other people. When a group or society is formed, each man naturally gravitates to doing what he does best, partly because he likes it, mostly because he can do it better and more quickly than others. He shortly finds that others want his product and are anxious to swap theirs for it. By swapping he can get whatever he wants with less effort than in any other way. A man would be very stupid to make any thing for himself, if he can buy it with something he can make with a smaller expenditure of his time and effort.

Specialization greatly increases the production of the whole society, for under it each kind of work is done by an expert who, by swapping, is in great part relieved from the general tasks necessary to support his life. Therefore he can spend all his time doing what he does better and quicker than anyone else. Since all the members of the society soon specialize, it is obvious that this specialization increases the production of every person in the society, and so of the whole society, both in quantity and quality.

Men's abilities vary with the individual. Those who have attained a higher degree of skill in some useful line than is possible for most people, because of their scarcity value, are naturally paid higher in a free economy for their more perfect production than the less proficient. Again, those who can produce more than others, or those who can organize others to produce more than they otherwise could, are also paid more than the less proficient, since pay is only the value in money of the wealth they have produced or caused to be produced. So great is all men's desire for wealth, "the object of human desire," that when left to themselves they show an extraordinary ability to get into those places where they can produce the maximum wealth for themselves and so for the general wealth of the nation.

Though specialization increases wealth, any form of enforced specialization is harmful because human needs are constantly changing, and a free flow of labor and capital at all times is needful to insure the greatest possible production of wealth by the nation at large. Any restriction of this fluidity of enterprise is harmful to the general production, as we shall see when we consider the guild structure in England. In Egypt, where specialization in trade was made hereditary by compulsion of law, and every man had to follow his father's calling, it utterly destroyed the economy and produced universal poverty.

Of course the income of a society or nation is precisely the same as the aggregate production of all its members. The same, in like manner, is true of the capital, or saved production, of a nation. In very primitive societies there is little difference between the national annual production, or income, and the total national wealth, because their type of wealth is not durable —their clothes and tents wear out, their tools break, and their cattle die. Even in the highly complicated and solidly built United States, its capital, that is the more or less permanent wealth saved from the production of the past, is estimated at only three-hundred-and-five billion dollars, or something like one and a half to five times the annual production. From this it will be seen that a nation can quickly build or rebuild its capital as soon as suitable conditions to encourage production are established. Experience has shown that the prosperity of a whole economy rises or falls together, as a unit. This is because,

when all parts are greatly producing, each part can readily exchange what it makes for what it wants. Whereas, if most of the
parts cease to produce, even those which continue to do so have
great difficulty in finding anyone with whom to swap, or sell,
their products.

Considering the above, it is fairly obvious that the prosperity of a society is entirely dependent on its production. The
more people busied at production, the more prosperous is the
society. Men's desire for material wealth is so insatiable that
they are generally keen to produce; for almost all men have
some skills or aptitudes, and when left to themselves, have
always shown an incredible ingenuity in applying their talents
to fulfill the wants of others—not altruistically, but in order to
get what they want for themselves in return.

Specialization also starts trade. In a trade, each party gives
something for something he wants more. Since only the two
parties can know what they want, the trade is their business
alone, and no concern of anyone else.

The prosperity, that is the production, of a society can be
increased by tools and machinery, with the aid of which men can
increase their individual production. Such tools and machinery
are, of course, productive capital. They cost ingenuity, skill,
time, effort and money to make. They must be paid for. That
payment can be made only with the savings from past production. This saving for productive capital is essential to increase,
or even, since tools and machinery wear out, to maintain the
prosperity of a nation.

The creation and maintenance of tools and machines have
become the main factors of production in our present highly
developed technical economy. They multiply our powers of
production enormously and may be said to be its main motivating
power. Yet it must be remembered that these tools and their
maintenance are merely the products of the savings of past production of the people, and that, since human nature changes
very slowly if at all, they are the products of the last part of the
savings of that production.

Quite often creative effort is misapplied, for one reason
or another, and something is produced that no one wants, and

that therefore is not wealth. Such foolish work actually destroys
wealth. It is more injurious to the national economy than would
be total idleness on the part of those engaged on it. For the
materials and capital used for it, as well as the energy and the
sustenance of the workers, are completely destroyed to no benefit or purpose.

A price is said to be "the fair price" if it includes the cost
of producing and assembling the raw materials, the processing
of them, the interest on the capital used, insurance for the risks
involved and a reasonable profit for the manufacturer's time.

In a free economy, because of the action of the natural
law of supply and demand, goods do not always sell at their
fair price. If too much of a certain type is produced for the
community to absorb, the makers have to reduce their price to
induce more people to buy it, and so have to take a loss of part
of their investment in order to free the rest of their capital
for future use. As making things at a loss is ruinous, the manufacture of this kind of goods ceases until the surplus is exhausted, when more can be profitably made and sold. Again,
if a great demand develops for something of which there is a
shortage, those who have the supply will make such great profits
that many others will manufacture it too. The shortage will end
and competition will cause the price to fall back to, or below,
the fair price again. Therefore, though the actual prices are
rarely the same as the fair price, they fluctuate perforce in its
immediate vicinity.

A good deal of nonsense has been written about supply and
demand by economic theorists, because they frequently confuse
"demand" with what is really "need." Demand is much more
closely connected with supply, for true demand is the desire
for a certain class of articles by a group who have the power
to purchase it by the exchange of other articles that they have
produced a "supply" of, for the purpose of exchange. Such a
group have a "demand" for the first class of articles. Another
group might need it more, but if they had created nothing that
could be exchanged for it, they could make no demand for it.

As examples, the population of the United States needs
rubber and has a great demand for it, since they produce much
that the rubber producers would gladly exchange it for. On the

other hand, the Navahoes, on their desert reservation, need almost everything, but they can produce so little to exchange for what they need that there is scarcely any demand for goods among them, though their need is pitiable.

Because of the greed, ambition and evil in human nature, wars occur at frequent intervals. War is the greatest destroyer of wealth. The wealth in the path of the fighting is annihilated. All those engaged in the war are taken out of production for the duration. The normal economy is completely disrupted. Those remaining in production are saddled with the burden of supporting the fighters. Their energy is turned exclusively to making war material, which is either expended, or at the end of the war is no longer wanted, and therefore ceases to be wealth. The dead and seriously maimed are permanently removed at the very beginning of their normal forty-year period of productive activity. Since the constant, normal, day-to-day production forms a large part of the wealth of any society, the whole effect of war on it is disastrous. Terrible as war is in inflicting physical and mental suffering on the peoples engaged in it, its most shattering effect is on their economy.

The economy of most nations can quite easily support a percentage of non-producers, though every one of them, whether he be a complete idler or merely engaged on some work that neither produces nor facilitates production, is a parasite on the economy. For what he and his dependents consume is destroyed, and he creates nothing to replace it. Therefore the percentage should be kept as small as possible, because the producers do, in fact, support the non-producers out of their surplus earnings, which they could use far better for themselves by turning them into productive capital.

Early in the history of any community, intellectuals appear. Intellectuals are men who can think more or less well, and who can express themselves admirably. They exert enormous influence over the thoughts, and therefore the actions, of men. Their power rests on the cogency and clarity with which they express themselves. It may be for good or evil, according to whether they have integrity and can think clearly, or whether they are

venal or muddle-headed. The former type, if they are masters
of persuasiveness, are valuable beyond price to mankind. Unfortunately the venal and muddle-headed are quite as often
masters of persuasion, and do incalculable harm. The work of
intellectuals must be regarded skeptically, for their power lies
in their skill in expression, not in the soundness of their thought.

Typical of the intellectual group are many college professors. Their constant practice in classroom lectures has made
them frequently masters of persuasiveness. Their sheltered lives,
authoritative positions, and lack of practical experience, are
rarely conducive to the soundest judgment. These gentlemen,
because of their lack of practical experience and because of their
academic habit of concentrating closely on one object of thought
at a time, mix themselves up terribly, and by their glib writing
and specious but high-sounding arguments, befuddle everyone
else. For example, in discussing the present subject, they usually
divide mankind up into producers, consumers, and, if they
remember it, taxpayers; as if there were three sets of people with
opposed interests who must be carefully brought into a just
balance by government; whereas every worker in the country,
except bureaucrats, are producers, and everybody is a consumer
and a taxpayer. All three names are aspects of the same individual, and to talk of him as if he were three separate people
results in consummate nonsense. Again, the academic economists
make statements such as: "What the country needs to recover
is more credit." Credit means the ability to borrow. Borrowing
always produces debt. You can't have an extension of credit
without an extension of debt. The two are different views of
the same thing. Yet if one of them said, "What the country needs
to recover is more debt," he would at once be branded as a
lunatic. But by using the other name for the same thing, they
are able to mix up themselves and everybody else. Economists
often say: "What the country needs to recover is to have the
farmers receive more for their crops," and they get great ap-
plause. Yet if they said, "What the country needs to recover is
to have everybody pay higher prices for their food," they would
be laughed to scorn. Yet the two statements are simply stating
the same thing in other words. These two examples are fairly
obvious. There are many more subtle ones. Economists say, for
instance: "Our manufacturers should be protected from foreign

competition by a tariff." This really means that everybody should pay more for the goods they buy for the benefit of the manufacturers, who, when foreign competition is eliminated, can sell their products at almost any price they see fit. Again, the economists say: "Dairy farmers must be protected against the competition of oleomargarine." To do this, laws are passed which practically destroy the oleomargarine business and everyone must pay more for butter so that the dairy farmer may be benefited. One should accept the dicta of economists only after thinking about their implications, for the words often express a one-sided and utterly incorrect picture.

A little consideration of the last chapters makes it plain that Government is primarily designed to give its citizens the maximum freedom from interference by itself or by other citizens or by foreigners. It is concerned with people's conduct and should have nothing to do with economics, for which its organization is not designed.

Economics has to do with the production of wealth. Since wealth is the object of human desire, everyone so greatly desires it that he will work unceasingly for it if left alone. This produces great individual, and so great national, wealth. History, we shall see, shows that the great increases in wealth have occurred only where something approaching a free economy has been permitted by Government. Yet no people have ever created a Government deliberately designed to permit a free economy.

A free economy is not a *laissez-faire* economy, for the latter permits the politically powerful to preempt economic privileges for themselves by statute and to impose legal restrictions on others and so destroy the freedom of the economy—nor does the existence of a free economy permit one member of it to use his economic power to ride down another member unjustly. Such an action is a question of his conduct and not of economics, and is a suitable and correct place for Government to stop his bad behavior; but it gives Government no right to interfere with his efforts to produce wealth.

CHAPTER 4

LESSONS FROM HISTORY

VERY EARLY IN THE history of all human Government, unfortunately, those with power in it have misused that power to grant to themselves and their friends special privileges of an economic nature, and always, of necessity, at the expense of somebody or everybody else. For others must always be handicapped that the privileged may be exalted, since privilege can by definition result only from the abasement of others.

Now an economic privilege can exist only by force of law. It is true, a producer in a free economy may acquire enormous economic advantages through his abilities, but if he does he will have earned them by his skill and the whole economy will benefit by his increased production. Meanwhile, all others are free to compete with him, and this competition will also increase the production and the wealth of the country. Eventually one or more of his rivals will outstrip him, again to the benefit of the general economy, and he will fall. But the situation is quite different when an economic privilege is given by force of law. In the first place, it is extremely unlikely that such a privilege will be given to the most effective producer. Its effect is always to exclude others from his occupation and so eliminate rivalry, to the loss of the general economy and to the loss of the opportunity of those others who wish to go into his form of production and are prevented from doing so by his legal privilege.

Legally granted privilege is, therefore, manifestly hurtful to the general production, wealth, freedom and opportunity of the society. Government can, because of its nature, create no

30

wealth. It can, however, by laws and privileges, directly check the production of wealth; and it can divert the fruits of that production away from those who earned it by their production, and into the pockets of others. The latter procedure, by destroying incentive, also greatly reduces the production of wealth. The only way government can increase the production of wealth is to leave its citizens free to produce for themselves; for man is so desirous of wealth—the object of human desire—that he will always go after it as hard as he can when left alone.

Though this truth is generally recognized, and though no honest government would deliberately try to slow up the production, and so the wealth, of its people, nevertheless, since government is in the hands of men, and men are selfish and not clear thinkers, it is constantly checking the production of wealth by seizing special privileges for its members or their friends, on the general theory that it is thereby benefiting the privileged and not hurting anyone else. This is done the more readily since the harmful effects of such laws are seldom immediately apparent. We have seen that most economies can support a number of non-producers, or drones, without visible harm, though the harm is there. In the same way any economy can support a certain amount of special privileges without showing signs of strain. But too many special privileges, just like too many non-producers, will break an economy.

Perhaps government has gone into the business of distributing special privileges because of the confusion that generally exists about the word "law."

The word "law" is used to express two distinct and entirely different realities. In one meaning, "law" describes a decision made and enforced by government. In the other, "law" means a general truth discovered from the observation of a multitude of related facts. For instance, the facts that the living die, that a hen's egg hatches in twenty-one days, that the area of a circle equals the square of its radius times 3.1416 +, are natural laws. The two meanings are utterly different, but, because they are both described by the word "law," they are confused in the minds of the unthinking who appear to feel that government can alter the one as readily as the other.

Indeed, there is a story that once a newly-admitted Western State passed a law that read:

Whereas much time has hitherto been wasted by children and
engineers in the State of .... by multiplying by
the absurdly cumbersome number 3.1416 +:

Therefore be it enacted that:

Hereafter in the State of .... the circumfer-
ence of a circle shall be three times its diameter, and its
area shall be three times the square of its radius!

To distinguish between these two meanings of the word
"law" in this work, the second kind will be called "Natural Law."

Economic laws are natural laws, since they are based on
observation of the ways men reason, work, covet, act and
react against one another and inanimate nature when in the
pursuit of wealth. They are inexorable and cannot be permanently altered. Sometimes they appear harsh since they often
are at variance with man's desires. But like other natural laws,
they are constant, can be determined, and man can learn to so
adapt himself to them as to mitigate their harshness and often
turn them to his advantage.

Economic laws cannot be reversed by statute any more
than can other natural laws, because human nature, unfortunately, cannot be so changed. But since economic laws are
based on observation of the actions of men, and since the actions
of men can be considerably influenced by statute, it superficially
appears that economic laws can be replaced by statutory ones.
Therefore government often tries to do this. The effect of it is
always odd. The statute generally appears to have considerable
influence immediately, (because it changes the way men have
been behaving) and momentarily checks the action of the economic law, which then behaves much the way a stream of
water does when checked by an obstacle. It first stops; then piles
up force, spreads out; and then either moves forward again in
approximately the same direction with greatly increased power,
or else seeps, as it were, underground for a way, and comes
up in an entirely unexpected place where it raises hob generally.

An example of the first effect is the Prohibition Amendment, which tried to stop the supply of alcoholic drinks in spite
of the demand. The habit of drinking was stopped for a few
weeks. Then it spread out to many people who had not previously been habitual drinkers, especially to women. Bootlegging

got organized. Then the drinking habit grew to an extent that had not been indulged in for decades, and was practiced by a far greater percentage of the people than ever before.

An example of the second effect was seen shortly after the First World War in New York City where some women's organization, to help secure the rights of women, got a law passed that the women who worked in the subway should receive the same pay as men. Men could do more and better work than women. The result of the law was that all the women immediately were fired. This greatly surprised the sponsors of the statute, though the economic law is that workers are paid according to their production. In this chapter we shall see how long series of economic disasters have been set going by attempts to replace economic laws by statutory ones.

A people once started on a course of interfering by statute with economic laws, is bound to it for a long time. For the result of each such statute passed is likely to produce a chain of unpleasant economic results that have to be coped with in like manner, if the principle of such foolish interference is admitted at all. The situation is well summarized in the Negro play "Green Pastures," where the Lord God of Hosts says to the Angel Gabriel: "Every time Ah passes a miracle, Ah have to pass fo' or five mo' to ketch up with it!"

There follows a picture of an economy wherein many of the forces that exist here today were at work, but in which their action may be seen more clearly against a simpler background, and free of the atmosphere of controversy which beclouds and befuddles all modern economic problems.

In the middle ages the people of England grouped themselves for mutual protection round some local leader. He organized their defense and governed them. He partitioned the land among them, so that it could be best worked for the joint benefit, and in return received from the people services and rents to use for the public protection and his own maintenance and that of his fighting men. In those savage times it was essential to safety that the control of the locality should not be divided, so the custom grew up that on the death of a local leader his duty and control passed undivided to his eldest son. As civilization advanced, the need of protection ceased, but the leaders thus relieved of their duties wished to retain their position, and since they formed the government, passed laws giving themselves title to the land, and to perpetuate their class, decreed the law of primogeniture which caused all a man's land to descend to his eldest son.

This law permanently congealed the land into great blocks which had to be farmed by tenants. Tenant farming is not an efficient method of production, as anyone who has had any experience with it knows. The tremendous increase in the production of Danish agriculture after 1863, when the farm tenants were allowed to become owners of the farms they had been working for generations as tenants, shows how greatly the former legal restrictions had retarded the agricultural development.

Had the law of primogeniture not existed, the passage of time would have broken the great blocks of land into pieces of reasonable size for owner farming, to the benefit of production; for it is unusual for a man to love his eldest son to the exclusion of his other children. The cruel practice of raising the younger children in luxury and leaving them penniless would not have developed, nor would the wasteful extravagance that existed for centuries in the great English country houses whereby the energy of thousands was turned into useless channels. Such a privilege as primogeniture, or any other assumed, will naturally and quickly evaporate if not held up by statute. If so maintained it disturbs the whole economy by diverting its effort into artificial channels.

In the eighteenth century the control of the government of England was still in the hands of the landed gentry. They, their tenants, their farm-labor and their hosts of servants and retainers, were entirely dependent on agricultural produce for their livelihood. The price of farm produce controlled the amount of manufactured and imported articles they could buy —all their necessities and luxuries except food, labor and livestock. Its price could not go very high because when it started to rise farm products from the Continent could easily be imported in quantity and would bring it down again.

It was only natural, then, that the landed gentry should use the power of government which they controlled, to help their pocket books. They did this by passing the "Corn Laws," laying a protective tariff against the importation of farm produce. This was privilege again. It raised the price of food, as was intended. Thus, part of the earnings of the rest of the population was unjustly and artificially diverted to the pockets of the agriculturists, for it took more manufactured products to buy food than an equal amount of capital and labor spent in raising the food naturally required. The tariff did not, of course, increase the production of England, but it gave the landed class a larger share of the income from that production at the expense of everyone else.

The Corn Laws also necessitated a Revenue Service. The men engaged in this service were taken out of production and also became parasites on the producers. A tax had to be levied on the whole population for the support of these men and their equipment.

As the price of food rose, the landed gentry found it profitable to cultivate more land and to pay a higher price to get more labor. They could afford the higher wages because of the artificially higher prices, and thus drew labor away from other trades where it would have created more wealth and, except for the effect of the Corn Laws, more money. They soon produced a surplus of food. This would have broken the price unless it could be exported. But since in foreign countries English food enjoyed no artificial benefit from the tariff, this could not be done at the new high prices. In fact, English food stuffs abroad could not be exchanged for as much as could any other form of English goods produced by an equal amount of capital and labor, but not protected by tariff. From this it is evident that the extra capital and labor so drawn into agriculture would have brought more profit to the country had it been applied to making any form of wealth whatever that was not artificially jacked up in price.

To overcome the difficulty of selling abroad, the landed gentry again caused the government to help their pocket books. A law was passed paying a subsidy on English food stuffs when exported, so that the owners would receive the same high price abroad as at home. This subsidy came from a tax which again fell on the whole people, and came out of their savings. The officials who administered it again were taken out of production and had to be supported by taxes.

Adam Smith, the great eighteenth century British econo-
mist, the soundness of whose thinking benefitted the world in
general and England in particular for nearly a century, expressed
himself on this matter. His phraseology now sounds quaint to
our ears, but time has dimmed neither the clarity nor the cogency
of his thought. He says:

"What is the species of domestic industry which his
capital can employ, and of which the produce is likely to be
of the greatest value, every individual, it is evident, can, in his
local situation, judge much better than any statesman or law-
giver can do for him. The statesman who should attempt to
direct private people in what manner they ought to employ
their capitals would not only load himself with a most unnecessary attention, but assume an authority which could safely be
trusted, not only to no single person, but to no council or
senate whatever, and which would nowhere be so dangerous
as in the hands of a man who had folly and presumption
enough to fancy himself fit to exercise it."

Industry in eighteenth century England was entirely in
the hands of the mercantile associations—the successors of the
guilds. A guild was a trade organization that controlled all those
engaged in a particular trade in a given area. Sometimes guilds
were national in scope, more often they covered only a city.
The guild membership was divided into three horizontal strata.
At the top were the Masters, who owned businesses of their
own, worked for themselves and might employ help. Below them
came the journeymen; the latter were graduated apprentices,
who worked for hire for the masters. They generally owned their
tools. They were recognized as members of the guild and might
become Masters as soon as they had acquired either sufficient
capital or enough customers to set up for themselves. Below
the journeymen came the apprentices. The apprentices were
those learning the trade. They generally worked for a period
of years for their keep, at little or no pay. Indeed, they often
paid a fee to their employer to induce him to take them. They
were only probationary members of the guild and might be
dismissed if unsatisfactory.

The guilds were obviously in the control of the Masters who had the money, and the power to hire and fire. The guilds controlled their trade in their particular area by means of bylaws of their own. No one not a member was allowed to practice the trade. Membership could be acquired only by serving the long years of apprenticeship. The number of apprentices was strictly limited, with an eye partly to the present needs of the masters for labor and partly to the danger of creating too many future rivals in the business.

At their faraway inception the guilds had been useful to society, for during the dark ages the population of Europe had sunk to such brutishness that any skilled labor was regarded as an art, and it took long training to teach the inept people the simplest industrial manufactures. But as conditions improved and the people grew more intelligent, they sometimes developed creative skills spontaneously and began to make articles for which there was a demand, even though they were not members of the guilds. Thus the guild members encountered rivalry, which was painful to them, for at that time all production except the crudest kinds of labor was regarded as the "art mystery and craft" of some particular guild. The guild bylaws, of course, controlled their own members only, and had no power over outsiders.

The guilds had become rich and powerful. They naturally wanted to remain so and to eliminate the new rivals. To accomplish this they had resort to government aid and obtained charters from the king (which had the effect of modern statutes). These made the guild bylaws the law of the land which all must obey. The object of the guilds in getting these charters was to eliminate rivalry and keep the price of their produce high. As this reason would scarcely have obtained the charter, they obtained this privilege on the false theory that guild organizations maintained the quality of the goods created, and so prevented the public being cheated. They repeated this false doctrine so often—the basis of all good propaganda—that it was generally believed, and is, in fact, still often remembered, though the true reason for the guilds' continuance has long been forgotten. False propaganda was crude in those days, but even then, harmful. Long practice with it has vastly increased its power for evil.

The privilege the charters conferred on the guilds injured the public by creating a monopoly which could hold prices up, and by limiting the quantity of each type of goods to the amount that those the guilds saw fit to admit as members could produce. This in itself was quite a weight on the production of the country. It also prevented all who were not members of the guilds from participating in any sort of production, and thereby forced them into the crudest kinds of labor or domestic service for a livelihood.

The charters were soon found to have put the guilds themselves in a sort of economic strait-jacket. If a great demand developed for the product of a particular guild, no more labor could be added because the guild rules forbade it. The guilds, therefore, lost a potential profit and the public suffered a lack. On the other hand, when the demand for a product slackened or disappeared, there was nothing its guild members could do but go on making and piling up unwanted goods in the hope that the demand would revive before they ran themselves out of capital and were reduced to starvation. They might not shift their energy even to a closely allied industry with small differences of technique which was booming beside them, and where profits and the demand for labor were great. The rules of their guild and the other guild, both given power by law, forbade it.

Today it seems incredible that the producers of a nation should have wanted to bind themselves with such laws. It is still more peculiar that any society should have tolerated them, for they held prices up at unfair levels, they considerably limited production, and they condemned all city dwellers, who could not get into them, to crude labor at low pay or to lives of miserable idleness and crime, all apparently for no sensible purpose. It must, however, be remembered that man is seldom able to see his own foolishness or the effects of it while he is indulging in it.

By 1775 some great manufacturers had developed among the guild Masters. They were making far more than could be sold at home, and were exporting. The price for their exports came back as imports. These imports were often similar to the goods produced by other English manufacturers and could be sold at lower prices. This was, of course, distressing to the latter, who turned to government and pressed for tariffs to protect their markets against the cheaper foreign goods.

They got their tariffs by urging the governing agricultural class to sacrifice its own interests to its patriotism for the alleged "good" of the country as a whole. Their argument was based on the false theory of "the balance of trade." All European currencies were then based on gold, silver, or both. The delusion that wealth and money were two names for the same thing was was then almost universally accepted. (Unfortunately it is still pretty generally accepted). Starting with this false conception they managed by some sort of muddled thinking to convince themselves that if a country had more bullion at the end of a year than it had at the beginning, it must have had what they called a "favorable balance of trade" and be somehow richer. Continuing, they came to believe that if they could sell goods constantly and not buy any, but get paid for them in bullion, they were becoming richer as a nation. Since high tariffs obviously discouraged importation of goods, and brought in gold instead, the merchants were able to persuade the agricultural governing class that it was to the interest of the country as a whole to have the tariff, which they really wanted in order to be able to sell at higher prices in the home market. They accomplished this in spite of the fact that thereby the agricultural governing class was raising the price of the manufactured goods it bought in comparison to the agricultural products it sold, to its own very great detriment.

It is indeed as absurd to judge the wealth of a nation by the amount of bullion it has within its borders as it is to judge the wealth of a man by the amount of cash he has in his pocket and his bank account. A merchant might start the year with $100,000 cash and no goods and, by the judicious purchase and sale of goods, end up the year with $200,000 worth of liquid merchandise and only $5,000 cash. Though he has $95,000 less cash he is obviously $105,000 the richer. Again, an injudicious merchant might start the year with $100,000 worth of goods and $5,000 cash, and end the year with no goods and $25,000 cash. Though at the end of the year he has five times the cash he started with, he is obviously $80,000 the poorer. It is the same with a nation, though it is less obvious. The relation of the amount of its present bullion to the amount of bullion it had at any certain date in the past has no necessarily comparable relation to its present national wealth as compared to its national wealth at that time.

A curious effect of this myth of the "Balance of Trade" occurred in Spain and Portugal. Both these countries had been prosperous and economic leaders in Europe, from the time of the expulsion of the Moors (about 1250), till the second quarter of the sixteenth century when they imported the huge quantities of gold and silver looted from Mexico and Peru. Under the influence of the "Balance of Trade" myth, the authorities forbade the exportation of this gold and silver. Since there was then a great deal more gold and silver than was needed in Spain, and since it could not be exported, it cheapened in price locally; that is, all other prices, including that of labor, went up in terms of gold. This automatically made the price of all Spanish produce inordinately high when measured in goods produced where gold and silver were scarce. Therefore the Spanish and Portuguese could not export their goods. Since there was no market for their surplus goods there was none for their surplus labor. So terrible poverty developed, together with the high prices. There was complete stagnation in trade. Both countries sank into poverty and have remained in it to this day—long after the gold and silver has been illegally smuggled out.

The restraints on the division of land, and thus on ownership farming, to augment the prestige of the gentry; the restraints on labor imposed by the mercantile associations or guilds; the restraints on trade and the raising of prices against the public, as well as the change in the natural distribution of the national income brought about by the tariffs and subsidies, formed a heavy burden on the economy of the people of England. The effect fell, as usual, on the least efficient, who were forced into abject poverty by the high prices and the laws which forced them to apply their efforts in the kinds of work which produced, and so paid, the least.

Notice the chain of economic results which followed:

The plight of the poor became so pitiable that it affected even the callous eighteenth century governing class. They passed a statute requiring each parish to support its own poor.

Immediately every parish ejected its poor on to its neighbors so that they would no longer be its own poor. The country at once became filled with homeless vagabonds of both sexes and all ages, in abject, penniless misery.

Another statute had to be passed establishing everybody as a resident of a particular parish and forbidding his being moved out of it, or even his voluntarily moving out of it, unless he had a very considerable sum of money. This anchored everyone where they were.

The effect of this was that no one could get work or get labor, except in his own parish. Therefore wages, and consequently production costs, varied from parish to parish. This seriously upset the entire economy of the nation. The parishes became labor-tight compartments, greatly aggravating unemployment where it existed, and holding down production elsewhere to what the local labor supply could produce.

By this time England's economic condition was apparently becoming hopeless, in spite of the wealth she had seized and was exploiting in her far-flung Empire. It was then that the wisdom of Adam Smith began to spread through the political and economic thought of the nation. The special privileges in England began slowly to wither away, till finally in 1849, with the repeal of the last of the Corn Laws, they had largely disappeared. There followed fifty years of the greatest prosperity England ever knew.* It was not till the beginning of the twentieth century, when the hog instincts of the business leaders had once more led them to grab off a large amount of special privileges by statute, and the Germanic ideas of the professors of Political Economy had brought about socialistic legislation (a very dangerous form of special privilege), that England started on the economic slide which has brought her to her present pitiable condition.

There was very little economic regulation in the early United States and there has been no instance in history where so great an increase in wealth and prosperity occurred in so short a time. In France in the third quarter of the eighteenth century almost all the power and wealth was in the hands of

---

* It may be plausibly argued that the condition of the London poor in the third quarter of the nineteenth century was pitiable. It was, by our standards, but it was a dream of bliss when compared to their condition seventy-five years earlier. It must be remembered also that today all the English—not only the London poor—are in want, discontent and poverty.

the nobles, who regulated nearly everything. The French began to starve in the midst of a rich and fertile land, well able to support them had their economy been free. The people had enough freedom left to revolt and destroy their government. In Russia, since the Revolution, all the wealth and all the power is in the hands of the Commissars. They regulate every phase of life and economy in what is probably the richest and one of the least thickly settled countries on earth. To date somewhere between five and ten million people have starved there as a result of the management for, and by, the privileged. The people have not even sufficient freedom left to revolt against their Commissars, who have all the privileges of wealth and power and who regulate everything. It certainly appears that the less privelege there is in a nation, the more prosperous its people are, and that the more the privileges increase, the less is the prosperity of the people, until finally the totalitarian state develops where the Commissars have all the power, wealth and privilege, and the people are mere starving slaves, exploited and completely controlled for the benefit of "The State," which is in fact the clique of rulers who control it.

CHAPTER 5

THE FREE ECONOMY

"The Land of the Free, and the Home of the Brave."
F. S. KEY.

THE ESSENTIAL QUALITY OF a free economy is that it cannot be planned. It leaves the solution of problems to the inspiration of the individuals in the untrammeled population. When something approaching a free economy has existed, it has always worked better than the schemes of any planners.

It is probable that there has never been an absolutely free economy, just as there has probably never been an entirely regulated one, for human relations are never governed by absolutes. At the time the Constitution was adopted, statutory privileges already existed in the United States in the form of state laws, and particularly of municipal ordinances. For instance, except in Pennsylvania, only citizens could directly own land. In New York City only "Freemen of the City" (i.e., those citizens who paid a substantial fee) could open a shop. These were protected in their privileges by various groups of inspectors nominally appointed to save the other citizens from being cheated. In order to protect those established in business, the number of apprentices a master might take was limited by ordinance and the apprentices could not set up as rivals in the city except under certain conditions, etc., etc.

However, except in the cities which were few in number, scarcely any such laws existed. The great majority of the people, who were then countrymen, were neither oppressed nor benefited by them. After the adoption of the Constitution the people assumed that they had achieved a free economy and freedom of

43

opportunity, along with the general freedom they enjoyed. As a matter of fact they had, if they had had sense enough to keep it; for the hog instincts of the politically powerful had not yet effectively urged them to preempt by force of law special privileges for themselves to the exclusion of others. During the debates which formulated and caused the adoption of the Constitution, there appears to have been no discussion of the dangers of special economic privilege; it was generally assumed to have been done away with. Actually titles of nobility, which had become the symbol of privilege because the nobles had been the chief beneficiaries of special privilege, were forbidden by the Constitution. Thus the symbol of the evil was destroyed, but its substance remained.

It is odd that there was no clear-cut discussion of a settled policy on legally granted privileges at that time. Perhaps its danger was not then apparent. Perhaps some felt that a certain amount of special privilege was necessary and desirable, and that it would be impossible to draw a limiting line. Perhaps it was believed that the machinery of government then set up was sufficient (which it was, had it been used) to enable the people to protect themselves from the growth of privileged classes in their midst. At any rate no dictum was ever spoken, no clear-cut policy ever defined, against the conferring of privilege by governmental action. Nevertheless, for fifty years the people grumbled loudly about the "Hamiltonian privileges" that quickly came into being, as will be seen in the next chapter. Even till this day, when the people are heavily hampered by the privileges they have granted through their legislatures, little attention is focused on the matter and no policy has as yet been formulated against them.

However, after the adoption of the Constitution most of the people believed they had a free economy, and did have it, in fact if not in principle. A free economy is not a perfect system —man cannot devise a system that will free people from the consequences of their own stupidity and wickedness—yet where it has been most nearly approached it seems to afford a pleasanter life, greater opportunity for self-development, and greater wealth than any modification of it that has yet been devised.

Let us look at the way Americans lived in the 1790's. By far the greatest percentage of the population lived on farms which were almost completely self-supporting units. A hundred acres or so of most American land will furnish everything a family needs if it is worked industriously. The great shortage was of labor, for at that time the immigration from Europe was a mere trickle. Therefore, since children were a potential source of labor, the families were enormous; as large as nature would furnish.

Meat, vegetables, heat, light, leather, shoes, tools, flax, wool, furniture, even the buildings, were provided by the men, and the women cooked, cured, preserved, spun, wove, and made the clothes. All this resulted in a great plenty, but it involved a tremendous amount of work. It also involved very careful planning and organization, for it is not easy for a householder to foresee all his needs and supply them each in its season, by his own family's labor. Those few who had not the gumption to create a home of their own, hired out to work for their betters. On the other hand, a surprisingly large number of householders achieved a very high degree of comfort, and even luxury, as can be seen from the many splendid homesteads and the beautiful furniture and utensils that have survived from that period.

The work necessary to accomplish all this had to be practically unremitting, but no one objected to it, for the workers enjoyed the full benefit of their labor. Much pleasure was woven into the life by skillfully turning a good deal of the work into play. House and barn "raisings," huskings, spinning, weaving and quilting "bees," sewing circles, etc., were occasions for big parties and much real enjoyment.

In parts of the country certain essentials were not available. Metals, salt, sugar were not found everywhere and had to be traded for. All pepper and spices, beyond the local herbs, had to be brought in. This was difficult because of the great distances and atrocious roads, but it was accomplished.

This type of life extended all over the North and West, except in the great cities, and all down the Piedmont region of the South, into which slavery had not yet extended. Where there was slavery in operation life was essentially the same, but the slaves did all the manual labor and the owners had to devote their time only to head-work and superintendence. Nevertheless, this kept the owners very busy, for it is no light task to direct twenty or thirty, much less two hundred or three hundred slaves, so that they produce from one's own acres a rude plenty for themselves and great luxury for their owners.

In the cities the life was different, but not nearly as different as one is inclined to imagine. There, the richer men were merchants who dealt in foreign trade, or members of the professions. The middle class were shopkeepers and the lower, mechanics, artisans, or workers. But the difference between the life of city and country ended pretty generally with the work of the men. The women, to a very large extent, bought the raw produce of the country, prepared and preserved the food, made the soap and candles, spun, wove, dyed and made their clothes, linen, and furniture covers. Shops, of course, existed, where finished goods could be bought, but comparatively these goods were expensive and even in the houses of the rich many of the needs were met by the industry of the women of the families, all of whom, in city and country, took great pride in, and were much admired for, their creative skill.

Again on the frontiers, life, though considerably cruder, was essentially the same. There, sufficient time had not elapsed to allow the people to create enough articles to give them much luxury. The transportation was so difficult that even the rich could not import any quantity. An abundance of necessities could soon be provided, but life was crude and somewhat hard.

Looking back on it one sees that the homestead economy of the early days required an enormous amount of work and provided a bountiful plenty and enough leisure for reading, contemplation, and the endless religious discussions (for it appears that many of the people got their mental thrills by imagining the horrors of Hell), but it did not produce much cash income. Without money the people were more or less bound to their homes and it was hard to travel, see things, and start new ventures. Money comes from trade and commerce. Trade and commerce require transportation, and there could be little transportation accomplished in home-made wagons over roads so terrible that travelers used them only on horseback. Therefore, in most of the country, though surpluses were produced, they could rarely be disposed of except by swapping with the neighbors.

Along the coasts and on the rivers, however, boats and ships furnished efficient transportation. A most extraordinary amount of amateur boat building went on. There was nothing required to build a boat but tools, and time to collect the timbers and fashion them. The maker or owner could then use it as a fisherman, or as a carrier, as he chose, and not be interfered with. Boats appeared everywhere, built by men alone, or in groups who owned them in shares, or by hired men who worked for the owners. Along the coasts every little harbor had vessels in the carrying trade. The same was true up the rivers. Albany, New York, and Middletown, Connecticut, became great ports. The produce of the river valleys was shipped to the coastal cities and even to the West Indies and Europe.

The most extraordinary developments took place. New York City's fuel was supplied from the scrub wood of the great barrens of Long Island and brought along the Sound in boats from every little cove. A man at Southampton, Long Island, built a boat in Tail-o-Creek, Shinnecock Bay, all by himself. He put his family, live stock and chattels aboard, sailed through Shinnecock Bay into the ocean, round Montauk Point, through Plum Gut, the Sound and Hell Gate, round New York City, up the Hudson, up the Mohawk, and finally abandoned the ship and settled in the Finger Lakes region. A group of men on the Ohio built a ship, loaded her with local produce, sailed down the Ohio, down the Mississippi, and clear to Europe. Along the upper Hudson it was the custom for the young men of sixteen years old or so, to put their first earnings into trade articles and go into the woods, trading furs with the Indians. The furs were sold to shipmasters bound for Europe and the proceeds reinvested for further trade. Three or four such trips successfully accomplished often enabled the trader to procure a ship of his own. He then carried furs to England, where he exchanged them for articles of luxury that were brought to the rich West Indies and, in turn, traded for sugar and rum for the home market. A very few of these triangular trips netted the venturer enough to enable him to sell his ship, buy a good farm, marry, raise a family, and live in considerable ease and style as a gentleman farmer for the rest of his life.

Fishing and whaling were also heavily practiced. All sorts of means were devised to get capital. The prospective profits of a journey were divided into fractional shares, called "lays," before the venture started, and a contract was drawn assigning

so many "lays" to the ship, so many to the supplies, so many
to the captain and ship's officers, so many to each member of
the crew, in accordance with each individual's skill. In this
way little initial capital was required and all were joint ven-
turers in the proceeds of the voyage, which not infrequently
were very profitable.

Soon a class of great ship owners developed in many of
the ports; men who owned and managed whole fleets. These
men had been seafarers themselves in their youth, but as they
aged remained ashore directing boats all over the world on all
sorts of many-legged voyages. It was not unusual for a ship
to start from Salem, go round Cape Horn to Alaska, there trade
for sea-otter furs (greatly admired in China), trade these for
Chinese silks and porcelains, proceed round the Hope to Europe,
and exchange them there for stuff in demand at home. These
trips took many months, but they were very lucrative. A smart
captain was worth his weight in gold to the owners and bound
to get rich himself.

Besides all the perils of wind and wave, these men faced
many others. Pirates were a plague in many parts of the trade
routes. France and England both preyed on our shipping continually during the Napoleonic wars, until our "Acts of Embargo"
stopped them, and the trading too, and reduced our ports to
stagnation. Corrupt port officials were pretty universal, especially
in China, South America and the Orient; and it was the captain's business to win their "friendship" and help by all means
possible (mostly bribery and corruption), but at a minimum
cost to the owners. These men soon became adept at "wangling"
benefits for themselves and were not above practicing their arts
on our own government for what favors they could get. With
all this trading our merchants formed the richest group of
America until about 1830.

Meanwhile, during the first fifty years of our Republic,
manufacturing was developing all over our north and growing
west. By the time the countrymen had supplied their homesteads with all the necessities, comforts and conveniences that
their women folk could think of, they found time on their
hands in the winters. They had then nothing to do except feed,
water, milk, butcher and tend the animals, clean the wood lots
and bring in the fuel, make the shoes, tap the maples and boil

out the syrup and sugar, and supply themselves with sawn lumber for the coming summer. This was not enough to keep them busy! Since everything they made brought them its full profit, and since there were no laws to prevent them from working at any line they chose, they threw themselves into every form of creative activity that appealed to them. Most families found they excelled in one particular branch of the many household arts, and built a little family factory to practice it, with a view to selling their product to, or swapping it with, their neighbors. If one studies a locality in one of the states that was settled at that time, one finds that such a "factory" existed at nearly every farmhouse. One had a tannery, one a smithy, a shoe, a furniture, a tool handle, a wagon, even a clock factory, a saw mill, a grist mill, a brewery or wine press, a number of looms, spinning wheels, or what-have-you. These greatly increased the production, and so the income, of the country. We began to grow rich.

At first, these were purely family concerns and their product was exchanged in the neighborhood only. Then, perhaps, the boy from one family would prefer the work at a neighbor's to that at home, and would go over and work for him at a wage. Thus some of the factories increased in size beyond the family class. Soon their production increased beyond the consumptive power of the locality, and before the spring plowing, boys would go off peddling with a wagon load of goods, selling it or swapping it wherever they could, and the great American race of peddlers came into being. Money began to appear on the farms.

All this, coupled with the natural desire of all farmers to dispose of their agricultural produce, led to a demand for good roads. Roads such as there were in America, except for the turnpikes or toll-roads, were a communal enterprise, managed by public officials. American public officials differed in essence from continental European ones. On the Continent, officials were supposedly superior beings, clothed with the infallible wisdom and unquestionable power of government, and imposed from above by a highly reverenced monarch. In America an official was merely a neighbor, generally selected for his known honesty and gumption at Town Meeting, and saddled, often against his will, with the duty of performing a public chore on the *per diem* wage for labor then applying. Incidentally, the

office let him in for little honor and a good deal of cussing.
He was truly a public servant.

Gradually the welter of family factories began to merge
into fewer, bigger factories. People began to work in them all
the year round. There was always a shortage of labor, which
Yankee ingenuity was constantly trying to make up for by labor-
saving machinery and organization. A great increase of inventions began and production increased to such an extent that distribution became the problem.

These factories grew till they somehow produced a new
type of human being, for a long time peculiar to the United
States, namely, the "salesman," who developed the ability to
convince people that they wanted and ought to buy what they
did not know they wanted. These gentlemen became in time
invaluable in using their acquired persuasive power to obtain
from government special privileges for their particular businesses.

Shipping developed much faster in the north than in the
south, where there was scarcely any manufacture at all. This
was probably an indirect result of slavery, for the planter class
were not trained to any sort of manual labor and looked down
upon it. Slave labor was unsuited to either seamanship or factory
work, and the general prosperity of southern agriculture, producing tobacco, cotton and rice, easily shipped on the many rivers,
removed all incentive to seek other forms of activity. Therefore
the upper class southerners who did not choose to be planters,
followed the professions or went into politics. Hence the great
numbers of excellent southern statesmen, jurists and soldiers.

But in the mercantile north and west, manufacturing developed with incredible speed and vigor. By 1830 the great
manufacturers were quite as rich, important, and powerful as
the great fleet-owning merchants. They were soon using their
wealth, prestige and persuasiveness to get for themselves all
sorts of privileges by legislative enactment. These laws somewhat impaired the freedom of opportunity and the share of the
nation's production that other people had had, to the manufacturer's great benefit. The privileges came mostly in the form
of charters conferring vast corporate powers, or in the form of
tariffs to help our "infant industries."

Quaintly enough these special privileges seem to have

acted on our national economy much as whiskey does on a human being. The first ones not only helped the beneficiaries enormously, but incidentally seem to have pleasantly stimulated and improved the whole national economy. Later it required progressively more privilege to produce the same effect. Much later, when almost every occupational group had succeeded in securing some sort of privilege, privilege seems to have become a necessity to enable the national economy to function at all. Finally, as we shall see, privilege is likely to tie up the economy so completely that it will bring its natural functioning almost to a standstill, just as whiskey affects a drunkard during his last days.

At first glance it seems curious that when the economy was practically free and anyone could make money in any way he chose, so long as he paid outward respect to the Ten Commandments, all the pressure groups' energy was expended to *get* additional privilege for themselves. There was scarcely any pressure group activity to *curb* forms of economic abuse, which might easily be supposed to spring up in a society where everyone was allowed to do about as he liked in making money. Yet a little consideration of the subject shows that in a practically free economy no man could continue unjust, or arrogant, long enough to become a public menace, no matter how much he wanted to. If an employer demanded too much and gave too little to his workmen they left him lamenting and went to his rivals. If a man got a momentary monopoly on a necessary commodity and ran the price too high, there were dozens to make or get a supply of that commodity elsewhere, and, stimulated by the sight of his profits, they would do so, and bring his monopoly to the dust. If a man became swelled-headed and arrogant and rode too ruthlessly over his fellows, those fellows would quickly gang up on him and crush him. In a really free economy a man can wield great power only because of his intelligence and judgment. Obviously, if a man with power goes against the public interest he shows neither judgment nor intelligence and is heading to his own doom. Therefore, while the economy remained free there was little clamor to destroy the powerful, for before they had done enough harm to have raised the clamor, they would have destroyed their own power. It was only when their power got to be upheld by government-granted privileges that it could be abused to such a point that public clamor demanded it be curbed.

Under a free economy all sorts of extraordinary things occur that could never be planned. Good burgeons from what any sane man would consider harmful. Childish toys, slightly changed, multiply the nation's wealth; hobbies, carried beyond reason, become great national industries against all human sense.

To show what is meant, a few examples follow. At the end of the Civil War, innumerable herds of buffalo roamed over nearly one-third of the area of the United States. They were unprotected by law, they were slow, stupid, awkward animals, easily killed. In a few years they were slaughtered to the point of virtual extinction for the couple of dollars their shaggy hides would bring as rugs, lap robes, farmers' cheap winter coats, etc. It seems at first a national economic crime. No group of planners could conceivably have arranged for it nor, had they wished to, could they have devised means to exterminate so many million wild animals. The unguided economy, still free in this respect, did so. The buffalo was a comparatively useless and very harmful animal to the white man's economy. His meat, though edible in parts, was not as good as beef, neither was his leather. He devoured the grass of billions of acres. He practically prevented the settlement of his vast range, for the constant movement of the herds obliterated fences and even lines of telegraph poles, and injured railroads. His extinction immobilized the hostile Indians who depended solely on him for food.

As his extermination progressed, the grass on his range, relieved of his grazing, was seen to flourish exceedingly. Even while the extermination was in progress, hundreds of men apparently observed this and began driving herds of cattle up from Mexico and selling them at a profit. The ranching industry was born. The packing industry followed. Settlement on the late buffalo range became practicable; ranches, homesteads, small towns, sprang up all over it. Agriculture and mining came into being on many parts of it. An inconceivable amount of employment and untold wealth to the nation resulted from the extermination of the buffalo. Beef became a cheap and common dish on everyone's table.

Another example: the great insurance business which has made Hartford, Connecticut, the richest city *per capita* in the world is commonly said to have started in this most surprising way. There was a man in town who had a mathematical bent and enjoyed giving himself problems to solve. He got playing with the laws of chances, and one day he figured out the mathematical chances of visiting farmers getting their teams and wagons back and forth to their farms safely. He enjoyed gambling, so he used to stand on street corners and, reinforced by the sheets of his calculations, bet with any passer-by that the latter would or would not get home safely—whichever way the farmer wanted. The genius, because of his mathematics, could offer odds either way that appeared attractive to the farmer but really were to himself, so he got a lot of bets and made money. In time he modified his scheme so as to bet in a disguised way with those who thought it wrong to gamble. He offered them a proposition whereby, if they got home safely, they were able to pay him a few cents, but if they got wrecked he agreed to pay for the damage.

Thus was the great Hartford insurance industry born. The man's betting sheets were its first crude actuarial tables. It is amusing to consider that if this genius, and really great public benefactor, had had his ideas only a century or so later, he would have been arrested as a common gambler, a public nuisance, and probably for obstructing traffic, and the great industry would have been smothered in the embryonic stage.

But in the youth of our country anybody could try to make money in any way he saw fit without let or hindrance by law. As every unimpeded man who is at all competent can always find something he can do or make, that others will be willing to pay for at some figure that will support him, there was no excuse or reason for unemployment. Almost everybody tried a variety of things at once, and either continued as a jack-of-all-trades or else concentrated on that form of effort which produced the most money. This complete freedom in the choice of one's occupation resulted in an enormous aggregate production of the objects of human desire, and so greatly increased the income and wealth of the country. It also led to the discovery of all sorts of previously undiscovered human desires that could be fulfilled, to the further production of wealth.

It was this latter tendency which altered the daily life of the nation and of the world, to the great increase of everybody's comfort and leisure. For instance, it led people from the old well and bucket to modern plumbing, from the huge scorching kitchen fire to the gas and electric stoves, from the iron shod log doing duty as a plow to modern farm machinery. This trend originated and brought about modern progress, and caused a greater change in the material functioning of life in a short century than had occurred in the untold aeons of man's previous occupancy of the earth.

It is inconceivable that all these benefits to the happiness and wealth of mankind could have been brought about by central planning. Sometimes it appears that the Divine Grace, the Will of God, finds it easier to function for human benefit in a free economy where it is not constantly opposed by the bright ideas of self-important men, enforced by statute.

It is unlikely that the material progress of the United States in its first century and a quarter could have happened in a society where there was a great deal of privilege granted by law, for the privilege of some automatically reduces the opportunity of the many. Furthermore, man's nature is such that he is generally diffident about starting new business ventures. If he is met at the outset by a maze of government rules and a tangle of licensing provisions that take a lot of study and cost a great deal of money to clear away, he is liable to stop, discouraged from his plan, and continue his ordinary work. He will not try to take a chance to enrich himself and, incidentally, the country, by trying out his half-formulated plan.

At any rate it appears that the free economy of early America was the only incentive provided here that was missing elsewhere, and which could have caused the tremendous burst of inventions and creations which we poured over the world. All the need and all the desire for these gadgets evidently existed in Europe, for the Europeans quickly imported or copied them to the extent they could pay for them. Obviously the natural intelligence of the Americans could not have greatly exceeded that of the contemporary Europeans, for they were of the same stock, and not by any means the most intelligent of that stock; for certainly those who were really successful in Europe did not emigrate. There does not seem to be any tangible reason for our unquestioned preeminence unless it was our form of government, which for several generations permitted a free economy that encouraged everyone to enrich himself, and so the country. This freedom of opportunity, though constantly diminishing as privileges were successively preempted, caused our great material wealth and prosperity.

Let us consider the picture here when the Constitution had been adopted. A form of government had been deliberately designed to avoid interference with individual liberty. An attempt had been made to distribute all freedom, all opportunity, equally among all the citizens, so that each man's strength, determination and ability set the only boundaries to his potential achievements.

The picture stirred the people's pulses. It animated their ambitions, called out their energies, as like freedom and like opportunity would rouse and reanimate our people today. They did not want security. Security is passive—a blessing, perhaps, to the old, the weary and the discouraged. They wanted and they had opportunity, the blessing of the young, the strong and the fearless. With it the people leapt forward into undreamed of prosperity. The past was squalid, poverty-stricken, horrible; but it was dead. The nation looked and moved forward. Anything, apparently, might be accomplished by the courageous and efficient. From an impoverished string of coastal towns and hamlets the great United States burgeoned and flowered.

Looked at in this way it seems like Elysium. At the time it did not appear to be. An enormous amount of work was necessary for success. Many men dislike hard work. The competition was terrific and, since human nature is as it is, people were always interfering with one another's schemes. Though the action of the free economy prevented any prolonged suffering from any one source of this, yet there was always some sort of suffering or irritation. The whole economy was a seething strife between the selfish, grasping, predatory instincts of the competitors. This may be the reason Christ did not recommend the pursuit of wealth as the road to happiness and salvation. But the white races seem to have chosen this path, and when they are allowed to follow it unimpeded they are unquestionably able to produce a great quantity of material wealth for themselves and their fellows. Many people take pleasure in this ever-changing struggle. The opportunities to get rich, the freedom to plan and act, the chances to be taken, the very competition itself, appeal to them. The whole country certainly benefits in a material way by the enormous increase of wealth.

Nevertheless, with all the opportunities to get rich, poverty existed. First, there was a sort of voluntary poverty that will always exist. There are some men who so greatly object to having anything interfere with their complete liberty that they will not even tie themselves down with a steady job. They gladly give up such wealth as they might acquire to preserve their freedom. Such men are not pitiable, since they get what they want out of life. Their families, however, if any, are likely to suffer. These men became the trappers and wood rangers of the old days when they often "went Indian"; the hoboes and tramps of a generation ago; the jallopy drifters of today. Such men will always be poor because they don't want to be bound down by either the acquisition or the possession of wealth.

Besides these, there was always the terrible poverty of the new immigrants from Europe, who generally arrived quite destitute and suffered fearfully till they got their start. This was really an imported European poverty. The individual immigrants usually passed quickly through this horrible period, but, since others were constantly coming, this imported poverty was a perennial sore spot.

The principal suffering from poverty, however, came intermittently as a result of the revolutions of the normal business cycle—good times, boom, panic, hard times—which followed one another rapidly in our early years. There were "hard times," or "depressions," in 1793, 1797-1798, 1801, 1807, 1812, 1816, 1819, 1826-1830, 1834, 1837, 1841-1844. Each of these was accompanied by loss of property, poverty, and suffering.

Business cycles are caused by the action of the mass foolishness inherent in mankind, and are apparently so inseparable from any economy which produces a degree of prosperity, that their periodical occurrence may be said to be almost an economic law. Their operation certainly deserves a little philosophic consideration.

In order to understand them, it is necessary to recall the fundamentals of banking, since banking has been practiced far longer than the United States has been in existence. After the fall of Rome money was always gold, silver or copper; the coins had their value in themselves. There was no credit, since no one could trust anyone else. By the time of the Crusades things got a little better. Rich merchants separated their specie geographically in the various cities where they did business, and arranged to make payment from their distant hoards by letter, instead of transporting the gold. Some of these men were honest and acquired a reputation therefor. Other people availed themselves of their organization when traveling, and instead of carrying specie with them at the imminent risk of robbery, deposited what they expected to need on the trip at the office nearest their home, and took with them a letter to the office where they were going, ordering it to pay them a like amount on demand—the first letters of credit.

Often the rich merchants had acquired more specie than they could use immediately in their business, and then they loaned it out at interest to someone who could use it, always taking from the borrower something—jewels, or land, or goods— that could be readily sold for more than the value of the loan if the borrower failed to repay, but to be returned if he did pay. Having arranged for the loan, the borrower was generally required to keep the money on deposit with the merchant until he actually spent it.

During the Crusades such an enormous number of people were traveling that vast sums of specie were deposited in the European coffers of the merchants, to be drawn on in the Orient. Soon the merchants noticed that because the individual deposits were drawn out slowly, and because others were always being made, a constant and large idle residue accumulated in their coffers. They began to loan this against adequate security as though it were their own. In time the unused parts of these loans they had made accumulated and became a constant fund as the other had done, and they loaned this also.

In this way credit banking was established. The potency of the bullion deposited was increased several times; the depositor was using it, the banker was using it, the first, second and third borrowers were also using it, all at once. It was as though the supply of money available in Europe had increased many times, and as the supply of money increased and there

was no increase in the other forms of wealth, there was less
need for the money; its value in other goods then declined; that
is, prices rose.

On the whole it has proved a sound plan but it is very
dangerous. At first it caused great apparent riches in Europe and
caused all sorts of industries to get started and a lot of real wealth
to be created. It had a good deal to do with enabling the fleets
of the merchants and explorers to set out, which brought into
Europe the wealth of the East and the looted gold of Mexico and
Peru. It benefited the peoples of Europe enormously then and
later.

The trouble with the credit system is that it is very elastic
and based primarily on human psychology, which is pretty generally unpredictable. No banker, let alone any layman in the
form of a government official, has ever been able to determine
how much credit a given amount of bullion will support. The
reason is fairly obvious. Doubling or halving the amount of credit
outstanding (now bank deposit currency) has theoretically much
the same effect as doubling or halving the amount of bullion in
existence. As it increases, its unit value decreases in relation to
other forms of wealth; in other words, prices rise. As it decreases,
prices fall.

Since this is true, there is a constant pressure to increase
the amount of credit while it is expanding, and decrease it while
it is contracting, because as it increases prices rise and it looks
as if more money could be safely loaned on the same goods, and
as it falls, the pledged goods have to be sold at lower and lower
prices to secure the loan, thus further reducing all values. A
banker would readily loan $6,000 on a house which, in normal
credit conditions (if there is such a thing), was worth $10,000.
If, over a period of years, the credit of the country greatly expanded, the house might become worth $20,000 and the banker
might well loan $12,000 on it. However, if the people got pan-
icky and credit was withdrawn, the house might well become
unsaleable, the owner lose it, the bank bust, and the depositors
be stuck with it.

A most illuminating case occurred in a small, remote New
Hampshire town in the early 1920's, which is quoted because
one can see principles clearly in small affairs and then apply them
to large ones. The town was doing pretty well in a small way

when the local rich miser died, leaving executors, an heir—his daughter—and $25,000 in cash in his house. The executors deposited the $25,000 in the local bank. A man owned a piece of unimproved land on Main Street and wanted to build on it but didn't have the money. Neither did the bank have the money to loan him, though it wanted to. As soon as the $25,000 was deposited, its president notified the lot owner, who borrowed the money, left it on deposit and hired contractors. The cellar contractor first ascertained he could borrow the money (the same money), then bought machinery, concrete, bricks, etc., and hired help. The same was done by the chimney builder, the boss carpenter, the plumber, the electrician, the plasterers, the painters. Each in his sphere. All on the same money. The new building was a perfectly sound business proposition.

Before it was finished the executor turned over the estate to the daughter. She had inherited her father's miserly instincts as well as his $25,000. She promptly withdrew the $25,000 from the bank and took it home. This cleaned out the bank. The banker promptly had to come down on the lot owner for his loan. He could not pay. Then the banker came down on each of the contractors for their share. They could not pay either. So the bank was bust. Furthermore, everybody of any importance in town was bust and the workmen were out of a job, could not be paid and were bust too. A complete picture of a national panic occurred in that small village, just as it would in the nation.

By the grace of God, the daughter had withdrawn the $25,000 late on Saturday morning. That afternoon the banker had time to figure out what had happened. Sunday he went to Boston and saw an old college friend who was president of a big bank there. He explained the situation; the building was a sound business proposition, the friend's bank loaned his bank $25,000, and the situation was never publicly known and was permanently saved. That, of course, could never have happened had there been a sudden destruction of national credit instead of that of a village.

Those two examples show the dangers of the credit system of banking. Its advantages are so obvious that this system was readily adopted in the new United States and has continued ever since. In fact, the government itself adopted it in part for its own use by issuing more paper currency than it had bullion to redeem, as it felt it would not be called on for all of it at once. We shall see how this trick of expanding and decreasing the currency and the credit, which has the same effect, has worked as the years rolled by. Now let us return to a consideration of the business cycle.

The cycle starts with everybody pretty frightened, a considerable shortage of goods, a complete lack of credit, little money in circulation and general poverty. In a free economy, since something must be done to live, the workers start producing for whatever they can get—often a great deal less than they had been getting. Employers and manufacturers sell their products for very little profit, or even at a loss, since they have to sell to free some of their capital to continue their business. Business starts slowly at this low level, but wealth begins to be produced in quantity. Things get better. As people lose their fear, money comes out of hiding, banking gets going again; goods are bought to fill the piled-up wants. Manufacturers can sell at higher prices. They can afford to pay their workmen more, when it is demanded, for they must keep them contented and producing, since their products are saleable at a profit. Thus the workmen can become purchasers. Thus the whole economy spirals up, full prosperity is reached, everyone who wants to, can get work, everything made can be sold at a profit.

When this point in the cycle is reached the whole world looks rosy. Everything undertaken appears to succeed. Every investment seems profitable. There is a lot of money in circulation. Banks and those with money are optimistic and loan readily on the basis of the risen prices, thus increasing the bank deposits or credit currency. Hired people who have received repeated raises believe it will go on forever. They develop new wants and buy luxuries hitherto undreamed of. They can't wait till they have earned the money to pay for them so they borrow, and pledge their future earnings for present luxuries. This creates a tremendous demand. More and more credit currency is created. Therefore prices rise. Manufacturers expand their plants, buy goods carelessly, pay any wage asked; for they can sell anything they produce profitably. Banks loan on the new prices. This brings them a lot of money.

All prices rise—commodities, land, interests in businesses

(or stocks). Because of the rapidity with which the money circulates and the credit currency increases, there appears to be lots of it. After the prices have risen for a while it appears more profitable to speculate than to work. Land is bought, not for use, nor for the rent, but to sell it again. Stocks are bought, not for the dividends, or to develop the production of the company, but to sell at a profit. This is pure gambling; it makes profits, but it produces no wealth. It seems, however, to be so profitable that countless people cease to bend their energy to efficient production, and go in for speculation (gambling), generally supported by bank loans at the risen prices. Factory owners get careless in their purchases and operation. Workers can make forty times their daily wage on one successful gamble, and as all gambles are for the moment successful, many stop working. No one can wait to earn the money to gamble with; it is so much easier and quicker to borrow it, and appears to be equally lucrative. So the production of wealth is slowed up; credit and prices are inflated beyond reason; almost everyone is in debt, having pledged their future earnings for present pleasures or new investments. Everyone is extravagant and wasteful, because money is so easily come by.

Suddenly something shakes public confidence. In a moment all the buyers become sellers. Prices plummet. The debtors sell like mad, trying to meet their debts by selling on the falling markets. No one buys anything except food. Factories can't sell their produce and close down. Money goes into hiding and disappears. Ownership changes all over the place and gets into the hands of creditors. Bankers get frightened and come down on their debtors. Because of falling prices, they cannot sell their collateral for prices that cover the loans. For as the credit vanishes, the credit currency vanishes too; as the amount of currency disappears and the rest of the wealth of the country remains the same, the value of the money increases in relation to everything else and prices drop steeply. All is chaos, terror, poverty; and starvation seems just ahead. Finally the banks themselves can't meet their creditors, and close. This is the worst that can happen in panics and it ends them—leaving the country jibbering with fear, to start the cycle over again with no credit currency to speak of, only real money left, and therefore all prices down to the bed-rock bottom of the true relationship of all the wealth in the country to the amount of real money there is. This man-made expansion and contraction of the amount of money available by adding to sound money the credit currency of banks—which is unstable and ephemeral, since it has no true existence except in the minds of men—is the true cause of our long succession of booms and busts.

Terrible though these panics are, it must be remembered that they destroy very little of the national wealth. True, they cause that wealth to change hands, rapidly and very painfully indeed to the losers. But every material object of human desire that existed before the panic is there afterward. It has moved, indeed, from foolish to wiser hands. Even the money is there, though the credit (which is after all a psychological, not a material thing) has disappeared. It is true, also, that the potential production, which might have occurred but did not, during the latter part of the boom and the early part of the panic, does to some extent reduce the national wealth.

Looking at these panics philosophically, one perceives they are merely another instance of the punishments meted out by the Laws of God—or, if you prefer, of Nature—to prevent excesses, and to compel all living things to act with wisdom and restraint, so as to avoid incurring greater evils. If a man overeats he has a dreadful bilious attack. He feels terrible. He does not want to eat. He gradually cures himself. If the chastening bilious attack did not come, a glutton might so overload his stomach that the piled-up food in it would rot and kill him. Booms are an excess; they have to be checked. They result from people trying to get rich at the expense of others, while creating no wealth. They bring about waste, gambling, dissipation of every kind, extravagance and idleness.

From the purely economic point of view with which we are dealing, the painful part of the business cycle was not an unmitigated evil by any means. It did not destroy any of the national wealth, the way useless work does. It merely caused that wealth to change hands. It stopped extravagance and waste very rapidly, if unpleasantly. It caused all business to reorganize —eliminating the unessential, speeding and cheapening production. It threw useless concerns into the discard, thus forcing their employees into beneficial lines of endeavor. It brought labor

costs into line with the wealth that labor produced. It stopped
people's speculating and made them keep their minds on their
jobs. It took the control of industry and business away from the
careless and adventurous, and gave it to the thoughtful, careful
and conservative, to the great benefit of the nation in the ensuing
era of prosperity. Though vastly unpleasant, these panic depressions were beneficial to the nation, just as the acute bilious
attack is beneficial to the character and subsequent health of the
glutton.

In our early days, people in the mass were about as foolish
as they are today, and good times, panics and depressions succeeded one another as they always have and will. But in those
days people had not completely deluded themselves into the belief that they could supersede economic laws by statutory ones.
So the panics and depressions came as soon as they were earned
by economic misconduct, and were not delayed and aggravated
by government measures intended to eliminate them. Therefore
they were more frequent but less severe than now. They were
severe enough, however. Almost all the people engaged as prin-
cipals in manufacture and business in those times went completely broke at least once in their lives, and generally more
frequently. Having done so, however, they could always pick
up the pieces and start again, because of the almost complete
freedom of opportunity. Their native ability soon carried them
back to approximately their old position. Many a one learned
from the bitter experience of going broke how the economic
cycle worked, and lived to profit by the knowledge. People did
not often stay rich for long, but there was plenty of opportunity,
and the future always was bright and an incentive to effort.

Even in the early days, the states tried to mitigate the
effects of the panics by passing laws forbidding the foreclosure
of mortgages, the sheriff's sales for debt, eviction of tenants, and
by granting poor relief. But in the midst of the distress of one
of them, John Quincy Adams said: "Government can do nothing
but wait for the two healers or destroyers, Time and Chance,
to bring either catastrophe or the cure." Somehow they always
brought the cure. And since bad times come from lack of wealth,
caused by foolish application of effort during the previous boom,
the cure was always the same: people pulling in their belts and

going to work hard, to produce what was needed and wanted at prices that could be afforded. Plentiful production of objects of human desire is the only possible way of creating wealth.

The free economy was always admirably adapted to this production. The whole population was looking for ways to get rich. The periodic "hard times" or depressions were stimulating them like goads. It was a certainty that some of the many searchers for wealth would find a way to make it. No one knew, or could have known, how the depression would be lifted. It was generally helped by some new discovery, invention, or form of business, which provided the fresh stimulus that brought "good times"—a new trade route, inventions, labor-saving devices. A horde of necessitous but untrammeled searchers were bound to find such relief. No board of well-paid planners, sitting down to a table in cold blood, could possibly have hit on the needed new industry.

Looking back on our early days, it superficially appears that there was a good deal of class distinction here. Those men who were outstandingly successful, either in the professions or business, were greatly admired and accorded great respect. They seem to have expected, or rather demanded, the latter. This makes the successful appear, as we look back through the mist of the years, to have been a class. They were not. They were merely a number of individuals momentarily enjoying the fruits of their particular outstanding abilities.

In 1798 Benjamin Rush wrote in his *Essays Literary, Moral and Philosophical*: "It is a singular fact in the history of the mechanical arts of this country that the same arts seldom descend from father to son. Such are the profits of even the humblest of them, that the sons of mechanics generally rise from the lower to the more respectable occupations, and their families generally ascend to the first ranks in Society among us."

As late as the 1880's, one of the guests at a very swank multimillionaire's dinner at Newport, said that if he had shouted "Low Bridge" every male guest present would have ducked! Thereby implying that every one of the great tycoons had worked in his youth as a bargee on the Erie Canal.

A very illuminating quotation may be taken from Harriet Beecher Stowe. She was born in 1811 and her book *Old Town*

Folks is a description of New England life at the time of her childhood. In the story, written in 1858, a young American becomes a British lord by the death of some of his relatives. In a letter back to America he writes:

> I have always as you know looked forward to the ministry, and to such a kind of ministry as you have in America, where a man for the most part, speaks to cultivated, instructed people, living in a healthy state of society, where a competence is the rule, and where there is a practical equality.
>
> I had no conception of life, such as I see it to be here, where there are whole races born to poverty and subjection, where there are woes and dangers and miseries pressing on whole classes of men, which no one individual can do much to avert or alleviate.

At that time there was much legally granted privilege in England, and very little in the United States.

CHAPTER 6

SPECIAL PRIVILEGES FOR EVERYBODY

OLD PROVERB
"Stone by stone was Rome built."

NO ONE HAD WORKED harder for the Constitution than Alexander Hamilton. Yet it had hardly been adopted when he himself, quite unwittingly to be sure, drove into it the thin edge of the wedge that was later to destroy the freedom of opportunity and the general freedom that it was chiefly designed to bring about. He wanted and got special privilege for himself and his friends. He caused the incorporation, by statute, of a number of companies. All corporations secure special privileges to their owners by statute, and these are enforceable by law. The modern world has gotten so used to them that it has almost forgotten that they grant privileges at all, or what those privileges are.

Corporations are a nineteenth century development, but an earlier invention. In the late eighteenth century they were in the embryonic stage. It is rather interesting that Adam Smith, contemplating them at that period, should have foreseen their future danger. He recommended that only those should be chartered which were manifestly of special benefit to the public and required a larger capital than an individual or partnership was likely to have—such, for instance, as a water company.

Corporations, being created by statute, are the product of political power. Government may, through corporation charters, divert an unearned portion of the national income into their corporate pockets. Sometimes when the political power of the sponsors is great, this diversion may become scandalous. For instance: between 1850 and 1871 the proposed transcontinental

66

railroads were sponsored by politically powerful men. Their charters granted them the alternate townships checker-boarded along their rights of way. In this way one hundred and fifty-five million acres of the public land were given to railroads and huge sums of money were also lent them by the Federal Government.

All those who start a business under corporate charter limit their liability at the outset to the amount they choose to put up. They are not liable to their creditors to the full extent of their fortunes if they fail in their venture, as they would be without the corporate charter. But if they succeed they enjoy the full benefit.

The corporate structure puts the power of the money contributed by all the stockholders, into the hands of the few directors. Sometimes the amount of this money, and so of this power, is colossal; far greater than a private person would be likely to acquire. The same men may become directors of many companies; and such men have been known to direct the business of several companies in such a way as to channel all their profits into the treasury of the one company in which they owned the greatest share themselves.

Directors can misuse the great money power they control, but do not own, to the detriment of rivals or the general public. Often corporations are so rich that they can eliminate rivals by selling their produce at a loss for sufficient time to bankrupt the rivals who must meet their price, and when the latter are eliminated, run up the prices with no fear of competition, recoup much more than their losses, and grossly overcharge the public.

The practice of buying up and then suppressing patents which would reduce the cost of a corporation's product but involve the purchase of new machinery, is not uncommon. In this way the danger of a rival's getting them is removed. There is no necessity for changing to new machinery. The company maintains its place in the industry. The public, of course, suffers, because it cannot buy the product at the lower price it could sell at, were the patent used.

Unscrupulous men can, under the anonymity of a corporation, do things that they would be afraid or ashamed to do in the open. Private mill owners in the early days were practically forced by public opinion to give their help decent housing, decent working conditions, and reasonable pay. The mills were

not huge. (They could not be, since they were in private hands.)
The owner knew most of his workers. Besides, almost everyone
the owners associated with also knew them, and if conditions
got bad, brought pressure on him that he had to comply with,
whether he wanted to or not. But as soon as the business was
incorporated, its president, formerly the owner but now generally
controlling by new capital and mergers far more employees,
could publicly deplore the living and working conditions of the
workmen but maintain that he was merely a trustee for his
stockholders' money and that bettering the conditions of the
employees was a work of charity and not of the business, which
unfortunately was not of an eleemosynary character. So he could
do nothing and get away with it.

For many years corporations used economic pressure to
influence their employees' votes. This control of votes, coupled
with the enormous money power that some had, led to the hideous
abuse of corporations controlling, not only individual legislators,
but whole legislatures, for their own ends. The creature thus
dominated its creator. Often such power was used to pass statutes that eliminated trade rivals, thereby creating a monopoly
that could charge the public higher prices than could have stood
with free competition.

Manufacturers—most of whom have operated as corporations—early brought all their political power to bear to get
protective tariffs passed. Tariffs for revenue had existed since
1797 and were not an unreasonable form of tax. The manufacturers wanted protective tariffs so as to obtain for themselves
a larger share of the national income than they had earned. To
obtain these they once more used as arguments the "Balance of
Trade" myth, but this they supplemented with the claim that
tariffs were needed to protect our "infant industries" against the
rapacious established industries of Europe. This argument was
used even after our industries had developed till they made those
of Europe look like the ones in a Mexican village. Finally it was
ridiculed into oblivion. The next argument was that the high
tariff protected the wages of the American working man against
cheap, exploited foreign labor. This is, perhaps, the only recorded
time that American corporations went on record as favoring high
wages for their employees! The fact is, of course, that the high
skill of the American workman, the ingenuity of American ma-

chinery, and our remarkable aptitude for industrial organization, enable him to produce a great deal more goods per hour than the workman of any other country. He can produce more goods at a lower cost per unit than any foreigner. Therefore he can profitably be paid more. If the protective tariff were the true cause of our high wages, then the wages of our farm workers (not protected) would be the same as European peasants! The fact that they are lower than those of industrial workers is due to the artificial redistribution of national income caused by the tariff.

All the evil effects produced by tariffs in eighteenth century England and already described may be seen in this country today. They have taken from the farmer a great share of his profits by artificially allowing a higher price for manufactured products than for agricultural ones produced by an equal expenditure of capital and labor. They have slowly strangled trade by hindering the importations that we receive for our exports and making it necessary for our exporters to take payment often in gold.

The control of wealth in the hands of big corporations and of trade associations has enabled them to undertake national advertising campaigns. They have at times induced newspapers and radios to undertake publicity campaigns to make the public "health conscious," or in other ways "educate" them, not for the sake of the public, but in order that the advertisers can, under the guise of protecting the public health by government regulation, obtain for themselves additional legally enforced privileges by which a larger share of the national income will be brought into their pockets. Examples follow.

The great vintner companies, using the widespread prejudice against the use of intoxicants together with the mania for "sanitary products," have had statutes passed requiring exorbitant annual license fees for the making and selling of wine. There is no real reason why wine makers should be licensed. If they make good wine it sells, otherwise it doesn't. If the wine is exposed to germs its alcohol kills them. Its quality depends on the grapes, the soil, the climate and the skill of the maker. Such high license fees cannot be to produce revenue, because thousands must forgo it for each one that can afford it.

When great capital and many vineyards have been assembled to produce hundreds of thousands of cases of wine annually, an enormous license fee is nothing. But such fees are utterly prohibitive to any small farmer who has time and inclination to press out five or six barrels of wine from his little vineyard, for local consumption. As a result, wine, which can be bought anywhere in Europe for a few cents a bottle, costs from one to five dollars a bottle here, and is almost universally of a nationally advertised brand. A multitude of small farmers are deprived of a legitimate source of income. Undoubtedly a great number of areas where excellent wine might be produced will not be discovered while this license is in force. The public buys distilled spirits because it gets more "kick" for the money. But the great vintner companies prosper.

Undertakers, or "Morticians" as they now choose to call themselves, under the guise of protecting the public health have fortified themselves behind statutory battlements to such an extent that for performing a simple, if unpleasant, service, they obtain a remuneration so huge as to be generally scandalous. After all, a human body is just so much meat (far less than a horse which is buried wherever convenient), and once it is buried there is an end to it. All the laws requiring embalming and metal coffins, and that no one but a licensed undertaker move a body after it has been buried, no matter how long, or build a coffin, are just pure flim-flam designed to swell their receipts at the expense of the public, and have really nothing to do with preserving the public health.

Along the same line, Cemetery Associations have for years made such great profits (though supposedly non-profit organizations) as to be generally a local scandal. On October 19, 1948, this scandal even broke on the front pages of the *New York Times*. They have obtained legislation requiring burial in licensed grave yards and thus eliminated the old-fashioned American custom of burying the beloved dead in the family gardens. The object of such legislation is, of course, to bring profits to the incorporators of cemeteries, though the reason given for it is a sanitary one.

Again, the small slaughter houses scattered all over New England have, under the guise of health regulations, caused laws to be passed forbidding any farmer to slaughter more than three head of his own beef per annum, and requiring, if the meat of these three is for sale, a form of inspection that is very difficult and troublesome for a farmer to obtain. Yet when a farmer slaughters, he does it in a field, keeps the hide for raw-hide or the tanner, the horns and hoofs for glue. The entrails go to the pigs. An hour after the butchering there is only a black stain on the grass that the next rain washes away.

But anyone who has passed within a quarter-mile of one of the small "sanitary" slaughter houses knows just how sanitary they are. The wet hides, horns and hoofs are thrown in piles. The entrails are kept in garbage cans till there is a carload of them for shipment to a fertilizer plant. They become a crawling, putrefying, stinking jelly that reeks for hundreds of yards. The floors are black, saturated and slippery with stale clotted blood. The whole place is loathsome. Also it is a fact that one still reads in the press of horse meat, and the flesh of animals that have died, being sold for human consumption.

This "sanitary legislation," sponsored by the slaughter houses, has had a curious effect, in New England at least. An eight or nine hundred pound steer, just before the war, could, because of it, be sold by a farmer only to the slaughter houses. These were few and closely banded together to hold prices down. The farmer received between fifty and sixty dollars for an animal. This was about enough to pay for its food. All the farmer got for his labor in raising and caring for it was the manure inci-dentally produced. On the other hand, the meat sold retail in the local stores for between one hundred and fifty and two hun-dred dollars. The hide, horns, hoofs and entrails went to the slaughterer. This utterly unfair division of the profits, from the point of view of the hours of work put into the animal, is typical of the effect of pressure group "sanitary" legislation. If there had been no interference, the farmer could have had forty dollars more for his steer, the consumers could have paid forty or fifty dollars less, and the retailer would still have had his fifteen to twenty percent profit. The result was, of course, that few farmers raised beef, that not all factory workers could buy it often, and that during the war there was a great, unnecessary meat shortage in the area.

Examples of this sort of thing could be multiplied indef-initely were it necessary, but any reader can, by a few minutes' thought, pick out his own. All are the product of legislation, falsely purporting to protect the public, but actually put through by business pressure groups to further their own hog instincts. Hog instincts of corporations or trade groups that strive to get more return for their own effort than other people can get from theirs, are at the root of them all, whether they are disguised as protecting the public health, public safety or public morals.

All the evils enumerated above arose from the practice of giving certain people privileges by statute. Under a free economy they could not have continued, but the force of government has upheld them. Many of the abuses rose from, and are directly or indirectly attributable to, the particular form of privilege given by a government through corporation charters, which were so loosely drawn that they gave rise to many unexpected abuses, in addition to giving the corporation the special privileges that were intended. These abuses became so outrageous as to cause public outcry that government should interfere. But instead of going to the root of the matter and revising or recalling the charters issued, the government has always reacted by passing further laws and establishing commissions to control the abuses it had itself caused by granting undue privilege in the first place. These regulatory government commissions are not often as efficacious as it was hoped they might be, and frequently by further legal tampering with economic natural laws, cause further havoc. For instance, the Interstate Commerce Commission, set up in 1887 to cope with the then outrageous abuses of the railroad corporations, has not in its sixty years of existence accomplished the primary purpose for which it was created, which was to establish the real value of the railroads so that fair and just rates could be established. But it has, by unfair, often stupid and arbitrary regulation, bankrupted railroads repeatedly and retarded the potential development of their service by keeping their earnings at a level that prevents in many cases their saving for capital improvements.

Again, the farmers of the country, who for years have been deprived of their legitimate share of the national income by protective tariffs, are now getting their own back by legally granted special privileges which are causing everybody to pay exorbitantly high prices for food and, incidentally, removing from production a small army of workers by making them inspectors, clerks, etc.

This is done by the government guaranteeing the farmers a very considerable amount as a loan on each crop. This loan is generally more than the price was before the war. As soon as a crop is gathered a farmer may pledge it with the government and receive the loan. If in the next few months the price rises, he may redeem his crop and sell it on the market. If on the other hand it falls below the amount loaned, as it usually does, the government is stuck with it and keeps it. This arrangement is the reason why vast quantities of farm produce are in the hands of the government and force it into such follies as the destruction of millions of bushels of potatoes.

Consider the effect of this. First, the taxpayer is soaked with the loss; second, the price of food and fodder is artificially jacked up against everybody to an absurd figure; third, the government is stuck with a product that it can hardly sell or give away at home without breaking the market; fourth, vast hordes of people are sucked into the bureaucracy to administer all this nonsense, thereby ceasing to be producers and becoming instead parasites on the producers; fifth, the farmers are encouraged by the high loan to grow another big and useless surplus and draw labor and money into this work and away from where they would create more needed wealth.

There are many other kinds of silly laws that have similar uneconomic effects, like the Fair Trade Practices Act which prevents cut-price sales of many kinds of manufactured products of which there are surpluses.

Instances of this kind of economic interference exist everywhere and complaints against them are frequent. Unfortunately they always appear as isolated instances of an abuse that adversely affects a small group and not, as what they really are, namely, symptoms of a general disorder that is destroying our whole economy because our government is trying to redistribute our income and changing the natural channels of production to put money into the pockets of pressure groups. This universal evil, though as yet scarcely seen by any of us, is destroying us all.

At the inception of the United States the favorite form of speculation was to buy tracts of wilderness from the government in order to sell them again in small pieces to future settlers.

Constructing roads that connected these areas to the settlements of course greatly increased their marketability, and hence their value. The roads also were indirectly very beneficial to the states and the country through which they passed because they speeded up its development and settlement.

At first the speculators built the roads to their own tracts, since this brought them profit. Soon they perceived the roads were incidentally doing good to the community at large. Being rich and influential men, they naturally had influence with the legislatures of their states, and by using the argument of the benefit the road brought to the public, they induced the states to contribute a share of the public funds raised by taxation to supplement their own in building roads to these remote areas.

The roads really were a great public benefit. During Jefferson's administration a considerable surplus of funds, mostly from the sale of public lands, accumulated in the United States Treasury. Jefferson decided to use this money to build good, through roads to the West in order to hasten the settlement and to develop trade and bring the products of the back country more easily to markets. Such use of Federal funds is not directly authorized by the Constitution, but as it seemed a good idea at the time and was certainly very beneficial to the country at large, it was carried out without objection. Thus it set a precedent.

If one section of the country might be benefited by the Federal Government at the expense of the whole United States, there was no reason why others should not. Improvement to rivers and harbors particularly benefited those who were living on them, and also indirectly the trade of the whole country. Therefore the practice grew widely and continued after the Treasury surplus had been exhausted and the money had to be collected by taxation.

It was soon noticed that the locality in which such an "improvement" occurred benefited not only from the improvement itself, but rather more from the money brought in by government to effect the improvement, most of which remained in the neighborhood in the form of payment for labor, material, team hire and board bills. This was discovered to be very pleasant. Therefore all congressmen were urged to get as large Federal appropriations as possible for their own district, and, being dependent on the approval of their district, complied. This use of Federal funds grew to be known as the "Pork Barrel." Con-, gressmen got their own appropriation by promising to vote for the appropriation requested by any other Congressman who voted for theirs. This was known as "log rolling." Today this practice is universal and in most districts the politicians judge the efficiency of their representatives by the amount of Federal "pork" he can steer into the district.

Now all the money for these improvements comes from the government of the United States, and the only place that government can get the money is by taxation, which falls on everybody. If one district alone received a Federal improvement that every district in the country paid for, it would undoubtedly get an advantage at the cost of everyone else. But when every district gets a Federal improvement at the expense of every other district there is manifestly heavy cost to all, and none get any special advantage in the form of something taken from someone else. In fact, in the average case each district pays far more than it gets, since its share of the universal high overhead cost of collecting the taxes and administering the appropriations, comes out of it also but does not return. Besides, a horde of tax collectors and administrators are taken out of production forever, to the detriment of the whole economy of the nation.

Furthermore, most of these Federal "improvements" have become pretty frivolous and are designed solely to spend money. Rarely is the improvement so useful that it would be at all likely to draw in private capital for its accomplishment, for then its cost would have to be justified by its future production. Rarely indeed is it so useful that the local people would directly vote their local funds for it. In fact, it is acceptable only as a gift, and that gift is made sweet, not by its result, but by the money wastefully spent in producing it.

Through this custom, we Americans, by our eagerness to use our political power to obtain something for nothing, that is from someone else, have assumed the burden of paying for a lot of almost useless work. We pay for it with our taxes, which might otherwise have gone into our business or pleasure. We pay for it by permanently diverting to government jobs a great number of officials who would otherwise be engaged on production and increasing the country's income and wealth. We also pay for it by the loss of the capital and labor applied to it directly, which in almost all cases would create more national wealth if applied by the taxpayers to building up their own businesses.

We have seen how corporations and industrial pressure groups have been able to secure special privileges by statute. They are not alone in this, for the hog instinct operates as well among members of the professions and organized "small business."

In the early days of this country's history anyone could be, or try to be, whatever he wanted. If a man hung out a lawyer's shingle or a doctor's sign, he was a lawyer or a doctor from that moment. To be sure, if he knew nothing about the job he was trying to do, he almost surely had to change it or starve to death from lack of customers. But if he learned his job he got away with it.

An example is the hand bill advertisement of about 1840, reprinted and widely sold a decade or so ago, in which the advertiser proclaimed himself below his picture:

Attorney at Law

Doctor of Medicine

Civil Engineer and Surveyor

and often assisting in fence-building and butchering.

All of us are familiar with the legend of the itinerant doctor with his rattlesnake oil and other Indian cure-alls. These men lived. They must have made a living.

Few people could have been injured by these charlatans for a man generally investigates a physician or a lawyer before employing him. Some very gullible people were no doubt killed or permanently injured by ignorant doctors, and others probably lost their legal rights through ignorant lawyers. Today gullible people still suffer in the same way! The real trouble in the old days was that too many of these self-styled professionals learned enough to get away with the practice of their profession by practicing it, and made a good living at it. Medicine and the law became overcrowded professions.

The more conventionally educated practitioners begrudged the business taken away from them by their less formally educated brethren, and organized against them. Under the guise of protecting the public, they had statutes passed requiring that licenses be granted by the State to those who would practice their professions. It required a formal education, certificates of character, etc. to pass the examinations necessary to obtain the licenses. It took a long time and much money to get them. Aspirants who had not the wherewithal turned to occupations less carefully fenced in. The medical and legal professions became temporarily less crowded, which was the real objective of those who pressed for this legislation "to safeguard the public." The standards of knowledge and ethics within the professions were probably somewhat improved. Perhaps the legislation was wise, though of course it did partly close the door to two fields of opportunity, and from the point of view of "safeguarding the public" it did not greatly improve things.

Today it may seem a very strange thing for anyone to boggle at the licensing of physicians or lawyers. Yet consider it for a moment. Almost every mature person knows of cases where shocking results have been brought about by the ignorance, stupidity or carelessness of doctors or lawyers. No one has ever heard of one of them losing his license for professional carelessness or ineptitude, and no doctor is ever publicly blamed for his carelessness by another, even where it causes death. In fact, that provision of the Aesculapian oath is the part doctors most closely adhere to. The license hardly seems to protect the public. Again, almost every family contains an amateur physician who doses everybody possible with aspirin, castor oil, sleeping pills, vitamins or whatever is favored. This is perfectly legal provided they make no charge for it. Yet if one of these amateurs, or anyone wise in the use of local herbs, should ask, or even accept, a fee from a grateful patient, he would immediately be criminally prosecuted by the county medical association on whose impounded practice he would be impinging. Therefore, are medical licenses for the benefit of the public or the doctors' professional income?

The same is true of lawyers. Every experienced business man of necessity knows the law relating to his own affairs. This knowledge he imparts to his associates and acquaintances as legal advice. Real estate brokers and income tax "experts" do the same to their customers. The latter, because they are working constantly and exclusively on tax matters, often give sounder advice than the lawyers. This is quite correct so long as they do not charge for their advice. The moment they do so charge, no matter how good their advice, they are likely to be criminally prosecuted by the local bar association. But nothing is ever done to a licensed lawyer who charges for advice that is foolish. Again it is the lawyers' income, not the public weal, that the legal license is designed to protect.

After a number of years, members of other professions saw the advantage that had accrued to the bar and medicine from legislation "safeguarding the public" and making these professions somewhat exclusive. One after another, and almost in the order of the average of the intelligence of their membership, the other professional, or rather occupational, groups banded together and obtained legislation excluding the general public from their particular calling unless a license was acquired. The acquisition of these licenses for new members was beset with as many difficulties as could be obtained from the legislatures. Today architects, plumbers, builders, real estate agents, insurance agents, librarians, barbers, tailors, restaurateurs, automobile mechanics, even "professional" clam diggers, and many others require licenses.

Once more, has anyone ever heard of a member of one of the above "professions" losing his license for inefficient or careless work? The air is full of complaints about the dishonesty, carelessness and inefficiency of plumbers, but none of them ever loses his license. Yet heaven help a gifted but unlicensed plumber who charges for his work in that occupation.

Every village has one or more restaurants. They are all licensed and inspected by a number of government inspectors, as the certificates on their walls show. Often the cooking is horrible; bits of neck or brisket are sold as "porterhouse" or "T-bone steak," many of their kitchens are a filthy, smelling welter of dirty dishes, garbage, grease, rodents and dirt. But the licenses on the wall are considered sufficient to protect the public health. On the other hand, if some capable widow who is a superlative cook tries to make a few dollars by selling clean and delicious meals in her house without a license, she is a criminal.

None of these latter licensed occupations require any special skill or training involving the public interest, although of course proficiency in them increases with practice, as it does in everything. However, the fact that one acquires a license often has little bearing on one's proficiency. In part of New England, for example, anyone willing and able to spend twenty-five dollars can obtain an automobile mechanic's license, whether he knows anything about automobiles or not, whereas the best mechanic in the world is legally barred if he be unwilling or unable to put up the twenty-five dollars.

In 1915 automobiles had just come to be distributed pretty generally into the hands of ordinary people. There was a "World's Fair" in the then outskirts of San Francisco. Daily, such vast hordes of people moved from the center of town to the Fair grounds and back that the street cars and taxis became hopelessly overcrowded. A great number of automobile owners conceived the idea of running back and forth from Market Street to the Fair and taking such chance passengers as hailed them. They charged a nickel for the ride and so were known as "Jitneys." They performed what was then an essential local service. They earned good money. They did no harm to the public. But they did cut into the profits of the local trams and taxis. Therefore, as soon as the urgent need of them passed they were put out of business by licenses. The practice spread to other places where again it was stopped by licenses. It seems to have had a beneficent effect on both car owners and passengers. What possible public good did it do to stop it for the benefit of the licensed trams?

Shopkeepers found that peddlers cut into their profits by selling goods like those on their shelves and often undercutting their prices. And so they obtained local ordinances requiring peddlers to be licensed, nominally to control them, but actually the licenses cost so much that peddling was practically stopped by them. Thus was eliminated one time-honored method used by ambitious young fellows to obtain sufficient capital to start in business. Thus also were local merchants able to band together to hold up their prices against their customers.

The stopping of peddling has had a very serious adverse

effect on farmers, and has added in a curious way a substantial cost to the distribution of food. Almost all farms keep a vegetable, or truck, garden to supply their own needs. They often produce a great surplus of some vegetable or of several vegetables or fruits which they would be glad to sell by peddling, but they rarely can produce a sufficiently large and varied supply to take care of a whole store in a neighboring town. They are forbidden to peddle. The town stores prefer to buy from one source and to be sure of being provided for. The result is that a farmer must, in order to sell at all, get hold of one of the itinerant food buyers who travel the countryside buying farm surpluses at far below production costs. The buyer takes his purchases to the nearest big town and sells to a wholesaler who in turn sells to a retailer, often in a town close to the original farmer. Thus there are three middlemen and an unnecessary double haul of forty to sixty miles between the farmer, who does not get production costs, and the consumer who pays exorbitantly for his product. All to save the shopkeepers from peddler competition.

The same is true of firewood. Most New England farmers have wood lots whose winter cleaning provides more cordwood than can be sold locally at cost. The fuel business of New York and most large cities is controlled by a handful of licensed fuel dealers who charge four or five times the fair price for firewood. So great is the price differential that farmers not infrequently arrange to sell a load of wood in a city at four or five dollars a cord under the city price, and illegally run in and deliver their farm truckload. Such a run from a distance of over a hundred miles, if successfully accomplished, before the war netted the farmer between $125 and $150. Why should the earnings of the farmers and the pleasure of those who enjoy open fires be restricted for the benefit of a few fuel dealers?

The benefit of licenses to the particular group given privileges by them is obvious. But the public is penalized for them by having to pay higher prices. A host of public officials are necessary to prevent infringement of the privileges they give. They throw the work and capital of the nation into unnatural and, therefore, less productive channels. They almost entirely prevent an energetic young fellow from trying several businesses at once, before throwing all his capital and energy into the most propitious line. It may not be in the true public interest to permit many of them, or any of them.

The exploitation of labor by the corporations, the low wages, long hours, bad working and living conditions, and the economic pressure used to swing their vote, all of these largely the product of giving extra privilege to corporations by law, soon caused the workmen to organize to try to protect themselves. This they accomplished because their voting power was enormous. Having obtained approximate justice, the workmen were no longer held together by pressure of circumstance, and their organization somewhat relaxed. It is likely that if left to themselves they would have broken down their organization altogether, its need being past. However, the "Labor Leaders" they had set up, enjoyed their work, salaries, and power, and wished to retain them.

The unions were organized by trades, and for the most part by the more important skilled trades. The leaders of each trade held their particular workmen together by promising to get for them higher pay than the market rate for work of like skill elsewhere. As each union obtained the desired increase, its workmen did not increase their *per capita* output. They therefore did not increase the national income or production; they merely preempted for themselves a larger share of the national income at the expense of everyone else. Their employers, whom they thought they were striking against, did not suffer very much, since they had a sound excuse for raising the cost of their product by a like percentage. It was the public who had to pay for their product who really suffered, by having to spend a greater part of their earnings than formerly for the particular product.

As trade union after trade union adopted this procedure, all prices of union-made goods naturally rose, and it became a very serious matter for the non-union members of the community. It must be remembered that it is not an easy or inexpensive thing to get into one of the highly-paid trade unions where there is a high initiation fee, and much favoritism is naturally practiced in the selection of candidates. Our unions today have much the same effect as the English guilds did in the eighteenth century. Many young men are prevented from entering the trade of their choice and are forced into less profitable forms of work.

Using their power to control great masses of votes, the labor leaders have acquired some extraordinary political privileges, relieving them from conforming in their conduct to established principles. For instance, the leaders were exempted from accounting to the members for the union funds in their hands, nor do the unions pay income taxes on their collections. Furthermore, all unions are largely freed from the binding effects of their own contracts, though management is bound by them, and they are also permitted the legal privilege of using coercion on other people. The above abuses could not stand in a free economy. They are the result of laws giving unions special privileges.

In the 1920's, organized labor took the bit in its teeth and made a drive to shut off foreign immigration. Labor had long objected to immigration as, from their point of view, it kept the labor market constantly oversupplied. Our immigration laws had long been a sort of national scandal, particularly since foreign powers had been making us a dumping ground for their offscourings. As soon as the first war ended, it seemed as if about half the population of Europe might want to emigrate, and Congress, under pressure from unions, cut the number of immigrants to be received from each country to three percent of those born in that country and then resident in the United States. This cut the number of annual immigrants to 309,556. In 1924 the law was again twice changed and it finally crystallized, allowing the immigration of 154,000 persons annually. This curtailment of immigration was primarily a measure for the benefit of organized labor, but the calibre of the immigrants who had been coming in the recent past was such that almost any kind of limitation or exclusion would have been welcomed by the country at large.

Yet was it, in the long run, a wise move? All Americans have been immigrants, or their descendants. Our whole economy has been built on immigration. Every economy must rest on a more or less broad base of cheap and unskilled labor. Day labor is a dreadful occupation. It is back-breaking and mind-stultifying. No one likes it. It produces so little it can never be well paid. Nevertheless, it is necessary, and like all necessary evils in this world, it must be faced and overcome. No one wants to do it except when he has to do it to live, and then only as a stop-gap till he can get some more productive, and so better paid, occupation. Americans, in particular, hate it. Politicians mouth about "the dignity of labor." It has no dignity. It is a horrible chore and anybody who has tried it knows this, as does anyone who thinks about it.

Ever since the foundations of the American Colonies, our people have been famous for the speed and dexterity with which they have gotten through their necessary initial period of day labor, risen to something better and passed the burden to the newcomers who were always more than willing to assume it in their period of initiation. They too, soon rose to better things. Furthermore, until we paralysed our economy by the network of special privileges, there was always plenty for everyone to do. Those in the lowest classes of society rose in the social scale always, often indeed through abilities superior to their initial occupation, but inevitably because a still "lower" class, the newly arrived immigrants, was shoved in below them.

Twenty-five years ago we shut off the stream of immigration. The necessity for the day labor remains. Few Americans will do it, most would rather go on relief. The less essential day labor is not done. The more essential is still done, but paid for at exorbitant rates. Anyone old enough can see by looking at the countryside and the cities how much such labor is needed, and how little is done in comparison with what was done before the first World War.

Furthermore, the successive rising of groups in the social scale has ceased; that of individuals has immensely slowed up. This is very largely the result of the other restraints by privilege with which we have bound our economy, but the stopping of immigration has a lot to do with it.

This can readily be seen if we look at Texas, now easily the most prosperous state in the Union. According to the magazine *Holiday*, November, 1948, in spite of the fact that it is illegal for Mexicans to emigrate from Mexico, the Texas Mexican population has increased from about 350,000 in 1920 to about 1,200,000 in 1940, mostly as a result of Mexicans fording or swimming the Rio Grande—hence their local name of "wet backs." So delighted are the Texans with this influx of low-class labor, that they not only encourage it, but jealously try to hold it in Texas and not let it flow over to other states that pay better wages. This they do by requiring hiring agents from other states to be licensed, and by more direct and less legal means.

The above Texas situation throws a high light of absurdity on our whole system of immigration. If we have, as we have, an immense amount of low-class work to be done at a price, and there are, as there are, thousands of foreigners eager to do it at that price, why should not they be welcomed and everyone made happy?

Another example of the beneficent effect immigration causes is seen in the vast improvement of Palestine since the Jews were allowed to enter it freely. Privilege, of course, is the answer; the privilege of the organized labor here to keep out the others. To this is added the fear that the newcomers may get out of work and on relief. Well they may, if we let them in and continue to practice our other foolish economic policies. Every time we indulge in an economic miracle we also "have to pass four or five more to keep up with it."

Yet is it fair to exclude the waiting foreign thousands who, bound down by their own absurd economic laws, are anxiously clamoring to get in and do for us the needed work we are unwilling to do for ourselves? Is it wise? How many capable, productive Americans are compelled to spend two or three hours a day on essential household chores that they would gladly pay to have done for them if anyone was willing to do them at a reasonable figure? Today a couple of domestic servants get about $400 a month and board, which amounts to at least $1,200 a year more. That is about $6,000 a year, the equivalent of the un-income-taxed investment-return on $150,000. There are few families indeed who can afford such service, and the result is that they have to do the work themselves, to the great injury of their potentially more productive efforts. Meanwhile in Europe there are thousands who, impotent and starving under their own more strangled economies, long to do this work for decent food and a tenth of the pay. Are we wise in preempting for ourselves the sole enjoyment of our less strangled economy?

A grotesque and sardonic twist has been given to the whole situation by the way our immigration law is administered. The idea behind the law reducing immigration to three percent of those born in each country and resident here, was presumably to ensure that we keep on getting the same kind of people we had been getting in the past fifty years, but in smaller quantities, though of all the types. However, our Jews, presumably by harping on the fact that they are discriminated against while seizing every special privilege for themselves that is possible, appear to have managed to get most of the positions on the Immigration Board. According to page 474, *World Almanac*, 1950, the percentage of Jews to our total immigration since 1925 has been as follows (the Jews for this purpose, of course, considering themselves solely as nationals of the countries wherein they dwelt):

1925	3.5	1934	14.03
1926	3.3	1935	13.84
1927	3.4	1936	17.21
1928	3.8	1937	22.59
1929	4.46	1938	29.07
1930	4.77	1939	52.35
1931	5.86	1940	52.21
1932	7.74	1941	45.85
1933	10.28	1942	36.86
		1943	19.83

There apparently are no later figures on the situation, though it is now commonly said in Europe that Jews have priority on our lists of acceptable immigrants. This is a bit tough on the other foreign nationals who want to come here. It is certainly contrary to the intention of the Congress which passed the act, and shows the way the bureaucracy can defeat the Congress. It is, perhaps, injurious to our economy, which needs cheap labor of a sort Jews do not furnish; for their genius resides primarily in commercial enterprise, and of this we have a sufficient native supply.

Since 1920 almost all nations, animated by the same motive, have forbidden or very greatly restricted immigration. This artificial restraint on permitting the people of the earth to move about as they want and are able to, has caused one of those curious situations where a checked economic law forces its way, so to speak, underground and brings up in a totally unexpected place. In this case it has caused a really strong incentive to start a war.

Let us study the matter for a moment. Looking at history, it is evident that nations experience tides of fecundity and sterility. In the 16th century the population of Spain and Portugal expanded suddenly and overflowed South America. In the 17th and 18th centuries that of France, England and tiny Holland did likewise and overflowed all over the world. In the 19th a similar wave struck the United States and caused our settlements east of the Alleghanies to populate our whole area to the Pacific. Later the fecundity of all these peoples dwindled to such a point that some suffered from declining populations. During the periods of expanding populations the people had to have somewhere to go, found places and went, to the great benefit of the economies of the places where they arrived.

In the 20th century these bursts of fecundity struck Italy and Japan and, to a less extent, Germany. After 1920, even the largely empty lands which had hitherto welcomed these peoples and been greatly benefited by them, were suddenly sealed off by legislation. The populations got too big for their national boundaries. They could not even better their condition by heavier industrialization because the universal protective tariffs prevented them from disposing of the wealth they so created. The pressure grew terrific. The solution appeared to them to be to take emptier lands by force and expand in them. Japan tried Manchuria; Italy, Abyssinia; Germany, Poland and Russia. We have seen the result.

Veterans feel properly that the country owes them a great deal for the drab and profitless years they were compelled to spend in military training, and for the terrible hardships and dangers in the campaigns. They want a large share of the national income allocated to them for their past services and they have the voting power to get it. This is a very heavy burden on the whole country. If they get anything like a free distribution, or bonus, or pensions, it is apt to weigh pretty heavily on the veterans themselves. There are now about 18,000,000 of them. That is, their number is about one-half that of the producers of the nation before the war, and about one-third of them today. Therefore each of them will have to pay between half and one-third of his own bonus out of his own earnings, besides paying one-half the cost of the government officials and equipment for collecting the taxes and distributing the bonus! Everyone must pay his share of public gifts of money. When the recipients, who also must pay their share, become so numerous, there is not much gravy in it even for them, and the economic disturbance of so great a payment to the country at large is very severe.

All these practices arose from the efforts of localities and occupational groups using their political power to force a larger share of the national income than they have earned into their own pockets. Their efforts have incidentally created an enormous body of public officials employed in enforcing the special privileges obtained by statute. In the past quarter century these officials have become a sufficiently powerful group to join in the national sport of trying to divert a larger and larger share of the fruits of the national income, or production, into their own pockets. Their methods have not been as direct and as unblushingly forthright as those of the other interests, but nevertheless, when they are considered they become sufficiently obvious.

There has always been a strong American tendency, inherited, perhaps, from our Puritan ancestors, to feel that we are our brother's keepers. This makes us feel that we ought to do good to our neighbor, whether he wants us to or not, and that we ought to compel him to do what we think is good for him, whether he wants to or not. We feel that we are benefiting him and it makes us feel virtuous.

Probably the best example of this type of thought took form in the Eighteenth Amendment and the Volstead Act. Those who did not wish to drink alcohol were not content to abstain themselves, but decided that such drinking was wrong in itself (Christ's example to the contrary notwithstanding), and that they would compel everybody else to avoid this sin, and abstain. The result was a vast number of persons taken out of production and saddled on the taxpayers as enforcement agents, and another vast multitude also removed from it to thwart the former by becoming bootleggers and racketeers.

It did not take the bureaucrats long to see the advantage to themselves which lay in the "do gooders'" tendency to regulate others. They encouraged them in their efforts because it brought into being more bureaucratic jobs to be filled. The results have been very costly to the country, not only in taxes but in time and money wasted by citizens in obtaining licenses, complying with frivolous regulations, and especially in loss of freedom. Here are a few examples.

Sometimes a perfectly sound and sensible idea progresses to madness in the hands of well-intentioned citizens and self-seeking bureaucrats. Most people believe that the public should in some degree assume the care of the insane and feeble-minded poor, and should keep them comfortable and treat them kindly. One state has recently completed a lunatic asylum, which cost for the building alone, without any provision for operation and maintenance, $10,000 per lunatic to be housed. In the same state the State Treasurer—a citizen of the finest type who had given great public service—dwelt with his wife and three children—all splendid citizens—in a house and grounds that had cost him, and was approximately worth, $5,000. It would appear that there is great disproportion here. A state, even with a bad case of "I am my brother's keeper" complex, cannot be justified in imposing on its taxpayers a housing cost for its feeble-minded and least desirable citizens, that is ten times as great *per capita* as that which one of its most desirable citizens feels adequate for himself and family. Of course an asylum with such elaborate and expensive living quarters calls for a host of state employees to keep it up.

Under the influence of "do-gooders" and public officials, a great deal of public money is spent and a great many public officials are employed in trying to avert disasters, such as the collapse of buildings, conflagrations, shipwrecks, etc. In many ways this seems to be wise. Yet proportionally, in spite of all the money and all the officials, buildings seem to collapse about as frequently, and disastrous fires and shipwrecks seem to be about as common today as they were in the early nineteenth century when things were left to themselves. No owner of a building or ship would knowingly permit a hazard to exist, for in the event of a disaster the damage suits invariably bankrupt him and he usually goes to jail. No system of public inspectors seems to help; in fact, we rarely hear of them except as extortioners. The insurance companies are generally the really effective inspectors. The disasters continue to occur with about the same frequency as they used to. As examples, take the Cocoanut Grove fire in Boston in 1942, and the Chicago and Atlanta hotel fires in 1946.

No public inspector was even arrested in any case, though if they had been on their job the loss of life would not have occurred. Is the army of inspectors and the great overhead of employees worth their cost in taxes and in people taken out of production?

Along the same line, all automobile drivers must have a license. Possibly a sound law. Certainly if all car drivers were careful and attentive it would preserve life and limb. Yet do the license tests do any good? They may insure the knowledge of the applicant regarding the necessary motions to make in driving; however, it is not lack of this knowledge, but careless hearts and wandering minds that cause the accidents. The licensing examiner cannot detect these. It is much more difficult to drive a team of horses than a car, yet no license is required. Of course it takes armies of examiners, inspectors and a great office overhead, to enforce these licenses. Pleasant jobs for lots of people who are taken out of production and settled on the taxpayers. The public has to waste a good deal of time and money taking the examinations and renewing the licenses.

All motor boats have to be licensed. To what object, in peace time, unless it be to give a large and expensive group of officials pleasant jobs? Again, it is illegal for pleasure-boaters to fail to carry a life preserver for every person on board. A great number of young men are publicly employed to go about and look for violators of this law. Pleasant for the young men, of course. But is it really any more the government's business that a man goes canoeing without a life-preserver than that he goes out in the rain without his rubbers? If he wants to risk drowning, it is not the public's business. The law is irritating to the individual concerned, costly to the taxpayers, and turns a lot of potential producers into economic parasites. Perhaps the manufacturers of life-preservers engineered its passage.

In the early part of the present century a general mania developed for "public improvements" designed to help the lot of the poorer or least efficient part of the population. The impetus for these improvements came from "do-gooders" and public officials. The bulk of them were carried out by the lower echelons of government and paid for by taxes on the local real estate.

Now it is delightful to have palatial schoolhouses, tarred roads to the remotest cottages, public water-mains, sewers and street lights all over the place, play grounds, etc., etc.—but unfortunately they have to be paid for. The payment falls principally on the land owners at first, which is hard on them. Every fifty dollar increase in taxation really decreases the value of the place taxed by a thousand dollars. That is not always realized, but will readily be seen if one considers these facts. Homes yield no income. The income from the money invested in the home therefore ceases. A man decides he can afford $1,000 a year for a home and so spends $20,000 in purchasing one, thus reducing his income at five percent by $1,000. Suppose when he buys it there are no taxes. Every time the taxes are raised $50 the income of another thousand dollars must be allocated to pay for the house. Thus a home (originally untaxed) which cost $20,000, would, if taxed $500 a year, use up the income of $30,000; $1,000 of it being the loss of income from the original $20,000 and the $500 tax coming from the income of another $10,000 that has to be used for this purpose. Therefore a subsequent purchaser desiring to spend $1,000 a year for a home, could not afford to pay more than $10,000 for the original one.

At first such taxes appear hard on the large landowners, and them alone; particularly since they usually get the least benefit from the improvements. The advantage seems entirely with the less efficient, who not having money enough to be landowners and having a strong voting power, enjoy the improvements and apparently do not have to pay for them. However they unfortunately do have to pay for them, and very heavily.

In the first place, the landowners always have to raise the rents to offset the taxes. In the second, home owners allot a certain amount annually to their homesteads to pay for taxes, maintenance, improvements and developments. The three last items bring work to the poorer people in the community and afford them their livelihood. They also increase the value of the properties and so the wealth of the nation. As taxes increase, the other three items have to be cut down. This is annoying to the landowners, but it is a real hardship on the workers, especially the less efficient who shortly find themselves unemployed.

Unfortunately an economic law is working here. Just as no family can thrive if it over-spends its income on luxuries, so no community can. When a community impoverishes itself by over-spending on luxuries, the greatest tribulation always falls on the least efficient. Therefore extravagant spending on public improvements, far from benefiting the inefficient as it is alleged to do, in fact saddles them ultimately with the greatest part of the hardship resulting from the foolishness.

The mass effect of all these regulatory laws, particularly those giving special privileges and redistributing the national income by taxes, by artificially holding up prices, and by precluding the general public from most kinds of lucrative work in order to protect those presently engaged in such work from competition, has tied up our economy, just as the eighteenth century British regulations tied up the economy of England. When the panic of 1929 occurred, it was no longer possible to cure it in the old-fashioned way, by everyone pulling in his belt and doing whatever he could find to do for whatever he could get, till production got going again at a lower price level and the depression cured itself. Many of those who lost their jobs were prevented by restraining regulations, from doing what they found to do, and were reduced to such jobs as selling apples in the street. Meanwhile government did all it could to maintain the inflationary prices of commodities. Dire poverty resulted.

Quickly the bureaucracy saw an opportunity to increase its numbers and power by administrating relief. Their propaganda departments got busy claiming that the depression was caused by over-production (as if a depression, or general lack of wealth, could possibly have arisen from the over-production of wealth!). Those out of a job were encouraged to go on public relief. Theretofore, Americans had been so loath to go on relief or "on the town" that they would do almost anything to avoid it, for they saw that in so doing they put themselves in the power of the public relief administrators, because where one takes pay one must render service. But now ballyhoo from government agencies in the form of public proclamations, etc., eliminated this dread and made many willing to take the easier path and become a charge on their neighbors. A more or less permanent class of professionally unemployed was established.

The unemployed and their families have a lot of votes. They feel that they are entitled to a sufficient proportion of the nation's production or income to at least maintain them, in spite of the fact that they produce no wealth themselves. Perhaps

they are right, since our unwise economic statutes, giving privileges in such great quantity, are chiefly responsible for their
being unable to support themselves. On the other hand, it must
be remembered that the true function of government is to establish a Rule of Law under which the people may carry on their
lives without undue interference from others; that it is the duty
of the people to support themselves, to watch their government
and hold it to its duty; and that it is not a proper function of
government to support its individual citizens.

Some of the unemployed, like the "Townsend Planners,"
feel that they are entitled to a large proportion of the income
created by the producers of the nation merely because they are
old, and in spite of the fact that they produce no wealth themselves. Others like the "boondogglers" feel that government
should pay them for doing what they want to do, even when
there is no demand for their work and it creates no wealth.
Most, like P.W.A. and W.P.A. workers, feel that they have
honorably earned their pay by raking up leaves in the fall or by
working on unwanted projects that were thought up by government officials, not because they were needed or wanted, but
simply to provide work for the unemployed. No nation ever
helped its economy, nor increased its production and wealth,
by plowing the sands or by building pyramids.

So firmly have the professional unemployed been able to
establish themselves as a class, that, according to the New York
Times of October 25, 1948, there were in New York City alone
137,131 persons on "home relief," that is living at home and able
to look after themselves, but not working, and so being supported by their fellow citizens at a time when every economic
form of activity was screaming for workers and the Times
itself had carried about ten pages of "help wanted" ads the
day before. In a free economy with no "home relief," wherein
the unemployed would have needed money, the whole unemployment situation would have adjusted itself in about a week,
and there would still have been jobs unfilled. But it is pleasant
to loaf on relief, and the professional unemployed are now a
well recognized and powerful class which must be reckoned
with politically. Hardly a week passes without a newspaper account of the discovery of some genius who has been supple-

menting his salary in a good job by collecting "home unemploy-ment relief."

More lately the Jews and Negroes have been busily engaged in arrogating special privileges for themselves by claiming that there is a prejudice against them and that, therefore, they are "underprivileged." By the constant reiteration of this plea, and by political pressure, they have had laws passed which make it a crime for an employer in New York to refuse to hire a Jew or a Negro because he does not like Jews or Negroes. This is a very special privilege. No laws compel an employer to hire an old American, or someone of German, Irish, Polish or Italian ancestry if he does not happen to care for any of those races, nor to hire a Protestant, a Catholic, an Orthodox or a Mormon if he dislikes those religions. A man hiring help should certainly be allowed to get the kind he wants, and to refuse those he dislikes, no matter how foolish the reason for his dislike. Laws of this kind exhibit the very essence of discrimination.

The aggregate result of this grab of special privilege by everyone has bound our economy and slowed down our produc-tion tremendously, if immeasurably. For it will be seen that these attempts to seize by statute more than a fair return for one's work or product result not so much in an increase of the earn-ings of the predator group, as in a reduction of the wealth that might have been produced for the nation.

Manufacturers of plumbing fixtures, or of optical lenses, for example, distribute their products to the public only through a class of retailers highly benefited by licenses, i.e. plumbers and opticians. These retailers are so few and so protected against competition that they are enabled to charge a retail price that is many times the wholesale price, and so apparently make exorbitant profits. As a matter of fact, their attempt at piracy does not result in tremendous profit for their trade as a whole, because the price they impose is so unfairly high that their potential customers are unable to afford it and resign themselves to curtailing their needs. Thus the retailers may get sufficient to live and do less work, as a result of the protection of the license law; but the customers are deprived of what they would like to have and could afford at fair prices, and the country's wealth is reduced by this reduction in the demand. The only beneficial effect to anyone is that the retailers get the same pay for less work.

Exactly the same effect results from the preemption of unfairly high pay by the members of certain unions. They may get higher pay for the work they do, but since the nation can only afford a certain percent of its income for each kind of work, their trade as a whole gets no more in the long run than it would at fair prices. Other citizens are deprived of the potential benefit of their work, since they cannot afford it, and the wealth of the country is reduced by that much, and, as less work must be done, unemployment is increased.

Let us summarize this chapter. It is manifest that the production of the country is the income of the country, and creates its wealth. It is a natural economic law that, when uninterfered with, a man gets an income about equal in value to what he produces. But here we have a picture of every trade, profession, business, locality and association trying by law to get for itself a greater proportion of the fruits of the national production than its productive efforts created. Because of the competition in this absurd and selfish struggle, it is doubtful whether any particular group actually gets more than it earns.

Every group in the nation feels that the government owes them certain favors.

Manufacturers feel it owes them protective tariffs.

Farmers feel it owes them subsidies.

Big business feels it owes them the corporate charters they acquired from it, as well as the other advantages.

Little business feels that by stabilizing prices it should relieve them from the dangers of competition.

Almost every profession, occupation and trade feels that the government should protect them by licenses from the competition caused by too many others getting in on their particular specialty.

Organized labor feels it should keep their pay and hours protected from the competition of those who have not got into their union.

The unemployed and unemployable feel it owes them a living.

The veterans want very special favors of it.

The ineffectives feel that government owes them unemployment and old age insurance and "security" in general.

The coastal regions feel that it should supply them with appropriations for rivers and harbors.

The mountain belt feels it owes them appropriations for irrigation projects.

Everybody and every section of the country wants favors, and the government tries to furnish them. The only place it can get the wherewithal to grant these favors is from the people of the country. Therefore, in order to give to all, it taxes and regulates all, till everyone is so regimented that much of the national enterprise has disappeared. The national production, which is its income, is so tied up it has been dwindling, up to the present boom which cannot last long. This makes the outcry for special favors the louder, and speeds the process along.

So little general opportunity is now left us in the United States, after so much has been preempted as special privilege, that each business and group would benefit if it gave up its own special privileges and received in exchange the general freedom that would come from a like surrender by every other business and group. Such action would restore a truly free economy and open the road to another burst of development such as we enjoyed in the last century. Furthermore, it would free us from supporting the enormous load of bureaucrats now engaged in enforcing special privilege, and change them from parasites on our economy into collaborators in increasing our national income and wealth.

As things are at the moment, the mass of special privileges is causing so many economic injustices and hardships which have to be corrected by giving further privileges (such as useless work to the unemployed), that the process seems likely to continue indefinitely. The logical end of such a course must be the complete regulation of everything and everybody and the general poverty found in all managed economies. In other words, a completely totalitarian state with the people turned into mere productive units, or slaves, to be used at the whim of the authorities, the whole under a Dictator with all privilege and all opportunity in his hands. Such states have been tried often in history, and of late very frequently. They do not appear ever to have been productive of human happiness or welfare.

CHAPTER 7

THE BUREAUCRACY

"Wheresoever the carcase is, there will the eagles be gathered together."

MATT., 24, 28

IN THE EARLY DAYS of our republic, we had a very light government. The enthusiasm of our citizens for it knew no bounds. This is evidenced in most of the writings and speeches of the time. In fact, the enthusiasm was so blatant it was frequently a subject of ridicule to visiting foreigners. By 1900 we were rather apathetic about our government, cheering for it, perhaps, on the Fourth of July, but not thinking about it much. Today we are crushed by it; and what most of our citizens say about it once or twice a week would have to be censored.

The bald government statistics in 1800 and today will show us why this is so.

In 1800, when the Federal government moved to Washington, all its officials and all its clerks amounted all together to 126 persons! At that time the states, counties, cities and towns had hardly any salaried officials. The officials they had were paid by the fee system; that is, citizens who wanted work done by a public official, paid for that work themselves at a fixed rate, and quite fairly. In 1800, the population amounted to 5,308,483. Disregarding the salaried state and local officials who were practically non-existent, there was then one salaried public servant for every 42,130 people in the country—a light weight to carry, surely!

Apparently there are today about 3,000,000 Federal employees of all classes exclusive of the Army, Navy and Airforce. The *Statistical Abstract* of the U. S. states that in 1942 there were approximately 2,000,000 state, county, city and village officials. That will have grown since. Assume the population of the U.S. to be at present about 140,000,000. Then there must be about one Federal employee to every 46 of the population. Almost 1000 times as many in proportion to the population as there were in 1800. If also the number of state and local government officials are figured in, there must be approximately one public official to every 28 of the population, counting the men, women and children, giving us a total bureaucracy 1500 times or 150,000 percent as heavy *per capita* load as it was in 1800. Only a handful of these people are producing anything; many because of their jobs are impeding production.

During the 1930's there were about 40,000,000 persons gainfully employed. If one in eight of these people was in government, it means that they were producing no true income for the nation, and that every producer, in addition to supporting his own family and dependents, had, through taxes, to support one-seventh of these bureaucrats as well as his family and dependents, out of what he produced.

Remember that each and every employee of government causes a double drain on the production or income of our economy. The first because his potential production ceases on entering the bureaucracy; the second because his salary is a levy on the income of the remaining producers. During the thirteen years immediately preceding the Second World War the cost of government amounted to 28 percent of the entire annual income of the nation. The employment of one-eighth of our potential producers by government reduced our potential income to 87½ percent of its potentiality. Cost of government took 28 percent of the remaining percentage, thus reducing our national income to 63 percent of its potential size.* With such a load, how then can the producers save enough to become rich and to prosper? From whence is to come the productive capital to develop new machinery for production, or even to maintain what we have, so that as a nation we may produce wealth, increase our income, and prosper?

* $1 - \frac{1}{8} - (\frac{7}{8} \times .28) = 63\%$.

Statistics are generally dull but the last paragraph will bear re-reading.

The last chapter dealt with the mania of every conceivable group in the nation to acquire as privilege, by force of law, a greater percentage of the national income than they had fairly earned. One of the by-products of this is the huge bureaucracy. It became essential, in order to enforce the myriads of laws giving special privileges to particular groups, to hire a vast army of public officials examining, licensing, recording, inspecting and enforcing these laws giving privilege. Each of these laws slightly restrained the freedom and opportunity of the many for the supposed considerable benefit of the few. Each of them required the hiring of public servants to support the privileges conferred.

We have seen that a few public officials are necessary to prevent the people's hurting and interfering with one another too much. (Unfortunately people can never be prevented from doing this somewhat.) These few are more essential than any producer, because they control and establish the conditions which permit all the producers to function without undue interference, and permit all to plan, shape and lead their lives unimpeded by others under "the Rule of Law." Beyond this bare minimum, every public employee is a parasite on the community, for he consumes what he and his dependents use (which others have produced), and gives nothing in return. Furthermore, if he is engaged in enforcing some law designed to give economic privilege to some group, as most of those in America today are doing, he is not only as completely useless as one who plows the sand, he is actually slowing up production by turning it into unnatural, and so less efficient, channels, and he is also reducing the freedom and opportunity of all. This is not his fault. It is the fault of us who hired him. It would appear from the first few paragraphs of this chapter that one-eighth of our potentially productive citizens are engaged on this destructive work at the moment.

We call our government a democratic one because at intervals we elect a few thousand persons to be our legislators, executives, and in some places our judges. These elected ones

have nominal authority over the five million odd appointed ones
who form our bureaucracy. But these five million are in almost
all but theory, our government. To be sure we do not elect them.
We have no authority over them. However, they have plenty of
authority over us. They regulate every phase of our lives, what
shall be the traffic rules, the sanitary regulations, how our business shall be run, etc. The higher bureaucrats, by the subtle
use of censorshsip and of propaganda, are very nearly able to
arrange what we shall think. We, as free citizens, are supposed
to have granted them our own authority to use over us. We
certainly have the privilege of paying them their salaries out
of our earnings. They are virtually our government, since they
govern us. What kind of people are they? Where do they come
from?

They are mostly awfully nice people. If you study them
you will find that nearly all of them come from the best families
in the localities, or at least have many friends among the best
families. For generations, and right up to now, it has been our
amiable custom to find a place in some government office for
any nice fellow we knew, or whose family we knew, as soon
as he had definitely proved himself incapable of making a decent
living in private enterprise. Everybody, of course, used to try
private enterprise first, with an idea of getting rich and bettering himself. But when any of the "right people" failed, we could
not let them and their wives sink to the gutter. It was manifestly
too hard on their worthwhile relatives to expect them to support
the fallen. In a public office they had a certain prestige, enough
salary to keep up a decent front, probably nothing much to do,
and it didn't seem to make much difference how stupid they
were. They probably could not do much harm. So into public
office they went, and seemed ideally suited for it. They are
delightful people, really; slow, easy-going, good tempered, kindly,
and many of them have great charm. Of course they have not
much business or financial sense or they would have remained
in private enterprise. Yet it is true that when a difficult problem comes up—one that we don't feel we want to cope with
ourselves, and say, "Oh, let the government handle that"—they
are the people who do handle it, and with our money.

Since a public official, or bureaucrat, in performing his
duties is carrying out the expressed will of the whole of society,

he must have authority within his sphere. This authority gives him a feeling of self-importance which is pleasant. After tasting it, a man's appetite for it grows. He seeks to increase it by getting more authority. He does this by explaining to anybody who will listen, the additional benefits that government (i.e., government as represented by himself) might confer, if it (i.e., he) had more authority. If his explanations are plausible and are accepted by the politically powerful so that he gets the additional authority, he generally finds that he is provided with assistants and that his pay is increased commensurably with his duties. This also is pleasing to him.

Spending money is an exercise of power. It is applying the stored energy of past labor to the problem at hand. If one spends one's own money, one is thoughtful and careful so to apply it that the effect of the energy expended stores up new energy for future use. Public servants are not spending their own money and, therefore, are largely relieved of this burden of thought and care. In fact, they find that the more of the public's money they can obtain authorization to spend for their work, the greater the salary they are given to spend for themselves.

There is a constant tendency for all governments to grow both in size and in authority, because the advantage of a big, powerful government, from the point of view of the bureaucrats, is personal, clear and ever-present to their eyes; and because the cost of it, not only in money but in freedom, which is lost by giving authority to officials, is vague and nebulous in the minds of the citizens whose attention is not focused on the government at all, but is directed toward other matters. Therefore, since the bureaucrats know exactly what they want and are working for their own immediate interest, and since the other citizens do not realize what they are giving up, and, in fact, have not their attention on the matter at all, it is obvious which group will prevail. That is why governments as they grow older become heavier, more expensive, more burdensome and interfering, until their weight is insupportable and the people are obliged at last to reform them.

This is true of all governments, but in the United States there is another force at work which considerably accelerates this process. We elect the higher executives in each stratum of government, the legislators, and, in some places, the judges.

These are chosen from among those whose ambition it is to hold office, as distinct from those who are best qualified to perform the office. A candidate has an enormous amount of work to do. First he has to convince the leaders of his own political party that his nomination will be more advantageous to them individually and collectively than the nomination of any of the other aspirants will be. Then he has to convince the majority of the electorate that his election will be more advantageous to them than that of the nominee of any other party.

The work involved in doing this, even for a fairly small office, is very great; much greater than any one man can do alone. He must rely on the work of other people. These may be friends who work from personal loyalty, but they have to be friends who know how to do the work, that is, politicians. Few men have many such friends who will work for them purely from enthusiasm. The great majority have to be paid for it in some way. Paying for this work in cash out of his own pocket is very expensive and unpleasant to the candidate, besides it savors of bribery and corruption. Paying for it out of subscriptions from well-wishers, that is out of campaign funds, involves two difficulties; the actual work and expense of the collection, and the fact that most of the subscribers tacitly expect political favors as a *quid pro quo* for their subscriptions. The most usual and the best regarded practice is for the candidate to promise jobs, i.e. salaried positions in the bureaucracy, in the event of his election. Such a job, if important enough, is sometimes promised to a particularly influential leader who wants it. More often the nomination of a number of appointments to small jobs is promised to a political boss or leader who will know how to parcel them out among his henchmen in such a way as to secure by means of them the maximum number of votes.

This system has two considerable advantages from the point of view of a candidate. First, the public pays his election expenses (though most of the public does not know it) and he is relieved of much trouble and expense. Second, the people who do the work are paid only in the event of the candidate's success. The remuneration is very large in proportion to the work done, as it always is with contingent fees. Therefore the workers are willing to work especially hard in order to achieve the contingency that will bring them so great a reward. This is peculiarly desirable to the candidate. It is also an advantage to him, because in the event of his defeat, he has practically nothing to pay and has sacrificed to his patriotism only his time.

Viewed from the point of the nation's prosperity, however, the system is not advantageous. For whoever wins, the public has an additional number of bureaucrats saddled on it to be paid for in taxes and removed indefinitely from producing wealth for the nation. Because of this practice politicians are always anxious to create new jobs against all sense and reason. The laws pre-empting privileges for occupational groups, the laws for the protection of the public, no matter how silly, were godsends to them as opportunities to create more jobs that needed filling.

It is the American fashion to laugh at the countries of eighteenth century Europe because their people were willing to support splendid, idle, worthless and parasitic courts out of the taxes on their earnings. But though the members of those courts lived in great splendor, and far more luxuriously than do our bureaucratic clerks today, yet their comparative expense was a mere drop in the bucket compared to the cost of our great, mid-twentieth-century American bureaucracy. In fact, aside from the expense, there was an advantage in the royal courts. They did no particular harm except to themselves, and their antics were a constant source of interest and amusement to the people.

There is a danger inherent in an army of bureaucrats that was absent from the great courts. It is the danger of too much government. Every bureaucrat has really two distinct kinds of work. His most serious, though unofficial, unstated and merely implied task, is that of getting and keeping a number of votes pledged to his patron, be that patron a politician or a political party. This, from his point of view, is his real job, as on it largely depends his success and advancement. All bureaucrats are ex-pected to do this, and each does it to the degree of his ability. Almost everyone will vote for anyone in order to help a relative or close friend to get a job or a promotion. This explains why members of large families find it so much easier to get political appointments and preferment than those who are comparatively alone in the world. They control more votes.

Their other job is the one they are ostensibly hired to

perform. Even bureaucrats have to appear to justify their existence by being busy. There are two requisites for a bureaucrat's promotion, the first, the ability to get and hold votes, the second, the number of subordinates he is able to keep busy. In fact, in the Federal Government the pay of a bureaucrat executive is proportioned by Civil Service law to the number of his subordinates. This leads to the rivalry in Washington as each petty bureaucratic chief tries to increase his "empire." Generally, in order to keep his subordinates busy the boss assumes an air of great importance and affects to be very hurried and under great pressure. He is very punctual at the office and insists that everyone else be. He then deliberately begins to multiply paper work, calling for reports on any subject connected with his job. He issues enormously complicated orders and memoranda for the organization of his office, requiring that all papers be so routed round it that almost every scrap has to be read by everyone in the office and discussed by a number of interlocking committees before it is acted upon. He requires that no paper be thrown away, but that all shall be cross-indexed and filed. He has anybody who can be tagged, interviewed, a stenographic report made of the interview and typed (often he has them mimeographed), and circulated to be read and initialed. By these methods it is quite easy to take an amount of work that could be done easily and efficiently by three men and two stenographers, and blow it up so that it can keep from fifty to two hundred people extremely busy, and yet fall far behind in its execution. Thus the uncompleted work gives him an apparently sound excuse for more clerks, who increase his prestige and his pay.

During the war there was a government department whose work—supposing it was worth doing, which is doubtful—could have been effectively done by about twenty people. It was run by a man with a bureaucratic soul. He asked written opinions from everybody on all kinds of subjects and had everyone else read and initial those opinions. He was always intensely busy himself, even at night; and he kept constantly increasing his department till he got it up to two hundred men and women. This made him very important. All the two hundred were so busy carrying out his regulations that they were in a constant sweat and confusion, had no time to think, and the essential

work in support of the war effort—supposing it was essential—
suffered dreadfully. He was rewarded and translated to a more
important job.

He was succeeded by a different character—a pleasant
gentleman of the old American type with a sense of humor and
of duty, who had little ambition and apparently not much regard
for the taxpayer, but who wanted the work done and to have
everyone contented. He spent about half an hour in his office
each morning the first week, as against about twelve hours a
day so spent by his predecessor. From 9:30 to 3 he walked
around the office talking and cracking jokes with the help. Then
he played golf. At the end of the week he fired about fifty of
the two hundred people, apparently at random. The work les-
sened considerably for the remaining ones. There was much
discussion of the upheaval and it was generally decided that
he had fired the fifty he was sure he did not like. Not a very
scientific way of eliminating surplus help, but it did lighten the
work.

About a week later fifty more were fired. This time the
axe apparently fell on those he thought he did not like. The work
for the remainder lightened enormously, though some of the
essential work of those dismissed was apportioned round silently
by those that remained.

Shortly thereafter about fifty more were let out. These, it
was said, were those he was not sure he did like. With three-
quarters of the force eliminated there was practically nothing
left but the "essential work," such as it was, to do. This was
done efficiently in about half a day by the fifty personnel remaining; far more efficiently than it had been done by the original two hundred. The fifty did their stuff and devoted the time
remaining—about half of it—to their own concerns.

The old gentleman, being now surrounded only by those
he knew he liked, felt he had done enough. He was generally
in his office from an hour or an hour-and-a-half a day. Then
he evaporated. The "work" was far better done than it had been,
people had time to think and were not in each other's way. It
probably could have been done by half of those remaining, but
that half would then have had to work about as hard as the
original two hundred had worked and there would have been
no benefit to anyone but the taxpayers. It is quite probable that

if the whole department had been eliminated the real "war effort" would have scarcely noticed it and not been harmed at all.

This is an illuminating story and could be advantageously applied, it is feared, to any part of the whole bureaucracy.

In order to show the present condition of the bureaucracy, an article, "Our Spendthrift Federal Government," is here quoted almost in full from *The Reader's Digest* of November, 1948:

> Determined to pare excessive Government costs, the House Appropriations Committee early this year sent a group of ex-FBI operatives into the federal agencies to ascertain why they currently require a budget of $43,800,000,000.
>
> They went, for example, into the State Department. They found there some of the reasons why that department had *11,000 more employees on its payroll than at the peak of the war.*
>
> To check on clerical procedure, the investigators took a letter at random from the department's files. It was a U.S. citizen's request that $100 which he enclosed be forwarded to the American Mission at Bucharest to pay his son's airplane passage from there to Prague. In any business office a clerk could have disposed of the matter in a few minutes. Tracing that letter through the department, the investigators found that it had gone twice through three buildings. En route it accumulated a multitude of initialings, forms, directives and copies. It underwent 35 separate processings. Before action could be completed, it consumed the equivalent of one person's time for an estimated 30 days!
>
> The State Department has paid 410 persons $1,449,000 annually just to plan and safeguard expenditures. Yet bills have been sent to only a few of the Americans who, on being stranded abroad, have been lent an estimated $22,000,000 since the beginning of the war so they might return home. More than a thousand of these debtors made overtures to pay. Their letters were filed without reply. Similarly, this division failed to detect a $100,000,000 bookkeeping error resulting in an overpayment to UNRRA. The Congressional investigators called attention to it!
>
> These are some of the reasons why federal expenditures

today are equivalent to 26 percent of all the privately produced income in the United States, as against about four percent in 1929 and less than 12 percent in the 1937 record New Deal year of deficit spending. Through direct taxes and higher prices which cover indirect taxes, the people last year spent nearly as much on the federal government as they did for food, two and a half times as much as for all their housing. Today there are nearly twice as many federal employes as at the crest of the prewar New Deal.

The Agriculture Department today has five different programs dealing with soil conservation. Its National Forests lands have increased only 11 percent since 1933, yet the estimated financial requirements for administering these have risen 280 percent.

The Navy soon should have surplus hospitals capable of accommodating 20,000 veterans. But the Veterans' Administration refuses to use these available beds. Instead it is spending a billion dollars for new hospitals. The cost—up to $23,600 per bed—is more than double that of the average non-Government metropolitan hospital. Furthermore, official records show that ills having no connection with war service account for 83 out of every 100 veterans already admitted to hospitals and 99 out of every 100 on the waiting list. Meanwhile, the Veterans' Administration payroll has grown to 192,000—one for every 15 living or dead veterans since the Mexican War on whose account compensation or pensions are being paid.

The theory always has been that public works should be expanded in bad times, contracted in good. Yet public works now are costing $2,000,000,000 annually—five times the price of the Panama Canal—with the bill going up a quarter billion a year under commitments for the future.

No less than 29 Government agencies are engaged in lending money, 34 in acquiring land, 16 in wildlife preservation, 12 in home and community planning, 28 in welfare, 14 in forestry, 65 in gathering statistics.

Sample surveys, made in two counties by the Council on Intergovernmental Relations, disclosed 36 units of federal government busy in Blue Earth County, Minnesota, and 106 in Henry County, Indiana. Ten federal groups were active in the public health field alone—the Public Health Service, the U. S.

Marshal's Office, the Food and Drug Administration, the Social Security Administration, the U. S. Children's Bureau, plus five branches of the Agriculture Department. All ten were financing projects on the local level. They not only trod on each other's toes but also competed with state and community organizations doing the same work.

Indicative of bureaucracy's attitude toward use of public money is a statement made by Interior Secretary J. A. Krug to the chiefs of the Bureau of Reclamation. "One of the most embarrassing things I have to contend with," said the Secretary, "is that every time we go over to the Budget and talk about our desperate and dire need for money, they lay up to us that you boys are sitting on the money bags. I would rather some year run over, and perhaps invite supplemental appropriations, than have these huge carry-overs we can't explain ... I am going to have a good look at the picture at the end of the year, and I am going to hold you fellows accountable. I don't think just because it is a desirable policy for the housewife or frugal father to have a big kitty in the bank that it is smart policy for the Bureau of Reclamation."

Hundreds of patriotic business men flocked to Washington at the beginning of the war in the hope they could help the war effort. Many of them retired shortly, completely baffled and confused by what they termed "the inefficiency of the people in Washington." They did not realize that the bureaucrats were extremely efficient in obtaining their objective. That objective was not the accomplishment of the work, which the business men generally and erroneously assumed it to be, but rather to employ as many men as possible in its accomplishment, and so to increase their own prestige and pay. In this they were highly efficient. Business men are trained to accomplish the maximum of work with the minimum of effort and labor, and they are paid in accordance with their ingenuity in accomplishing results with the least expenditure of time and money, because they are always up against the natural economic law. Bureaucrats are trained to use as much help as possible in accomplishing their work, so that thereby they can line up as many votes as possible. The objectives are quite different.

If a bureaucrat's office regulates private enterprise, he can further increase the work of his department by constantly issuing questionnaires to the businesses controlled, and by frequently changing the forms of the reports required. This gives much work and requires a great deal of help in his department. Incidentally, it drives the business men distracted, and keeps the bulk of their attention on making the reports, and not on their business, to the great detriment of the latter. Furthermore, it necessitates that each large business keep a small army of statisticians constantly answering these questionnaires at great expense.

The cost of these statisticians and record keepers (and there are legions of them scattered in great and small businesses all over the country) should be regarded from the point of view of the national economy, as government expense. For although they are paid by the individual businesses, they are made necessary by government, they are taken out of the production of wealth, and their cost is in truth a form of tax imposed by the government on the concerns that must maintain them.

Another method that bureaucrats practice to gain power and prestige is to inch out of the territory over which statutes have given them supervision and control, and to encroach on the freedom of citizens remaining beyond that area, to the further destruction of liberty. This is a very easy thing for bureaucrats to do. As a case in point, in 1942 there was a graduated income tax practically confiscatory on incomes above $25,000 a year. There was also a heavy tax on gifts to individuals. A good many rich people paid this tax and made gifts to their children of sufficient capital to support them on the income, in lieu of paying them an allowance. After the gifts had been made and the gift taxes paid in accordance with the laws enacted by Congress, the bureaucrats of the Treasury Department ruled that, since the individual had to support his children anyway, the gift was an evasion of the income tax, and that the donor must in future pay the tax on his own income plus that on the income of the gifts! This was later somewhat modified by the courts.

Bureaucrats, like most of the rest of us, associate chiefly with people in their own line of business. Also like the rest of us, they are apt to talk a good deal about their business and how to improve it. From their point of view, improving it consists in increasing the amount of government "service." They constantly hear one another say that the public needs and wants some additional service, until they get to believe it. Then they go about working for it and saying with full sincerity (for they have heard each other say it so often) that the public "demands" this particular additional government service. Their sincerity and the evidence they offer thus often bring it into effect.

Bureaucrats often talk about economy; for they know they must keep within their appropriations, and that further appropriations are sometimes hard to obtain. Their views on economy, however, are sometimes quaint. It is not unusual to hear them say, when discussing a prospective new bureau designed to regulate and license some additional business, that such a bureau "will pay for itself." They mean by this that no general tax need be levied to support it because the cost of the license fees will carry the new corps of public officials and their overhead. They do not appear to realize at all that the cost of the new licenses must be passed on to the public by the licensees in the form of higher prices, and that these higher prices are a concealed form of tax, nor that the regulations issued by the new bureau constitute a further grant of privileges and so a further curtailment of liberty and opportunity that must be borne by the general public and its economy.

For a long time our bureaucracy was operated under the "Spoils System." This name is derived from the classic slogan: "To the victor belong the spoils." In former days all appointments to the bureaucracy were made by the political party in power. When that party was defeated, all the bureaucrats in office were immediately thrown out and their places were filled by faithful heelers of the victorious party. It was not a very noble system. It was not conducive to efficient governmental administration, for it often got people who were clerically incompetent into office, and besides, time and again, at about the time the new incumbents had learned their jobs, they were thrown out by the next election. It did have certain virtues, however. It prevented anyone from becoming a bureaucrat for life and so losing completely the point of view of the man on

the street. It also permitted the elected officials to reward their
political workers by *changing,* instead of *increasing,* the bureaucracy.

Its defects, however, were so glaring and annoying that
as time went on Civil Service laws were passed. These required
that, in addition to receiving an appointment, a candidate for
the bureaucracy had to pass a mental examination and have
certificates of character, etc. Once installed in the bureaucracy
under the civil service, the incumbent was there for life, or
during good behavior. He need worry no more about his economic status. These laws, however, made it more difficult for
the elected officials, because in order to reward their political
workers, they now had to devise new jobs for them instead of
merely turning out the incumbents of the opposing party and
filling their jobs. The result, of course, has been a great increase
in the number of jobs, and thus in taxes, with the accompanying
increase in the restrictions on the freedom and opportunity of
the citizens. Furthermore, since, under the Civil Service laws,
appointees became members of the bureaucracy for life, the
bureaucrats were given a strong incentive to organize and form
a powerful bureaucratic lobby. Because of their political influence this became very powerful indeed.

With all these human tendencies clandestinely at work
and no conscious effort being made to control them, the bureaucracy grew fairly rapidly. By the beginning of the First World
War it was far too big and economically wasteful, but it was
not the enormous economic burden it has since become, nor had
it reached the stage of being a great power in the land—a
crushing incubus. In 1916 the number of Federal employees
was 480,327 in a population of about 100 million, or one for
every 208½ citizens, instead of one for every 43 as it is today.

There had been all along one brake on the growth of the
bureaucracy that very considerably slowed it. People hate to pay
taxes. Up till the First World War they were very loath to
create a public debt. Therefore, whenever public officials got
rambunctious, hired a lot of people and spent a lot of money,
taxes rose at once. This made the voters mad and they "turned
the spenders out" and put in an "economy administration." This
restraint held the bureaucracy within reason. It was shortly to
be removed.

In 1913, the Sixteenth Amendment to the Constitution was adopted, giving the Federal government authority to tax incomes directly. About this time some states also imposed an income tax. The full evil effects of the income tax on the national economy will be discussed in the next chapter. Suffice it to say here that one of its effects was to remove a great part of the cost of government from the backs of the general public and to settle it on a comparative handful of very rich men who were numerically so few that they had virtually no political power whatever. Their howls of protest evoked only howls of laughter. Thus the greatest restraint on the growth of the bureaucracy was removed, and it proceeded to grow and spread like a jungle vine. The figures of its growth are too tedious to quote in full, but readers with statistical minds will find them, for the various years, in the *World Almanacs* which can be consulted in any village library.

The income tax was a bonanza for the bureaucracy. When it was coupled with the Civil Service law, it was a gift from heaven. The job holders had been too many, but still, politically speaking, they had been comparatively few. They had, up till these laws, held their positions temporarily, until a change of party at election threw them back to earn what living they could in the production of wealth as ordinary citizens. They had not been a class—merely a group of people temporarily doing the same kind of work. The Civil Service law gave them a life tenure of their jobs—welded them into a class. The income tax permitted the elected officials to increase this class vastly, and without serious protest, by paying their political workers with jobs. The bureaucracy had vast funds to spend. Therefore vast power. They were the boys who had accomplished the election of the legislators, "put the buttons on them," to speak vulgarly. This did not detract from their power to get legislation favorable to themselves. Shortly they organized themselves closely and efficiently.

Soon the bureaucrats as a class began to get unpopular with the citizens, who did not like the way they were being restrained and ordered round by public officials. The bureaucrats dimly sensed this and very quietly began organizing "publicity bureaus," that is, propaganda bureaus, to "educate the public" into believing in the divine wisdom and beneficence of the gov-

ernment (as represented by themselves) in managing everything
and everybody. These official propaganda agencies developed
enormously during the Second World War when, of course,
it became "necessary" to build up public morale and teach the
public the high purpose of their leaders and the necessity of
self-sacrifice. Propaganda bureaus disseminate true information
when it suits their purpose. They suppress or distort it when
it suits their purpose. They fabricate lies that have no basis of
fact, when it suits them. Then they publish this assorted mixture
as THE TRUTH, under the authenticating stamp of government.

Now the axiom on which the theory of democratic government is based is that the majority of the people can always decide
on the facts what is to their best interest, better than anyone
else can. What, then, becomes of democratic government when
the facts on which the people must base their decision are suppressed or distorted into downright lies, and promulgated as
the truth? This question will bear considerable thought, for
without free access to knowledge of the truth no democratic
government can function. In March 1947, according to the New
York *Journal* the Federal Government was spending $75,000,000
of the taxpayer's money per annum on this sort of deception,
and employing some 43,000 bureaucrats on the unsavory work.

In the United States there have always been different
hierarchies or organizations of bureaucracy. Because of the way
our country developed, we have many largely autonomous kinds
of government—districts (school, fire, water, etc.), villages, cities,
towns, counties, states and Federal. All of these, except the
districts, were designed so that each one could function practically alone. In the old days this made sense, because distances
were so great because of the then modes of travel. Therefore
each has most government functions—the administration of
justice, the police, the maintenance and building of roads, the
care of the poor, of criminals, of traffic and of other regulatory
laws. The authority of each overlaps the other, causing much
duplication of effort and confusion, which is sometimes somewhat simplified by gentlemen's agreements between the officials
of the various echelons. In each echelon the bureaucracy has
grown inordinately as time passed. Each police unit, road unit,

etc., etc., has to have its own set-up, its headquarters, its record files, its clerks and its administrators. The confusion and over-lapping of functions is almost inextricable. Few bureaucrats thoroughly understand it even in their own departments. It is doubtful if anyone completely understands it. From the point of view of providing jobs for the maximum number of faithful political workers, the set-up is, with its innumerable central offices and overhead departments, a masterpiece of efficiency. Furthermore, the whole system of all these overlapping government units forms the most intricate sort of maze, a maze into which all the bureaucrats can retire, and so befuddle the public, as to the responsibility for any particularly unpopular or out-rageously wasteful expenditure, that no one can be punished.

All bureaucrats, of every echelon of government, work together for the benefit of their class. They are all members of the same lodge, so to speak. The ones in the larger government sections try to gain control of the smaller ones so they can employ more people in drawing up orders for them and pre-paring questionnaires for reports from them, and tabulating the answers and filing the whole mess. The smaller ones are nothing loath, as they in turn can also employ more people carrying out the orders and answering the questionnaires.

Some time in the early part of the century, some bureau-cratic genius invented the system of having the larger echelons of government bribe the smaller ones to incur heavy expenses by offering to share part of the expense. For instance, the State Board of Education will tell the school districts that if a school district will build a schoolhouse of a certain expensive type, and hire a certain number of teachers of a certain designated class, janitors, etc., the state will then meet one half of these expen-ditures. Of course, in exchange for this bounty the state demands certain rights of supervision and control, and a great many reports. The principal of the school will put this proposition up to the citizens of the school district in such a way that it appears to the citizens that they are getting something for nothing, and they generally vote for it with enthusiasm. No mention, of course, is made of the fact that the citizens are taxed for half the increase in expenses as residents of the school district, and for the other half in their capacity as citizens of the state, (since every other school district is doing the same thing) and for a good deal besides in the shape of the tremendous overhead built up. The citizens forget this detail in their enthusiasm! They do not get something for nothing; in fact, they pay exorbitantly for what they do get. They also forget that, generally speaking, government functions that are run most directly by the people close by, serve their interest best, and that the more remote the control the more inefficient the service. Many of us have seen the high school girls in country school districts being taught typing and stenography under state controlled education, but not taught cooking; while in the district where most of them will probably continue to live, there are not ten typewriters outside of the school, and yet everybody eats, and country cooking is often deplorably poor.

Again, the citizens forget that all public school teachers have gradually become bureaucrats, and have learned all the bureaucratic tricks to increase their pay and comforts. The teachers are better organized than most, on a nation-wide basis, and have probably the strongest single bureaucratic lobby in the country, since they are somewhat more intelligent than other office holders and can effectively get their propaganda to the voters through their pupils and through Parent-Teacher associations. Unfortunately also, the teachers are generally using their power to further their own interests and that of the bureaucracy generally, and not particularly for the good of the children. They are for the most part shortsightedly throwing their influence against free enterprise and free opportunity, though both these are advantageous to the bulk of the citizenry and apparently necessary to create wealth for the country as a whole. So blatant have they become that, according to the New York *Times,* at a meeting of the American Council on Education on May 3, 1947, the president of one of the subordinate teachers' groups demanded that seven percent of the country's entire income be spent for schools, thus doubling the present apportionment!

School districts are not the only small units of government that are so bribed by larger ones on the theory that they are getting something for nothing. The racket is especially virulent in the building and maintenance of roads. Villages, towns, counties and states are so bribed by town aid, county aid, state aid, and even Federal aid roads. In a more subtle manner, local relief work is being taken over by higher and higher echelons of government, without the taxpayer being given an opportunity to vote on it. In the same way county agricultural agents are being controlled and absorbed into the control of the Federal Department of Agriculture.

This system of the higher echelons of government getting control of the lower ones is new in this country and not fully developed as yet. When it started, the public authorized it, believing that as citizens of the lower governmental echelon they were getting something for nothing, and not realizing that they were paying for it in full, and a great overhead besides, in their various capacities as citizens of the lower (grantee) echelon as well as citizens of the higher (grantor) echelon of government. It is a system that is admirably adapted to unifying and organizing the whole bureaucracy into a coordinated whole with a centralized hierarchy of command, for each higher echelon's bureaucrats give favors, work and money into the hands of the bureaucrats of the lower echelons, and by the same token take command of them.

In this way the 5,000,000 bureaucrats in the country are being closely organized into a single force, a mighty army, as it were, under the command of one man; for the bureaucrats of the higher echelons of government are coming to control those of the lower, and the bureaucrats of the highest echelon of government, that is the Federal Government, are, so far as their power is concerned, completely under the hand of the President of the United States.

Before it is too late it may be well for us, the American people, to check this novel and growing system of ours. Five million people, all in the government and all under the control of one man, is quite a severe threat to our liberty. It is virtually giving absolute dictatorial power to one man. Stalin, with 3 million party members, controls 180 million Russians, their lives and deaths, their work and amusements, their manner of life, their very thought. Could not an American president, if he were of the wrong type of character, enslave us through command of five million bureaucrats already in the government? There are only about 140 million of us.

Before closing this chapter, it is well to remind ourselves

that the conditions it describes are not obsolete and did not end with the war. It appears that the number of our state and local officials increased from 1,934,800 shortly before the war, to 3,858,000 shortly after it. And we must add to this the 3 million in the Federal service. This vast horde is engaged primarily in restricting and taxing every group in the country for the alleged benefit of each group in it. Is it worth it? Robbing Peter to pay Paul has been legalized by statute, but a higher Power once said, "Thou shalt not steal." It looks as if the Pauls were suffering quite as much as the Peters.

CHAPTER 8

THE INCOME TAX

IN 1913, THE SIXTEENTH Amendment to the Constitution was adopted, giving the United States Government authority to tax incomes. About the same time several states imposed income taxes. The income tax is a European invention imported to our shores. The arguments for it are perfectly logical, but like most abstract logical arguments applied to human nature, they have proved not entirely sound. The theory ran that the richer a man was, the greater was the benefit that he was receiving from our government, and so the more he could afford to contribute to it. Therefore it was no more than just that he should contribute according to his means. This was so logical that the amendment was adopted with little objection.

The first income taxes were very light. They varied from $20 on the first $3000 of income to $119,800 on incomes of $3,000,000. They applied to corporations as well as persons, so that anyone owning shares in a company paid two income taxes, one on his share of the company's earnings and a surtax on the dividends he received as income above the minimum tax bracket. The tax on the companies was at first much lighter than on individuals.

In 1915 the United States internal revenue receipts looked like this: (*World Almanac*, 1918, p. 256).

Ordinary only	$283,410,138.71
Emergency and other......................	52,069,126.29
Corporation income tax....................	39,155,596.77
Individual	41,046,162.09
Total receipts	$415,681,023.86

Of this the income tax furnished $80,201,758.86, or approximately 19.3 percent.

The same 1918 *World Almanac* (p. 257) gives the number and class of income payers as follows:

Above $100,000 a year income 3,829
           25,000 "   "   "   27,972
             3,000 "   "   " 336,652
           Total Income Tax Payers......................368,453

There were then about 100,000,000 people in the country. So the income tax payers were about one-third of one percent of the country, though they paid 19.3 percent of the taxes.

The fruits of the income tax put great sums for spending in the hands of public officials. Spending money is a source of power. The officials liked it. They soon noticed two facts. First, that most people did not particularly notice that the corporations in which they had shares were paying income taxes, and made little objection to it. Second, that the very rich were extremely few but paid in a great many dollars. In 1917 the law was changed; those with incomes of $7,500 or less—the vast majority of the taxpayers—continued with no increase in taxes, but on incomes above that the taxes rose enormously, until those with $3,000,000 income paid a tax of $1,800,000. The squawks of distress that the very rich emitted were found highly amusing by the public officials and the public at large. The slogan, "Soak the rich," was in common use, and evoked much spiteful laughter.

This was an almost perfect example of taxation without representation. As soon as the government could spend the vast amount of money it could collect in the aggregate from all the rich and politically powerless, it did so with avidity. No one whose voice counted, objected. The bureaucracy used this money to increase its numbers, strengthen its organization, and so entrench itself in power that nothing short of a major effort on the part of an indignant and united public could dislodge it. This it could never have accomplished without the income tax.

Following their usual custom, the bureaucrats inched out into new territory. Today, anyone with more than $600 a year must pay income tax. A surtax starts at 17 percent of the first $2000 and goes up to 77 percent on incomes of $200,000 and over. The corporation tax is almost as heavy but too complicated to describe. Today the income tax is no longer an affliction of the rich alone, though they still pay a disproportionately large share. The public is saddled with the cost of a huge Federal bureaucracy which had grown from 450,000 in 1913 to 3,000,000 in 1946. Its number had increased seven fold, and its power, unfortunately, many times as much as that.

It is interesting to notice that in 1945 the total United States Government tax collection amounted to $43,800,387,-575.90. Of this colossal sum $35,061,526,200.36 was collected as income tax of various sorts.* In other words, the government collected in 1945, 437½ times as much money in income tax as it did in 1915. Meanwhile the estimated wealth of the United States has increased from $253,552,000,000 in 1912 ** to $305,-000,000,000 today. That is, by only about one-fifth.

Now it is all very well to "soak the rich" so long as one remembers that almost all the money which provided our productive capital came from the rich. They furnished, not only the necessary labor-saving devices, machinery, and tools that permitted our *per capita* production (and so our national income), to increase so phenomenally, they also provided the venture capital that tried out new industrial devices and ideas and established them, if they proved profitable, to be new wealth producing industries that enriched us all.

We have seen that it is the nature of man to use the first fruits of his production for his daily life, and the second fruits for such unproductive capital as will make him comfortable and his life worth living. It is only when these wants have been amply supplied that he devotes the remainder to productive capital—to investments that make him, others, and the country, richer. This is as true of the rich as of the poor. Therefore, when the rich are hit by the enormously high taxes of recent years, they continue to live as much as possible as before. They pay their taxes out of the part of their income that would formerly have been invested as productive, or venture capital, and they do this the more readily since no increase of their wealth can benefit them; for the government practically confiscates all the income they receive over $25,000 a year. Their mode of living

* *World Almanac*, 1946, p. 661.
** *Statistical Abstract of United States,* 1912.

is not greatly affected by their taxes, but the rest of the country is very seriously affected. The money for productive capital and the increase of *per capita* production is diverted to pay the expenses of the bureaucracy and so lost as a means of increasing the income of the nation. The drying up of this only source of productive capital has had an obvious and increasingly serious effect on the production and income of the country during the past twenty-five years. Since it is impossible for the individuals of the country, and therefore for the country, to make the necessary savings for productive capital, the final result must be declining national production, declining *per capita* incomes, absence of prosperity, the road to ruin.

The income tax has produced some very interesting by-products, as do most laws drawn to divert the fruits of production from the producers into the pockets of others.

In any productive economy, very able business organizers arise; men who have the intelligence to see their business as a whole, how its production can be improved and its product cheapened, so that it may be enjoyed by ever more people. Such men generally have the ability to force their visions to materialize. They are of tremendous value to the prosperity of a nation, for they are able to organize many men and put them profitably to work, creating wealth. Thus they sometimes can create employment for thousands, and riches for many of their employees, while showering over the country the wealth that their organization creates.

Such men are invaluable to the prosperity of a country because their ability and leadership greatly increase its production, income and prosperity. Their ability is recognized in Russia where they are stimulated and coddled with high pay, tax exemption, state honors and tremendous privileges, to encourage them to further efforts. In this country, however, of late everything is apparently being done to discourage such men.

These great business executives are much like the rest of us in that they work primarily for their own and their families' benefit—in other words, to make money. Their work is, however, much more exhausting than that of most people, for it takes far more out of a man to inspire great effort in others than merely to work hard himself. Since this is so, since such men are rare birds, and since the increase in production they cause is tremendous, they are paid very large salaries. Such salaries, though great, are as nothing to the increase these leaders bring about in the production or income of the country. The rest of this income is shared by their collaborators, for it must always be remembered that no one, except a pure gambler or a thief, can grow very rich without also enriching a multitude of others in his organization. These men, though they bring so much wealth to their associates and the country as a result of their efforts, are by no means altruistic in their intentions. They, like the rest of us, work for what they get out of it themselves. They can always make money in any organized society that countenances private property at all.

Today in the United States almost all these great industrial leaders have laid by enough capital to furnish them with far more income than the income tax permits them to retain for themselves. Therefore any salary or pay they receive for their work of giving employment and greatly increasing the income and prosperity of the country, is, in fact, taken away from them by the income tax for the benefit of the bureaucracy. In the last fifteen years, many and many a highly-paid executive of this type has suddenly awakened to the fact that the net pay after taxes which he is receiving for his Homeric efforts is less than he pays his stenographer! A very few of them, on making this discovery, have continued working for the joy of the work. Most have simply quit and gone home to enjoy themselves by playing golf or gardening, and live on what the government leaves them of the income of their invested capital. Thus is the country deprived of the fruits of their genius, of the increase of wealth, of income, prosperity and of the enjoyment of others that their abilities might have brought about. Personally, they probably have a pleasanter time on the links at Palm Beach, but the national prosperity suffers from the waste of their unusual ability.

All that has been said of the income tax is quite as true of the confiscatory inheritance tax. There is no sense in piling up a fortune if the government is going to take nine-tenths of it; so there is no incentive to work for one's children. The natural heirs, who are not unlikely to have inherited some of their father's skill as a great producer, have to sell his properties to pay the taxes and are at once reduced to economic insignificance.

The purchasers of the properties use money that would otherwise have gone into new productive capital, so that only the old
is retained and nothing new is added to develop the country's
wealth. The money paid in taxes is paid out to the bureaucracy
which creates nothing and so is economically wasted. This waste
of the inheritance tax differs from the waste of the income tax
in that it does not merely prevent the current saving for productive capital, which is now so much needed; it actually diverts
what savings the income tax has left, from new enterprise into
the older ones that are being sold; it does so for the benefit of
the bureaucracy, and nothing new is created.

The second by-product of the income tax is its effect on
the youth of the nation. Business *per se* does not greatly appeal
to the average young man. Its fascinating interest does not take
possession of a man till he has spent one or two years in it and
achieved a modicum of success. Almost all young men used to
go into it, however, because it promised the surest and quickest
road to the personal riches which gave that independence and
freedom to live without financial worry, which everyone craves.
Until recently, business could promise every intelligent, energetic and industrious young man at least a competence, if not a
fortune, on which he could live as he chose. This is no longer
the case. Because of the income tax it is almost impossible
for a young man, no matter how bright, to build up a sufficient capital to live comfortably on its income. Therefore, young
men of ability are turning from a business career to others
which, from the outside, look more interesting.

An unnoticed effect of the income tax is that it has been
silently and subtly congealing our population into classes, in
the European sense. It was because any young man of intelligence and enterprise had the opportunity in the United States
to get really rich, that there were no classes in this country.
Anyone, who was able, could rise to any height, and most wanted
to and were rising. Therefore no one had any feeling that he
belonged in the laboring class, or the white collar class; he felt
that he was merely getting the training of that kind of work on
his way up. Now the income tax has pretty effectually blocked
the way up. A sudden lucky or skillful coup does not enrich
a man any more, nor does a great earning power; for most of

the fruits of these are taken immediately in taxes and diverted to the bureaucracy.

The bureaucracy accelerates the tendency of young men to go into activities other than business by government propaganda, which is continually holding up "Big Business" (i.e. the producers of the nation) to ridicule, obloquy and contempt. So we see our bright young men flocking into such occupations as archaeology, teaching, or the bureaucracy itself. No nation can make a living by hunting dry bones or teaching one another, nor yet by governing itself!

After all, and whether we like it or not, it must be remembered that it was the business men of the United States who made its greatness, and caused its development. From the first tobacco planter on the James River to the last great industrialists whose equipment enabled our soldiers to win the Second World War, it was the business men, the producers of material wealth, who made our nation great. In fact, when one looks back on our history, it is surprising, considering our numbers, to see how pitifully few really great men we have produced who were not primarily business men. It ill becomes the bureaucrats and politicians who are living off the produce of business and are pushing us to ruin, to hold up the nation's greatest producers to contempt.

A third unexpected and very harmful effect of the income tax has been on the institutions of our country. Our great industrial and business geniuses were almost universally lavishly generous, and great public benefactors. They were the people who gave the funds to establish our colleges, universities, hospitals, museums, zoos, scientific foundations, dispensaries, beneficial foundations, and the thousand and one institutions that have so greatly improved our national health, productive and scientific development, culture, knowledge, learning and intelligence, to the lasting benefit of our own people as well as the rest of mankind. As a rule the great business geniuses, the very rich, gave them, the moderately successful supported them and everybody enjoyed them.

Of late this vastly beneficial practice of founding such institutions has perforce stopped. Even the support of them is drying up. Most of them are putting on drives for funds constantly, but running bigger and bigger deficits. Some are closing up. The reason is simple. The income taxes have left no one with sufficient money for philanthropy. They have even eliminated the prospect of making it. It is true that gifts to such institutions are free of tax if not exceeding ten percent of the donor's income, but the fact of the matter is that almost everyone today needs every cent of the income he can keep, either for his own expenses or to help impoverished relatives and friends, and has little, if anything, left for voluntary benefactions.

If the present trend continues, there is no prospect except that the state will take them over as is done in countries with totally managed economies. Then will come the curses of state control: the appointment of the officers and employees for political expediency; state control of college education, because the state pays for it; state control of hospitals, though many people would rather run the risk of dying than go into a state hospital. The habitual slackness and lack of energy typical of all bureaucrats will be applied to every kind of institution. Our museums will become dark, untidy morgues like the European ones. Few people here want this to happen, but the income tax will bring it about shortly unless the present trend is reversed.

In sum, the situation appears to be this. The income tax amendment, which established a sort of taxation without representation, has permitted the bureaucracy to grow beyond all reason and acquire great power. The potential income of the country has been reduced to 63 percent. Therefore there can be virtually no saving for new productive capital and hardly enough to maintain what exists. Without new productive capital we must grow constantly poorer. Every obstacle is set out to induce our great producers, the men with the "golden touch," to retire from business. Further conditions have been created by the bureaucracy to discourage our young men from entering business by preventing them from amassing the means for leisure. Is it any wonder that our production or income is not sufficient to make prosperity, and is, in fact, declining slowly toward poverty?

As production declines, the public is distressed and turns for help to the bureaucracy as the bureaucracy has taught it to do. The bureaucracy can do nothing to increase the production or national income, but it can, and generally does, redistribute the income artificially, thereby increasing its own numbers and aggravating the evil.

Like all vices, this vice of too much government is developing faster and faster. Unless it is checked by public opinion, which alone can do it, it will grow worse and worse until the producers get tired of working for the bureaucrats and quit in masses. Then will come dearth and starvation, and the "man on horseback," "the Leader," who will undertake to form a totalitarian state. The bureaucracy will give him the power. Everything will be taken over by the state. Freedom will be gone. Opportunity will be gone. There will be "youth movements," flags and cheering, and the people will become numbered "productive units" of the state, working at what they are told, where they are told, as long as they are told, for whatever portion of the national income the Leader chooses to allot them.

CHAPTER 9

MANAGED ECONOMY: SEED AND FRUIT

"As the dog returneth to his vomit."
II PETER, 2, 22

HUMANITY, EITHER AS INDIVIDUALS or nations, rarely directs its life by carefully weighed judgments. The trifling decisions of the moment, which build up habits of thought and action, have far more influence. The habit of always driving oneself to finish one's work correctly, which is formed by constant repetition of an effort of will, is likely to produce a great man. The habit, momentarily insignificant, of relieving one's weariness with alcohol, is apt to produce a drunkard. This truth is obvious on all sides when mature people are observed. For instance, it would have been as difficult for George Washington at fifty to pick a stranger's pocket as it would for an habitual petty rogue of the same age to have accomplished what George Washington did in the remainder of his life. The accumulated force of a lifetime of habit had bound each to his own line. It is the same with nations. The force of national habit, or the chain of circumstances, have far more effect on the policy of a nation's government than has any carefully worked out, widely discussed, and deliberately chosen, policy.

In the United States the government has for many years been giving particular groups many special business privileges. These have forced the productive effort of the country into all sorts of unnatural channels, deprived many groups of part of their earnings for the benefit of others, checked the profits in certain lines of endeavor, limited the choice of occupations, and thus reduced the possible production of the population to an extent that must be enormous.

126

In the late 1920's we got the first instalment of our come-uppance. The United States was seized once more by a mania for gambling. This time the vehicle was the stock market. This seemed a very significant fact at the time, and Wall Street, the Stock Exchange and stock brokers were greatly blamed for the subsequent crash. But the blame was misplaced. It is true that when the mania for gambling came, Wall Street provided the facilities to meet the demand. But when the spirit of gambling hits people, they always get someone to provide the facilities, and the true blame lies with those who create the demand, not with those who meet it. As examples: the great European seventeenth century panic was caused by speculation in tulip bulbs! In the two great eighteenth century crashes the speculation was in land in the Mississippi Valley and the South Seas—areas then as remote, unknown and unreal as fairyland is today. In all our own numerous early panics, real estate was where the speculation occurred. It is true that the last half-dozen panic depressions have been preceded by inordinate stock market speculation. This is a symptom, not a cause. Most of the time—the time when one does not hear of it—the stock market is quietly performing a most valuable service to the economy of the country.

The speculation that preceded the panic of 1929 reached a frenzy previously unknown. Stock prices rose almost constantly for nine years. They became the conversational topic "A" of the country. Intellectuals wrote books proving that a "new era" had dawned and stocks would rise indefinitely. Everybody "got into the market." Insane things occurred. The stock of the National City Bank of New York rose till it was selling at twice the book value of all its assets and *all its liabilities!* The rise seemed to be going on forever.

The duration of the steady rise in prices was unusual in pre-panic booms. It came from two causes. First, the government then taxed capital gains as income. Because of this, legitimate investors, who had seen their stocks double and quadruple in price in a few years, were loath to sell, for they would have had to pay over 50 percent of their profits to government as income tax. The other half, that they were permitted to keep, they would have either had to let remain idle, which is unpleasant, or had to invest in some stock, which because of the frenzy had risen quite as much as the one they had sold. Therefore these legiti-

mate investors—many of whom knew their onions—preferred to
let their profits run till the last possible moment and then get
out of the market and stay out, living on their capital till bottom was reached. This attitude of mind took the vast majority
of the country's available stock out of the market and "into
boxes." The small quantity of free stock—that which was available
for market purchase and sale—thus acquired a fictitious scarcity
value, for it was all there was with which the gamblers could
slake their speculative thirst. Therefore it was bid up by these
crazy men to prices far higher than could possibly have been
reached if all the stock in the country could have been freely
sold without thought of the confiscatory taxes. Therefore, also,
when the corner was finally turned and stocks started to plummet
in September 1929, all the legitimate investors, who had been
waiting for this moment, dumped their holdings as fast as possible and infinitely aggravated the terrific decline.

The second cause lay in the fact that government had by its
credit policy through the Federal Reserve Banks removed the
only brake that had ever previously stopped a pre-panic boom.
Hitherto, when too much money was drawn into speculation, the
supply became so short that interest rates rose inordinately. It
cost so much to borrow that it did not pay to speculate. This
time government, in its efforts to modify economic laws so as
to make them pleasant for everybody, tried to eliminate the
bugbear of tight money by arbitrarily fixing interest rates at a
low level and offsetting this by emitting large quantities of
unjustified Federal Reserve Credit and encouraging money to
be loaned at low rates on stock at inflated levels. From 1924 to
1928-29 the amount of credit (Federal Reserve Notes) it put
out rose from 996 million to 1505 million—almost enough to
finance the rise of the stock market. Thus the natural brake on
the boom, the obvious warning signal of the impending crash,
was removed by government itself.

Hardly were the first two months of dreadful panic over
when government, under the lead of President Hoover, tried to
prevent all the unpleasant but salutary economic hardships
which, as we have seen, normally if painfully cure panics and
depressions. It advised all employers not to retrench, especially
not to reduce wages; to keep on employing everybody they
could, even if no profitable work could be found for them, and

not to reduce prices. Private charity was encouraged to give "relief" by hiring men to do useless work at high pay—selling apples on the street, or preparing expensive books like *The Great Mansions of Eighteenth Century America,* etc., etc. The Federal, state and local governments were urged to launch all sorts of projects that were neither needed nor wanted, simply to give work to the unemployed at the previous high wage scale. It must be remembered that by this time the thousands and thousands of special privileges given by government in the form of licenses, and the power of the trade union organizations, had pretty well tied up our economy. People who lost their jobs as a result of the panic encountered numerous legal obstacles if they tried to take up a new kind of work, or even if they tried to continue in the old line at a lower rate than they had formerly received. Legal difficulties also interfered with the necessary reduction of prices. Thus it may be said that the government had done everything possible to eliminate the old salutary economic effects of the panic. The Reconstruction Finance Corporation was started to loan money to corporations which had been so foolishly conceived or wastefully managed that no privately owned bank would lend them any more money.

In a word, everything was done to prevent the normal salutary effects of a panic on the economic body—elimination of speculators, foolish enterprises, high costs and unduly high wages. All was done with the best intention in the world, but it stopped the purgative effects that panics are designed by God or nature to cure. It was like forcing on the victim of a bilious attack more of the rich foods and drinks that had caused the illness. The effect was to delay the crisis of the depression and even of the panic, but no one single horror of the previous panics was evaded or even mitigated. Instead of going into the normal V-shaped trough that is fearful but soon over, we started on a slow, three-and-a-half year economic slide that whittled away all values: stocks, bonds, real estate, businesses and pay envelopes. No effort seemed to produce any reward. Bankruptcy perpetually loomed, a nightmare fear for everybody.

People were so frightened they hoarded money and it disappeared from circulation. The government tried to alleviate this by printing money. They dared not do this openly; for the example of Europe's inflations was too fresh in people's minds.

They resorted to the subterfuge of saying that since the Federal Reserve Bank had long been able to issue money against the security of goods in transit, it should now be able to issue it against the security of government bonds; for nothing, they said, was as secure as a United States Government bond. Thus they befuddled the people, who would not even then have stood for fiat money. They made fiat money by running the government printing presses twice: once to print the bond, a second time to print the money secured by the bond. By these means the Federal Reserve increased its credit outstanding from $1,505,000,000 in 1928, when business was whirring, to $2,077,000,000 in 1932, when it was stagnant, and the money in circulation from $4,496,000,000 to $5,328,000,000 in the same time. Yet the people hoarded so much that there appeared to be very little money in existence.

Of course, in all this the Government bureaucrats had tried to do what was in the best interest of the country. First, by keeping the interest rates artificially low so as to keep the boom going, they had removed temporarily the only brake on it—high interest rates—and the boom had proceeded to madness. Then, when the crash came and the bank credit currency or deposit currency had vanished, they tried to make up for the loss of it by supplying in its place printed currency with nothing but "credit" behind it. This policy delayed the crisis of the panic for three years and the recovery indefinitely.

So greatly did the government's efforts slow up the normal operation of the business cycle, that three-and-a-half years intervened between the stock market break and the closing of the banks, which normally is the termination of the panic, instead of the usual few months. No phenomenon of panic was avoided. All the horrors were experienced. But the delay was so long and painful that the morale of the people was destroyed by the long years of unsuccessful effort.

The last three-and-a-half years of Hoover's administration were devoted by his bureaucracy to planning for an economic recovery. The people got sick of these bureaucratic charlatans and were calling for a return to free enterprise, but the bureaucrats had an answer for them.

If anyone who believes in free enterprise objects to a new plan, the answer always is: "Very well, what is your plan?"

The objectors must remain dumb. For the very essence of free enterprise is that it can have no plan. It is supremely illogical. But the fact remains that great material progress has occurred only in those countries where free enterprise, or nearly free enterprise, has been permitted. Besides, it is the only system that frees the individual from interference and coercion by government.

For a century we Americans have been drifting from an economy of free enterprise into a managed economy which few of us want, simply through bad national habits. From the beginning we have never clearly realized that the function of government is to regulate the citizens' conduct toward one another, and not to try to fill the pockets of some groups at the expense of others. When government regulates people's conduct toward one another, it creates a rule of law under which individuals can plan and a free economy can function. When it attempts to put money in people's pockets, it is on the road to managing the economy.

It may be argued that there is a difficult line to draw in practice between making men behave justly toward one another, and diverting the proper income and emoluments of one group into the pockets of another. There is, but it is never an impossible line to draw in a given specific case. For instance, a tariff is a perfectly correct way for a government to raise revenues, but the moment it is used as a protective tariff to divert the earnings of one group to another, it is a tool of a managed economy. A requirement that factory owners should have safety and sanitary devices is a rule for their conduct, even if its result is to eat the factory's earnings. It is a rule of conduct exactly like that forbidding people slapping one another's faces. It should be handled by government in the same way, not by a horde of inspectors, but on the complaint of the aggrieved party. The difference between a rule of conduct and a privilege given a group is always present. It can be seen if it is looked for. But if the principle that it is not government's function to interfere with business, either to augment, diminish, or redistribute its profits, is not recognized, it will be violated all the time. It has not been a clearly recognized principle in the United States. It has been generally violated.

The constant violation has forged a chain of circumstances

that is dragging us to a managed economy. It is of the essence
of a free economy that it shall be free. Every man must be
permitted to do whatever he wants and create whatever he
wants, as long as he does not unduly interfere with others. When
a man is not free to do this, when he meets with governmental
obstruction in many, if not every direction, the economy is no
longer free. Ours is not, and it is going lame now. It will go
lamer and lamer as time passes and the obstructions increase. If
we persist in our present course, the time will come when so
much of the producers' income is diverted from them to other
purposes that whole masses of the producers will get discouraged
and quit—as many of the able business organizers have already
quit. They will prefer the freedom from worry of life in the
bureaucracy, or on public relief, to the arduous and little rewarded labor of production. There will be a shortage of production and too little income to go round, no matter how divided.
Then starvation, chaos, and "the man on horseback."

Lincoln said that a country half free and half slave could
not exist. It is even more certain that an economy half free
and half managed cannot exist. The free part is constantly
upsetting the plans of the government. The government is
thwarting free enterprise. The result is general discontent and
stagnation so great that the situation cannot last. The bureaucracy, which has most of the power at the moment, is pushing the
rest of us, who are thoroughly confused, into a managed economy
against our will. All this has arisen from our indulgence in bad
national habits. Now let us look at a theory that developed simultaneously and parallel with our own progressive indulgence.

To do this we must digress and consider Germany.

In 1648, at the end of the Thirty Years' War, Germany
was prostrate. Her social and governmental organizations were
practically gone, her property was mostly destroyed. It is said
that in places the people were reduced to cannibalism. Strong
men set themselves up, as they always do, and started to whip
the conditions and get things going as best they could. As a
result, a myriad little separate governments got started, each
ruled by its local strong man or lord. For the most part these
tiny states continued for a hundred-and-fifty years, though some
of them amalgamated, and Prussia, Saxony, Bavaria, Baden,

Wurtemberg and the Hesses were of reasonable size and efficiency fairly soon. Nevertheless, up to the time of Napoleon, Germany was divided into some 350 practically independent states. Most of these were ruled by an absolute lord, "for the good of the State," which was pretty generally the good of the lord. The average level of government and of economics was incredibly low. Everything was taxed. The common people were in misery and practically slaves. Some of the laws were fantastic; one lordling, for instance, who wished to practice polygamy, turned all his subjects and his state Mohammedan!

Napoleon did most of his fighting in Germany. Nevertheless, he did her a lot of good, for when he was through the country had coalesced into but thirty states, each with a fairly enlightened ruler. The mere removal of so many governing units with their stupid laws restraining the liberty and business life of the people so as to give privilege to the ruler and his friends, was of extraordinary benefit. This was augmented by the wisdom of Adam Smith, which began to have influence in northern Europe at that time, and by the example of the United States, which showed to the astonished eyes of Europe a nation risen from an impoverished beginning to wealth and prominence in a few decades, evidently as a result of not having any economic regulations at all. At the same time the Industrial Revolution was getting going. Almost as soon as Napoleon was out of the way, the Germans added a fifth tremendous stimulus to all business and industry by putting into effect the Zollverein, or "customs union," which abolished the intricate tariffs on both imports and exports that for centuries had stifled all trade between the numerous states and cities within Germany.

Under the influence of these stimuli, Germany's business and industry increased extraordinarily. The increase in her standard of living, wealth and prosperity in the second and third decades of the nineteenth century, would have been one of the phenomena of history, had it not been eclipsed by the even greater increase along similar lines that occurred in the United States at the same time.

Of course, Germany's new prosperity did not reach all sections of the population at once. Some felt it almost immediately, others lagged far behind the rest. These latter groups became very pitiable objects in the eyes of their more prosperous brethren. Their condition was not in truth any worse than it had been for centuries, but against the drab background of the former general misery, it had not been very obvious. Now, in contrast to the considerable new prosperity everywhere apparent, it was thrown into high relief.

The nineteenth century Germans were a kindly, leisurely, people. They liked to be happy and to have those around them happy. They were distressed at the misery and poverty they saw. They are a philosophical people. They enjoy reasoning logically. They are an orderly people and have great respect for the State. They have one very serious fault. They are not a very observant, perspicacious or understanding people. Therefore they do not always select the true premises on which to base their profound logic. Arguing logically from false premises produces, of course, nonsense—frequently a dangerous form of nonsense, since it creates the illusion of truth. This defect in the German national character is perhaps more than anything else responsible for the apparent national madness which has afflicted them in the present century.

Let us see how they worked out their economic philosophy.

Germans, because of their militaristic nature, had for centuries kept themselves divided into classes, such as princes, nobles, knights, professional men, burghers, farmers, employers, artisans and laborers. These classes became fixed by custom and habit, in some respects even by law. It was very difficult to move from one class to another—either up or down. Therefore the German mind became convinced that classes were an immutable fact in nature, that men were born with the fixed qualifications of their class, and were, therefore, bound to remain in it.

They had not enjoyed the enlightening contact with the wilderness that had taught Americans that a man's ability alone determines his position in the world at maturity. Here, where nearly every business leader has passed up through every department of the business, we regard the type of work a young man is doing as part of his training to get him to the top. This was not true in Germany. There the type of work a young man started on was generally the result of the position of his parents, and once started on, very generally established his position for life. The idea of immutable classes, in spite of the occasional exceptions like Krupp, was accepted as a fact. It was accepted as a premise by the German political economic philosophers, particularly by Karl Marx, who in the light of his own distorted nature, believed that the classes should hate one another, and whose doctrine fomented such hate. Its acceptance was one of the causes which sent German economic philosophy haywire.

Furthermore, the Germans had observed that their great burst of national prosperity had occurred shortly after the somewhat enlightened governments that had succeeded Napoleon had removed many of the absurd governmental regulations which the earlier German rulers had imposed on business. They therefore credited government intervention with the new-found prosperity and developed the idea that government, by regulating business, could improve it. They were not sufficiently perspicacious to see that business had cured itself, once the restrictions imposed by the earlier governments had been removed. In their minds they confused the removal of economic regulations by government with regulation by government. This was the second false premise from which the German economic philosophers reasoned themselves into unreason.

A free economy, as we have seen, is a most illogical affair. Since it is a dynamic body formed of contending forces, no one can foretell the direction of its movements. It is full of temporary injustices, due to the evil and stupidity inherent in human nature, but it is so fluid and changeable that none of them can last long. It is full of opportunity. It produces more wealth—the object of human desire—more hope and more energy than any other type of economy yet discovered. Though it often causes pain, it works beautifully for everybody in the long run— and no one can tell why! It is so illogical that it is almost terrifying for an orderly mind to think of.

The Germans have orderly minds. It appeared to them that if such great and obvious good as they had witnessed had been brought to their country as a by-product of the fierce disorderly struggle of her citizens to enrich themselves, a far greater amount of good would come to the country if the struggle were scientifically directed from the top for the benefit of all. A most logical conception, and difficult to combat. Therefore German intellectuals began to think up ways of using government to force the free economy into lines more beneficial to all. These intellectuals were theoreticians, not efficient producers. They believed that government regulation had caused the rise of prosperity. They believed that men were immutably divided into classes. They saw the evils of free enterprise. They were kind-hearted. They were active-minded. Above all they were logical, and expressed themselves admirably. They talked themselves into such power that their governments began to regulate their economy along the lines proposed by the theorists. The economic regulations of the intellectuals—the professors of their own theories of political economy—came to be substituted for the economic regulations of the princelings—for the public good, of course. "The burned fool's bandaged finger went wobbling back to the fire."

Now the chief trouble with a free economy is that in it there are always some people too rich and some too poor. They are not always the same people, to be sure. The workings of a free economy are always pushing individuals up and dragging individuals down. But the fact remains that though not the same people, there are always some too rich and some too poor. This the intellectuals abhorred and they undertook to have the government take the wealth away from the rich and give it to the poor. They did not see that great wealth is the product of skillful management, and that when it is taken out of able hands it cannot be distributed but is destroyed. As Mr. Baruch has recently said, "Government cannot distribute wealth, only poverty." They also saw, or fancied they saw, that if certain industries developed more rapidly, it would benefit the country. They therefore framed laws to help this development.

Thus they started in Germany the chain of circumstances leading to a managed economy. Once started on this course, Germany proceeded far more rapidly than the United States has done. This was due to management being there a deliberate policy, and to the innate respect the Germans had for the wisdom of their political officials—something which was long lacking here. Pretty soon the inefficiency of a partially managed economy caused the German intellectuals to think about a totally managed economy. They did so, and found their thoughts agreeable.

Theoretically, a government might be able to establish rules which would cause every individual to perform exactly what would best serve the general interest. But to enforce such rules the ruler would have to possess all knowledge, all wisdom, perfect integrity and complete power. There are no men like that. Furthermore, all the citizens would have to be unselfish, well-disciplined, and wholly devoted to the public good. There are no men like that either. If there were, any government would work—and none would be necessary, for the Kingdom of Christ would be in operation.

These necessary conditions are impossible at the moment; nevertheless the idea of a perfectly regulated economy is a delightful subject for an intellectual to contemplate and theorize about, for it is a large philanthropic subject and one adapted to extremely orderly and reasoned thought—very different from the subject of a free economy. German intellectuals thought about it, evolved closely reasoned theories, and German professors expounded these theories. Professors of other nations took them up. They were fascinating subjects to teach. They were altruistic in motive and sounded possible of accomplishment if one did not think about them too critically. There were a few errors in them; for instance the somewhat touching belief that by changing the form of government you were changing the heart of man, and that by having everybody as a Government official regulating and spying on each other you were making everybody happy. But such details as these were not emphasized as the theories were taught. Though changing the form of Government does not change the heart of man, any Government can give any man great power over any others. The less of this that is done, the better for everybody.

Soon the realists in the movement realized that no people would willingly submit to the discipline necessary to carry the theories into practice; that the people would have to be forced into submission by government. Forgetting that this ideal government had to have perfect knowledge, wisdom, integrity, as well as power, and that it was unlikely such a government could be found, they finally talked themselves round till they were practically back to the philosophy of Count St. Simon, the first of modern advocates of a socialized state, who, as a reaction against the disorderly license of the French Revolution, recommended a state organized entirely for production and run by the great industrialists. He advocated that those who did not conform to this rule should be "treated like cattle."

The exponents of managed economy all put the state's welfare as the greatest good. They entirely forgot that the state was the creature of individuals, erected by them for their convenience. Impliedly, and generally unconsciously, they denied Christ's doctrine of the importance of the individual. But because their theories were logical and easy to teach and learn—very different from the subject of a free economy—they were studied and expounded by intellectuals everywhere. Gradually, over the years, a body of men has developed in every country who sincerely believe that totalitarian states with fully managed economies should be brought into being. They realize that few people would want such a monstrosity. But *they* do. It is difficult to analyze the thought processes of such men. Some of them are undoubtedly muddle-headed altruists. Some may be those who hate to make up their own minds, and want to be looked after and told what to do. But the bulk of them are the type who crave power and are willing to do anything to get it. Their mentality, even at that, is queer, for understanding the functioning of a totalitarian state, they must know that no one in it can have either security or freedom. Such a state, to function, must be a close-knit hierarchy like an army. Each man with complete power over those beneath him—but each subject to the whim of his superior and dependent on it, not only for his career but for his very life! Even the dictator has no bed of roses, for though his power is absolute, he must know that, as the head of such a pack of power-hungry wolves, if he makes one slip he is done. This uncomfortable feeling accounts for the ruthless vengeance all the dictators have taken on those who opposed them.

Economic planners of this kind know that no partially free people would willingly impose a totalitarian dictatorship on themselves unless driven to the ultimate of discontent. Discontent is, therefore, essential to these power-hungry ones. Discontent is the result of poverty. Therefore their first task is to produce poverty. Since no great nation was suffering acute poverty between 1850 and 1914, the power seekers had no opportunity to put their theory into practice, until the First

World War brought Russia to bankruptcy, and Germany and Italy to the verge of it. For decades, all three had been swiftly following the same road to economic ruin that the United States is pursuing so eagerly now.

When the income of a nation is reduced so low that there is general want, and starvation is near or present, its people are easily beguiled into all sorts of foolishness by promises of universal ample wealth. This is particularly true when the promises are accompanied by blueprints of a huge and complicated machine that no one understands, but which looks as if it might accomplish the object it is said to be designed for.

A totalitarian government puts all power in the hands of the state, and the state in the hands, first of a small group, then, necessarily, of one man, so that the lives and the energies of the citizens may be forced into closely organized production until wealth has been created to provide an ample sufficiency for all. That is, at least, its avowed objective. Its real one is more apt to be to give its organizers enormous wealth and power.

The prime need of any totalitarian government is a leader, since it is organized like an army. The leader must have a great lust for power (or he would not wish to become one), considerable intelligence, and above all a charming personality. He must be a most persuasive speaker. To be successful he must, unfortunately, be ruthless, have little regard for truth, supreme faith in himself and a well-concealed contempt for everyone else. A dictator must have absolute power and subordinate everything and everybody to his will. Therefore he must abandon all ordinary morality, or fail.

In order to impose a totalitarian government on a state its proponents must have a plan. It is hard to get six people to agree on a detailed plan for the simplest course of action. It would, therefore, be impossible to draw a detailed plan for taking over the management of a state, all its business enterprise and the direction of all its people, that more than a handful of men would agree to. Since the future dictator must have a plan that all may rally round, and since a detailed one is impossible, one so vague and general must be adopted that it means nothing; but it must be so worded that each hopeful individual who wants to can read into it all the good things he desires for himself.

Having the leader and the plan, the next step is to get

the political power. To accomplish this the organizers must pose as great democrats and lovers of the people, make vicious attacks on all existing monopolies, all existing evidences of selfishness and injustice, and laud to the skies their leader and "his plan" through every means of publicity at their disposal.

Since, unfortunately for them, the conditions consequent to the over-managed economy that has brought them into power have also created a great yearning for freedom in the hearts of the people, they must laud freedom. Not that they have the slightest intention of permitting it in the ordinary sense of freedom. Their consciences, however, are elastic, and they advocate special kinds of freedom: "New Freedom," or "Economic Freedom"—which means that people need no longer worry about their economic life, since the government will now take care of them and tell them what to do. They also advocate freedom of planning, which means that the government should be allowed to plan the lives of everybody without interference by anybody.

They must also maintain elected legislatures, since legislatures are a symbol of democracy in the public mind, and since, in the incipient stages, totalitarians claim to be nothing if not democratic. Legislatures are no serious impediment to them. Legislatures were designed to draw the regulations of conduct that establish the rule of law. They were well devised for this. But they are utterly incapable of regulating the business of a country. This is readily seen when one considers the difficulty of getting a small group of partners, who know all about their own business, to agree on a plan to regulate that business for six months. How then could a legislature of several hundred members agree on detailed plans to regulate all the various businesses of the country about which they know little? This difficulty confronted legislatures very early in the history of government's interference with business. They met it by providing committees of experts under the executive branch of the government to draw up the rules for the regulation of business, and by giving to these regulations the force of law. Thus most legislatures have already abrogated the function for which they were designed, and it is an easy matter for a leader to reduce them to the position of a mere reference committee—not even a coordinating one. Theoretically, even under totalitarianism the legislature has power to make the laws, but once in the saddle a dictator has such control that he can cut off the livelihood or the life of anyone, and the individual legislators are so afraid of being purged that they always confirm his acts, and the legislature becomes a mere rubber stamp.

To get political power the prospective leader makes his appeal primarily to the stupidest classes in the country. This is because their stupidity has given them little discrimination and they are therefore most ready to accept a vague plan without considering the effect of the details. Also he appeals to youth, many of the young not yet having developed discriminatory powers, and all being easily beguiled by youth movements, parades and government financed vacations, guest houses, etc. No other large groups of the population are so easily coalesced round vague doctrines, so blind in their partisanship, or so violent or intolerant. Such groups are necessary for a leader, in order to build a majority around them.

It is difficult to unite large bodies of people for something. It is absurdly easy to unite them against something. There is always a popular "pet hate" that can be fanned into flame and the great majority united against, on the "they" and "we" principle. So served the Jews in Germany, the kulaks in Russia. Great majorities could be rolled up against them. It is also a great advantage later to have created a public whipping boy on whom anything that goes wrong can be blamed.

Once the leader is elected to the control of government, he must at once get control also of all means of publicity, so as to control the thought of the country by propaganda. The next chapter of this book is devoted wholly to propaganda, therefore suffice it to say here that its object is to kill all criticism, to make by constant reiteration everybody believe that the leader's plan is everybody's plan, and that if any single group or coterie be opposed to him it is unique, small and therefore powerless.

Having got control of the machinery of government and of propaganda, the leader must secure complete economic power. The economic disturbance preceding the establishment of a totalitarian dictatorship is very great. Government control of business and heavy taxation have so discouraged producers that most of them have stopped working, and thereby have created the shortages of everything which resulted in the discontent that caused the dictator's election. It takes an appreciable length of time for the compulsory production of a fully managed economy to get functioning. So there is a period of great want at this stage. It is then that the dictator confiscates private property, for then such action is likely to have widespread approval from the masses who expect to have the benefit of the property confiscated. The assumption of property helps the dictator get the country through the difficult period, since it gives him control of all the nation's wealth. Furthermore, the confiscation beggars everybody, and people totally without property are virtually enslaved, for to be free they must have at least enough to live on till they can get themselves into a position where they can make more. Most people have forgotten that the institution of private property is the greatest source of individual freedom, but dictators have not—and are against such freedom. Individual freedom cannot be reconciled with a single national purpose— the dictator's purpose—of making everyone and everything fit into a blueprint map of a planned national production set-up.

The seizing of private property and putting it into the dictator's hands gives him the complete economic power of the country—a power almost inconceivably great, to the minds of those who are used to something like a free economy. Totalitarians argue that all the economic power existed before in the hands of the private owners and that transferring it to one pair of hands does not increase it. This is an utter fallacy. In private hands the economic power of each owner was pulling with, against, or across that of every other owner, and the various pulls neutralized one another and held the whole in an almost powerless balance, much as the centrifugal and centripetal forces in the solar system hold it in balance. When all the power is in one hand, however, and pulling one way, its force is irresistible. As examples, if an employer gets angry and fires a workman, the latter can get a job with a rival owner at little inconvenience. If a totalitarian government, in its economic aspect, gets angry at a workman and discharges him, that workman starves to death, for there is no other employer. If an owner or several owners make something foolish and neglect to make something necessary, they go broke but no particular harm is done. Other owners will have made the necessity and the foolish ones will scarcely be noticed. On the other hand, if the dictator makes a mistake and forgets to provide for the manufacture of a necessity, the whole nation goes without that necessity. A very few such mistakes lead to starvation.

In Russia, where there had never been either freedom or much public opinion, private property was simply taken over. In Germany and Italy, where there had been some freedom, and where public opinion had weight, and where they had the horrible mistakes that Russia made as an example before them, control of private industry was taken over very gradually, and at first largely by a system of rewards and penalties. In all three countries, however, every grab of power, every new form of coercion, was always accompanied by paeans in praise of liberty from every unit of the government-controlled, propaganda-publicity department. Thus were those who longed for liberty soothed down.

To manage the state either in its governmental or productional departments, a dictator has to get people behind him and shouting for him. To accomplish this, he gathers round him a corps of disciplined workers, either party members or men in the public pay who thoroughly believe in the totalitarian theory and in the leader and his plan, and who are willing to do anything for the cause. These men are of the bullying type, who like to order others about. They are willing to obey orders themselves, for the fun of passing them on with additions of their own, and of enforcing them. They are ruthless men, held in line by "honors" and emoluments, supplemented by punishments. They must act on the principle that the end justifies the means. The nature of the job is such that only the most brutal and arrogant part of the population will take it.

These men are used by the government to get further control. It inserts one or more of them into every possible group in the population. They are inserted clandestinely as spies; they get intimate with their fellows, and denounce any they see fit, for anti-government statements or sentiments. The accused are then summoned before authority and offered a sort of suspended sentence if they, in turn, will act as spies and informers. In this way a huge unpaid army of spies is formed by blackmail. This system results in no one ever trusting anyone he associates with, and therefore completely prevents any organization for resistance. It also results in the worst and most brutal getting to the top; for in Russia, for example, no party worker can receive any promotion until he has betrayed at least two of his "friends." It is from such men—the "discipline under leadership" set— that the leader picks his henchmen and lieutenants. They are the ones who enforce the rules, rally everyone behind the leader, and stir up the hatred against the public "whipping boys." It is their moral outlook that accounts for the depravity of the totalitarian states and their leaders.

The leader must be foresighted if he is to exist at all. He must train up children to be good party men in the future. This is comparatively easy as the state has long run the schools everywhere. It is not hard, with the assistance of uniforms, bands and youth movements, to build strong party organizations among the very young. This leads to children, as party workers, spying on their parents, and when momentarily disgruntled, reporting them to the party, breaking up homes and other pleasant things.

As soon as the leader has all the political and economic power, he has to make the whole thing operate. The "discipline under leadership" gang are all right to do the shouting and bullying, but it is the bureaucrats on the committees who must make the system work. This takes all the fun out of being a bureaucrat. Before dictatorship, the bureaucrats had great authority and no responsibility. Under a dictator they have full authority and full responsibility, a very sadly different thing. Many a kindly, old, self-confident, bureaucratic bumble-puppy was jolted out of his "security," his job, and sometimes his life, because he could not make the plans he had made, work. It had been so easy to make plans for other people—if you didn't have to make them work.

When a legislature has been reduced to the function of referring all problems to appropriate committees and endowing the regulations of those committees with the force of law, the government has to be carried on by those committees. There must be a committee of "experts" on every conceivable business, putting out rules to govern that business. Experts proverbially disagree, but that makes little difference as disagreement can be ironed out in the committee. The trouble is that each committee approaches its problem as if it were in a vacuum, and as all economic problems are inextricably intertangled, the rules of each committee contradict the rules of about a dozen related committees; then coordinating committees have to be set up for groups of related industries, and, as their rules conflict with those of other groups of related industries, another set of super-coordinating committees has to be established. So echelon after echelon of coordinating committees are created, capped at the top by the leader himself, who has the final say on everything. This is why there must always be one leader, for such an organization can work only with one man at the top. Often the most trivial matters have to wait decision till they go through several echelons of coordinators, and an infinity of time and effort is wasted in bottlenecks at the top. Also further hosts must be taken from production and put into government to manage things.

When a government-controlled economy is compared with the decentralization of a free economy, whose adjustments are automatically brought about by the price of materials and labor, it is so clumsy it is a joke. This is clearly borne out by the starvation standard of living in countries with a managed economy. But even supposing a managed economy could amply supply the needs of a nation, even then it would prove a stagnant economy. New industries are ever likely to evolve from the toys of the rich that are unpopular and jeered at when new. The plumbing, automobile and airplane industries are of this sort. Many people now living remember the unpopularity of the early automobiles: the signs saying, "Automobile Speed Limit, 8 Miles an Hour!" The yells of "Git a horse!" Many more recall the raucous laughter that greeted those who thought men could fly. "Darius Green and his Flying Machine" was a nationally known comic poem while the Wright Brothers were experimenting at Kitty Hawk.

Since this is the normal public attitude toward anything new, it is highly improbable that new industries would develop under a managed economy. In a managed economy the whole initiative is in the hands of the dictator, or leader, alone; and it is extremely unlikely that the genius of a Stalin, say, and of a Thomas Edison should ever be found united in a single man. Then, too, the possible inventors could afford no time out of their regimented lives for the necessary experiments, nor any money from their regulated salaries for the materials that they would find hard to obtain. Furthermore, with the possibility of personal gain removed, they would have no incentive for their efforts. The bureaucrats, whose job it is to supply the public with what it knows it wants, would be loath to divert goods and effort to building a new toy, especially an unpopular one, when all that was in sight for them was more work and no benefit. The economy would stagnate.

Under a managed economy there can be no rule of law, for when the government takes over industry it must decide everything, and take sides for and against individuals. If it runs bus lines it must decide between what points they will run, who shall make the busses, who drive them. Each decision is necessarily in favor of one individual or group, and against others. Therefore there is no rule of law under which people can plan their lives. No one ever knows where he stands. He is a toy of favoritism.

When formal justice gets in the leader's way, he establishes courts of "socialized law" to interpret his views as law. That is the end of justice enforced by law, for by giving the executive branch of government sufficient power, its most arbitrary and unjust act becomes legal.

So much for the set-up of government in a fully managed economy. Now let us look at it from the point of view of how it works on the producers.

In the first place, there is absolutely none of the vaunted security in the ordinary sense of the word, since each man is entirely under the orders and at the mercy of his immediate superior who can move him about, promote or demote him, even dismiss him and take away his character so that he can get no further work at all. There is, however, "full employment" for those in good standing. They can have work of such a kind as government assigns them, at the pay, for the hours, and at the place government assigns. They may be moved about to different places (even whole populations may be moved from place to place) at the dictate of the bureaucracy. Not only can a man in good standing have work—he must have it—and have it on whatever terms the government orders—or he will be allowed to starve. There is no difference between this and old time slavery. If any there is, it is in favor of slavery. Slaves were allowed generally to retain the food they grew and the gadgets they made in their spare time. That part of the national income at least, was theirs. That is not true in a totalitarian state. There, one finds, farmers are being constantly prosecuted for putting up food for themselves instead of turning it in to the state. The passion for reapportioning the national income is very strong among those working to produce a totalitarian state, probably because it is such an excellent tool with which to distribute misery. Anyone clothed with this power can enrich any favorite, irrespective of what the favorite produces. He can also reduce the wages of any group of producers to such a point that they will cease to produce. In a state approaching totalitarianism but not yet there, those who won't work are always supported anyway.

Judicious use of this power can quickly reduce the whole income of a nation to nothing, and so mentally prepare it to submit to dictatorship. Such use is now being made of it in England, where the coal miners lately were supported in semi-idleness and neither made to work nor made to allow others to work. Therefore the economy of England is reaching a standstill. England is full of self-pity at the moment, and claiming that she was always an importing nation and now cannot import because she is so poor. Everything she imported in the old days she paid for by the wealth she created herself, and exported. She grew rich in this way. She earned every cent she got until recently, when she found it pleasanter to become a pensioner of the U.S.A.

Russia is the only country that in modern times has gone to the logical extremes of a managed economy. There, in spite of, or rather because of the complete concentration of political and economic power, the execution of workers for inferior work, etc., the whole system failed so frightfully that 15,000,000 people are reported to have starved in a land that is naturally one of the richest, and certainly one of the least populated, on this earth. The one-time German and Italian dictators, therefore, never pushed things to anything like the same extreme, and Russia herself has receded from it considerably.

The Russians had such trouble with their workmen and their production that they came to value most highly the men who could inspire others with enthusiasm for their work, or organize them efficiently so as to increase the general production—the men of the same type as the great industrial organizers in this country, whom our government is now doing its best to discourage by income and inheritance taxes.

John Scott in his illuminating book, "Behind the Urals," quotes Stalin as saying: "Inequality of incomes is the key to industrial efficiency." Stalin is right in that. By putting this theory partly into practice he brought the Russian people from general terrible starvation to a low subsistence level. Scott gives a snapshot of how the internal economy of the Soviets works. According to him there were in the great steel center of Magnitogorsk, about 200,000 people. The unskilled workers drew 125 rubles a month, about $50. The bulk of them lived in tents, cellar dug-outs, or four in a room in wooden barracks. If they left their job against orders they were likely to be shot, or at least deprived of their cards and made ineligible for another job, so they would starve. The manager of the plant drew 2000 rubles a month salary, an additional 2000 rubles a month production bonus, or $1,600 a month all together. He was also provided with a chauffeur, an automobile and its maintenance, a 14-room house fully equipped with furniture, with grounds and a small deer park, and all valued at 250,000 rubles—equal to the total earnings of 166 unskilled workers for a year. The equivalent cost of such an establishment in America, measured by the pay of 166 unskilled workers' gross earnings for a year, would be about $850,000. Furthermore, the house was equipped with servants and the grounds with caretakers, at the expense of the plant. The manager had received, as most have, some Soviet Industrial Order that exempted him from paying income tax. He was permitted to buy scarce luxury articles at a very low price. His children also, for a low fee, but a prohibitive one to most of the people, received a high education. He and his family got vacations in first-class hotels at a nominal fee. The subordinate officials received proportionate benefits, according to their grade. The Soviet, indeed, cherishes and preserves its industrial managers. Of course, if the manager of a Russian plant is caught in a really bad mistake, he is shot and not simply kicked upstairs to be chairman of the board, as the president of an American corporation would be.

It would seem from this picture that the dictatorship of the proletariat, after putting the Russian people through a blood bath, mass starvation, a great destruction of property, and tremendous suffering, has achieved nothing for the proletariat. The inefficient among the producers are much worse off than under the Czar, though the propaganda machine tells them they are not. The efficient, on the other hand, are about as well off as before. A curious result, certainly, and an end that would have surprised the early revolutionists, could they have foreseen it.

So much for the producers of the managed economy, which must manage not only production, but also the saving-for and building up of the productive capital or factories of the country, and manage the national consumption and export as well, that the whole economy may be in balance. From the point of view of the people, the management of consumption is quite as unpleasant as that of production.

In the first place, it is obvious that since the government produces everything and owns everything, everyone must buy from it with what it allows him as wages. This means that people can buy only what the government wants them to, because only that is produced, be it food or clothes, books or games, tools or material. Also government takes most of the fun out of leisure by directing it, and by permitting or withholding the materials used in it. Compulsory consumption is quite as depressing as compulsory production.

Not only are production and consumption, the work and play, of the people completely controlled by government and channeled into lines that the government thinks will be helpful to itself, but an attempt is also made to control thought. Of course thought can never be controlled except by the thinker. But there are today a myriad aids to thought in the shape of books, newspapers, plays, movies, radio programs, which furnish "food for thought," and without which thought must be of a very high and abstract kind indeed, or else degenerate into mere day-dreaming. All this "food for thought" the government can and does control "for the best interest of the people," which is really the best interest of the leader and his henchmen.

This thought control is directed to eliminate subversive ideas and all information that might tend to make the people discontented with their lot, by maintaining that their lot is the best. (Note the surprise of the Russian troops at seeing "the excellent" living quarters of the workmen in Berlin, Budapest and Vienna.) It is also directed to making the people believe they are contented and happy as a whole. Each group in the land, of course, actually knows its members are fed up and want a change, but are afraid to say so. The government is well aware of this, but builds the illusion that all the other groups are well satisfied and strong supporters of the regime. Thus each group is afraid to start anything lest it should have no backing. Not that any or all the groups could do anything much, for they have been deprived of their arms and are, therefore, about helpless. All but the army, that is, and that group is kept really well contented.

Life for the ordinary citizen of a totalitarian state must be sheer hell. Since everyone everywhere on earth craves freedom from interference, particularly government interference, and longs in his heart for a government that would keep others from interfering with him and leave him alone itself—Americans particularly would resent an authoritarian state because of their traditions and national memories. Yet stone by stone, and quite unwittingly, we are building a prison wall round ourselves by trying to improve the economic laws—the natural laws—the laws of God—by statute, by trying to legislate ourselves rich. Those prison walls are high now, but the prison is not closed. We are not slaves yet. We can still get out if we act in time. But remember, the convinced believers in an authoritarian state—the discipline under leadership gang—are standing around waiting for the proper moment to lock us in forever. That moment will come when our economy, which we have bound as the Lilliputians bound Gulliver, by a myriad threads, can no longer function and breaks down. Breaks down to an extent where there is not enough income to go round, no matter how divided, and real want occurs.

CHAPTER 10

PROPAGANDA

"You can fool all the people some of the time"
ABRAHAM LINCOLN

THE THEORY OF DEMOCRACY is based on the presumption that the majority of the people of a nation can decide from the facts before them what is to their own true interest. "Facts," as used in the above sentence, is synonymous with "Truth." So Pilate's unanswered question, "What is truth?" is ever present. Long experience has shown, however, that the majority of the people can decide pretty clearly what the real facts are from the host of conflicting reports that arise. Therefore it is generally assumed that the majority will be able to select the true facts from the welter and act on them intelligently to their own best benefit.

If, however, all the reports of a set of facts are suppressed, so that the people do not hear of them all, or, if only one report of the facts is allowed to go to the people, and that one a deliberately or accidentally falsified report, it is obvious that democracy cannot function at all, since no majority can decide what is best on a basis of no facts or of distorted ones. Therefore it is essential that there should be complete freedom in reporting any facts and in disseminating those reports, except when doing so would endanger the safety of the country to a foreign enemy.

We have seen that by the time the panic of 1929 arrived our people had set up a huge bureaucracy which could control them rather thoroughly. Many of the bureaucrats had by then

151

come to feel that the government was an entity by itself, set over the people, and in some of its interests rather opposed to them. The old idea that government was set up for the convenience of the people and was their servant, had become very dim. Some of the bureaus which felt themselves unpopular, had set up propaganda departments under various subterfuges, to gain popularity.

By that time also there had come into being over here a small but highly intellectual and active group of believers in the German theory of managed economy which leads to the totalitarian state. These men were inspired to a large extent by articulate college professors, and many of them, following the rules to bring about revolution as laid down in many books of revolutionary theory, had got hold of a great many means of publicity, and were using them to spread propaganda.

Propaganda is defined as "Any organization or plan for spreading a particular doctrine or system of principles."

In 1929, the majority of the bureaucracy had no very clear particular doctrine or system of principles they wanted to spread —except, perhaps, that they wanted to be popular and increase in size. But those who believed in the theory of managed economy promulgated by the German professors had a very clear one. They wanted to set up a totalitarian state. To do this they had to destroy free enterprise, and the capitalism which accompanies it, because both were weapons that defended freedom, and a totalitarian state manifestly can tolerate no freedom. They knew that they were a small and unpopular minority, and that freedom, capitalism, and free enterprise were highly prized by a vast majority. They could attack them only obliquely and indirectly by twisting the meaning of words and by disparaging certain of their aspects by ridicule and obloquy. At first these intellectuals were acting as a loosely-knit private group. Later, when the New Deal put them in control of the bureaucracy, they could use the bureaucracy's propaganda bureaus and the great prestige of government. Even then their task was not easy. At the beginning it was immensely difficult. Nevertheless, they did it admirably.

Let us study briefly the high spots of their method. We must remember they were helped all through by two attributes of the American character. First, everybody hates to think deeply.

It is an awful effort that few people will undergo unless absolutely forced into it. Second, all Americans love a "wisecrack"— a witty, though superficial summation of a subject. When they hear one our people are momentarily entranced; they are consumed with a desire to repeat it, and their minds forthwith cease to grapple with the problem so snappily disposed of.

The intellectuals' first opportunity came with the panic-depression beginning in 1929, which had arisen, as we have seen, from a mania for gambling, and had been greatly aggravated by the government fiscal policies described in Chapter 9. Furthermore, the interlocking network of conflicting privileges held the whole economy entangled in its meshes, so that no part of it could voluntarily give way. The attention of each particular business had, for some time, been focused, not on increasing the production—or income—of the nation, but on impounding for itself the largest possible share of the fruits of the existing production. This had led to all sorts of agreements—wage agreements, trade agreements, "gentlemen's undertakings," agreements to purchase raw materials at high figures in exchange for some favor, etc. All these held prices high above the fair level, yet none of them could be violated without a breach of business ethics, and many of them were legally enforceable under privileges given by statute.

What the economy needed was a good old-fashioned purge in the shape of a panic-depression that would squeeze out the inflation. People had been able to pay the high prices when everyone was working overtime and making gambling profits as well. But when the crash came and some businesses stopped "broke," and many people were out of work, the prices charged by businesses, still continuing the old high scale that their privileges and agreements had bound them to, appeared perfectly exorbitant, and few people could or would buy their output. Therefore such of the businesses as could and did go on operating could not sell their products and piled up great inventories, much needed but unsaleable because of their price.

Taking note of these frozen inventories the propagandists came out with their first great slogan: "The depression is caused by over-production." As if the general lack of wealth, which was the depression, could possibly have been caused by an over-production of wealth! This was a wisecrack, however, and it

saved thought, so it was accepted by millions who longed for
necessities and luxuries held at a price they were simply without
the means of attaining.

Those old enough, will recall that a year after that depression started almost every family would have gladly and wisely
spent a year's income (had they had it) in replacing worn-out
necessities and refurbishing their homes. The need was there.
The supply was there. But the demand was not, because the
prices of the supply were artificially held up to a point few
could afford. Therefore there was idleness, no production, general lack, because the prices of the supply were artificially held
up to a point the need could not touch.

As the surpluses piled up, factory after factory had to close,
because of the union wages, the lack of new equipment and the
privilege-bound economy that prevented them from selling their
goods at a price that was acceptable. Thus the situation was
infinitely aggravated.

In order to inject an element of despair into the picture, the
idea was fostered that the depression would be permanent. Much
was written about technocracy—a hifalutin word to describe
the condition wherein machines would become so efficient that
they would throw nine-tenths of the population permanently
out of work, to starve without recourse. This chimera was nothing but a re-evocation of the old bogy that walked at the very
start of the industrial revolution, when the first spinning and
weaving machines were invented. Prior to that time, almost all
women were busied preparing and making cloth by hand. The
machines threw them out of that work. But instead of starving,
they rapidly found more profitable uses for their time than
spinning and weaving. This worked to their great benefit, the
while all were benefited by the great cheapening in price and
improvement in quality of textiles. Something similar will
always result from improvement in machines; for the desire of
mankind for material possessions is so insatiable, and the ingenuity of people in finding work for which there is a demand
is so keen, that left to themselves and unhampered by restrictions, taxes and captious regulations, men will always ferret out
new ways to create more wealth.

Had the depression been left to itself, it must have resulted in a general breakdown of all costs and prices, and the situation would have been cured in the old-fashioned manner after a few tough months. But government leapt in with cure-alls.

A false conception was carefully built up by propaganda that if factories could be started producing as fast as they had in the previous summer, and everyone received his former pay, everyone would again spend as he had been doing, so that all the produce would be bought once more and everything would again be lovely. To accomplish this, the government was to spend Federal money, the product of taxation, or of government borrowing which had to be met by taxation, and distribute it lavishly to the people in order to build up their spending power, as if taxing and spending could create wealth! This maneuver was labeled for public consumption as "priming the pump" and caught on like wildfire, for it suggested that a little additional spending would quickly start a flood of prosperity again.

The Reconstruction Finance Corporation was put into operation to loan money to companies which had been run so wastefully that they were too near to bankruptcy for commercial banks to loan them more money. This was done on the theory that these bolstered outfits would furnish employment at the old rates of pay. The result was, of course, to maintain the uneconomic rates of pay, the absurdly high cost of the products and the highly watered capital of the improvidently run companies—all of which would have been automatically greatly reduced by the natural action of the panic to a level that could have met the pocketbooks of the frightened and impoverished population.

Furthermore, a great ballyhoo was raised by a number of government agencies that there was no disgrace in going on relief; that anyone who needed it at all should apply; and that those who took it would not be going on the charity of their neighbors as the government would furnish suitable work to all at which they could honorably earn their pay. Then the government proceeded to furnish such work as raking up leaves, cleaning ditches, building over-elaborate athletic fields and parks, acting, singing, dancing, etc., at the public expense. Almost all such work produced no wealth whatever, but was rather a complete economic waste of effort; and since it was done at the old high wage rates, automatically prevented the one essential required, to wit: cheap and rapid production of wealth to fill the great national lack of it.

All these government palliatives were at the expense of the taxpayers and therefore further reduced the wealth of the country and produced nothing in return. All of them hindered, rather than promoted, recovery. But for all that, they were not in the least foolish or inept from the point of view of those who put them over. Those who believe in a totalitarian government need two things; first, general and continued poverty to discourage people sufficiently to make them accept such a form of government, and second, the lodging of great further power in the hands of government. All these devices promoted waste! One put the "rescued" industries under the control of their creditor government; the other put the reliefers largely at the mercy of the government, for it was perfectly easy for the bureaucrats to pick and choose who were entitled to relief and who not.

All this was swallowed by our gullible people because of that splendid shibboleth, redolent with old America and mornings on the farm—"priming the pump."

Simultaneous with this "priming the pump" effort, the slogan that "the depression was the result of overproduction" was worked to a fare-you-well. The bureaucrats bought and killed the famous 3,000,000 little pigs, bought and plowed under every fourth row of cotton, and paid farmers for not raising crops. They collected the nation's wealth in taxes or by borrowing against the future, and used that money to buy the wealth they destroyed and obliterated. This was not at all foolish from the point of view of those who believed in totalitarianism. By destroying much of the crops they put a scarcity value on the rest which raised the price beyond what those unemployed and not on relief could pay, thus forcing more people on to relief and so gaining their support. They saw that the farmers who supported their policy got paid the most, and the most readily, for not raising crops; and by wastefully destroying great blocks of the wealth of the already impoverished nation, they continued at an accelerated pace the waste and extravagance that had caused the depression in the first place, and that it was designed by God or nature to cure.

The long-drawn-out panic-depression had caused an infinity of financial worries. The people longed for surcease and peace. The totalitarians capitalized on this longing by saying there was a great public demand for "security" and that they would supply it. The unthinking mass of the public heaved a sigh of relief and cheered.

Security is defined as "freedom from apprehension, anxiety, or care; confidence of safety or power." A moment's thought shows that such a security for any individual has never lasted for more than a brief period; furthermore, in the strifes and changes in this vale of tears it can never last longer. No one could possibly have it whose course of life was dependent on the action or whim of another. Therefore it is an utter impossibility in a totalitarian state, where everyone is at the beck of a government official.

Many people do not think of the true meaning of security at all, but vaguely regard it as a stable continuation of the pleasantest conditions they ever enjoyed. Obviously this is not possible. Even if it were, it would not be desirable, since variety is the spice of life, and the long continuance of any given method of life, no matter how pleasant at the moment, would shortly become insupportable; the more so as, if it ever could be carried out, it would necessarily cause everybody to be frozen into the conditions society was in at a given moment.

The nearest approach to anything like a general security on this earth can come only from the complete freedom of opportunity that comes in a free economy. Because only there, where no man or no government can interfere with his actions or conduct so long as he does not injure others, can a man be confident of supplying his needs and desires by his own efforts.

The believers in totalitarian government, however, had no idea of working toward this true security. Their nostrum was to forcibly collect a part of everyone's earnings as premiums for a sort of term insurance to supply a fixed dollar annuity at a future time—when a man was too old to work. The system was really one of forced saving, but the saver was deprived of all use of his savings except that prescribed by the government. Having collected this mass of forced savings from those who earned them, the government did not use them to create new wealth, as corporate insurance companies would have done, but dissipated, wasted, and destroyed them in present governmental expenses, and gave the saver only its promise to supply the payments at the future date. As government has for the past decade and a half been lowering the purchasing power of the dollar, and hence of the future payments, by issuing money in quantity and by reducing the wealth of the country by interfering with production, it is a good arrangement for government.

It is a hard one, however, for the forced savers who are unable to use their savings in their own behalf to increase their wealth as opportunity presents itself, and who can get at the end only what they are given, and say thank you. Furthermore, the savings so paid in are not used to create more wealth, as they would be in private hands, but are dissipated in current expenses, leaving only a future debt to be paid by taxes or further inflation. This to the general further impoverishment of the country, and to the general injury of the prosperity of us all.

It is interesting to speculate on what would be done to the officers of a corporate insurance company who managed their business in this manner.

Benjamin Franklin said: "Those who would give up liberty for a little temporary security deserve neither liberty nor security." It looks as if we in the United States might get our desserts.

After the Roosevelt administration came in and those who believed in the theory of managed economy as promulgated in Germany had taken over control of our government, a great many bankers objected to the highly uneconomic laws and edicts that were being put into force. The objections were on economic grounds solely, and failed to consider the political ones. It was natural that these objections should come from the bankers. As long as our economy had remained at all free, the bankers were, perforce, the key men in that economy; for they controlled to a large extent, and guided the use of, the savings of the people, which are the life blood of such an economy, the means which, discreetly handled, can create the maximum wealth for its owners and so for the country. They were in effect the leaders of the vast community of American business men whose united efforts have created the greatness of the United States.

It is sad that the objections the bankers raised were instinctive rather than clearly thought out. They were made against specific acts of the government that the bankers saw were economically unsound, and incompatible with the operation of free enterprise. No banker, unfortunately, thought over the whole situation and expressed his thoughts on it with sufficient clarity to gain a following. Perhaps in the harassment of that hour no one of them had time to.

At any rate, many bankers did object violently and vociferously to a great number of the changes which government was forcing on the bewildered country. Immediately all the vituperative force of the various propaganda bureaus was turned on them. By this time those who believed in the German philosophy of managed economy had gotten control of a very large percent of the means of publicity, and, as advocated by every classic primer of revolution, were using it to hold up the nation's natural leaders to ridicule, obloquy, and contempt.

All the means of publicity accused the bankers' group of being the sole cause of the panic-depression. They were, in fact, not wholly innocent of this charge, since many of them had been gambling, just as had many in every other group. Proportionately, they were about as responsible for the cataclysm as was every other group in the United States—no more and no less—but the propaganda made them out to be solely and completely responsible for the whole mess. Those who believed in the theory of managed economy could not attack free enterprise directly; it was too popular in the country. But they could attack its leaders and so indirectly the whole system, and they did so with rare ingenuity, by labeling the bankers "the money-changers in the temple." This phrase, which if considered dispassionately is utterly unjust in its application, conjured up a picture so hideous that many began to hate all bankers *ipso facto*. In a short time its meaning was extended to include all powerful business leaders believing in free enterprise. From then on, for a number of years "the money changers in the temple" became the whipping boys in the United States, just as the Jews were in Germany, the kulaks in Russia. Whatever went wrong in the country, particularly whatever went wrong with the new regimentation being imposed, was immediately and viciously blamed on "the moneychangers in the temple." Thus was the system of free enterprise, the foundation of our greatness, vicariously held up to ridicule and contempt.

Soon the restrictions became so onerous to the people that propaganda had to be put forth to soothe them. This was done by two distinct methods. First, the meaning of words was subtly distorted so that unpleasant acts were made palatable by giving them a pleasant name and *e contra*, thus changing the meaning of words. The second method was by deliberately taking people's minds off what was going on in the government by forcing their attention on some new or impending evil. So a series of dummy chimeras were built up in the shape of "crises" and "emergencies," later to be overthrown or forgotten as seemed expedient, with a view to keeping the public mind dancing about like a pea on a hot shovel, and never focused anywhere.

Let us look at a few examples:

A "liberal" is a man who believes in liberty, absence from interference, a light government, and toleration of his neighbors. A delightful thing to be, surely, and one which everyone feels he would like to be. Yet very shortly the word was used exclusively to designate those who believed in the Germanic theory of the centralized authoritarian state and a managed economy. Those who admired and wished to emulate the present Russian system called themselves, and were called, "liberals."

Freedom is the absence of interference. Yet all the means of publicity directly began cheering for "economic freedom," which apparently meant the promised absence of worry in a state-regulated economy, where rules are laid down to keep everyone at work at such place and for such hours and pay as government directs. Freedom of planning shortly ceased to mean "the right to plan for oneself without interference," and came to mean "freedom for the bureaucracy to plan everyone's life for them and force them to conform to those plans."

A "Tory" was a member of a British party that in the reign of King George III wanted to create a highly-centralized totalitarian state. It was against the "Tories" that the American Colonists revolted. Now the term "Tory" was scathingly applied to those who strove for less government and more freedom. By the same token, those who wished to manage their own business without government interference were labeled "economic royalists." Finally—God save the mark—those who did not willingly accept the German theory of the totalitarian state and the managed economy were publicly, scornfully dubbed "un-American." This deliberate and absurd misuse of words by those in authority so confused the public mind that for a while it sank into puzzled apathy.

Let us look now at the false chimeras, the crises and emergencies used to beguile us.

In the summer of 1933 there was a severe drought in the Middle West, as there rather frequently is. This drought was accompanied by great dust storms, as is the standard order of procedure. Immediately the propaganda experts took our minds off what the bureaucrats were doing to our government by raising a hullabaloo about the terrible drought that was destroying the United States. According to their statements, it was caused by bad farming methods, by the wasteful breaking up of the prairie grass-lands, which had caused "soil erosion" to such an extent that the fertility of the soil was lastingly injured. All the ballyhoo was accompanied by photographs showing dilapidated farms in the melancholy appearance they usually have after a dust storm and before it rains. There were also photos of eroded gullies, to show the effect of the bad farming practiced under the free enterprise system. Both sorts of photographs were generally pointed up by throwing a cow's skull into the middle foreground to produce an aura of discouragement, devastation and death. One particular cow's skull with a curiously crumpled horn was used against so many backgrounds that many of the reading public acquired quite a friendly feeling for it. All the propaganda was accompanied by special efforts at relief, the more expensive the better. It was even suggested that belts of trees should be planted across the plains where they had never grown or could grow, to prevent further erosion!

Now the facts are that the plains of the Middle West have always been subject to very dry spells. In fact, in the early '80's there was much discussion as to whether they were habitable at all, for this reason. Terrible dust storms were common from the earliest days. The first cowboys on the Chisholm Trail wore kerchiefs loosely knotted around their necks to cover their mouths and noses quickly when the dust storms came. The United States Army had to provide similar kerchiefs for its cavalry uniform. The eroded gullies, known as arroyos, gulches, coulees, etc., have been there as long as white men have, and were always considered by the army in its tactical dispositions against the hostile Indians. In other words, the conditions of 1933 in the "dust bowl" were little different from their normal. They were blown up into a tragedy to remove the peoples' attention from what the partisans of a managed economy were doing to our government structure.

In contemplating the curious indirect ways in which the propaganda for the totalitarian state is applied, one should bear in mind the enormously difficult tasks its propagandists are confronted with. They are animated by the class hatred enjoined by Karl Marx and they want to have everything managed. We, on the other hand, are animated by a spirit, if not of brotherly love, at least of friendly cooperation, and want to be let alone in an economy of free enterprise. The two objectives are completely opposite. Yet to persuade us to adopt their form of government they must use arguments that appeal to us, which almost automatically points them against themselves. With this fearful disadvantage it is extraordinary that they have done as well as they have with their propaganda. Of course their main reliance must ever be on causing general discontent among us, by inducing us to ruin ourselves by huge government expenses and by turning us ever further toward state management and away from free enterprise.

Let us take one more example of holding up free enterprise to ridicule and, if not impoverishing the country, at least preventing it from enriching itself.

After the "Lost Frontier" gag had been used for a while and was growing stale, someone, who was foolish enough to take the subject matter of the propaganda seriously, "discovered" publicly that there were still 175,000,000 acres of unoccupied land available for settlement in Alaska. It was also "discovered" that "the taking up" of this land was hedged in by so many rules that, like the Czar's lands in eighteenth and nineteenth century Siberia, no one was willing to take them up. These rules were said to be "to conserve the country's natural resources," and a great smoke screen was laid down describing how "under the free enterprise system our lumber, mineral and soil had been wasted to the great detriment of the nation." A sin that was never to be repeated; and so the development was stopped.

Let's look at the record. In 1600, the area now comprised in the United States barely supported 2,000,000 naked savages.

It had vast forests, untold millions of fur-bearing animals, no mining, almost no agriculture. Its surface was as unbroken as on creation morn. Today that same area supports a population of 143,000,000. The fur-bearing animals are gone but they were mostly predatory and have been replaced by millions and millions of the animals most useful to man. A lot of the trees have been cut down, but a lot of houses have been built, and a lot of land put under the plow. A lot of minerals have been dug up, but a lot of railroads, factories, automobiles and machinery have been made from them. There has been a lot of bad farming, but even that is a whole lot more productive than no farming at all. If turning a howling wilderness into the most prosperous land on earth is "waste" in the eyes of the German political philosophers, then we need more of that "waste." It used to be called "making use of the bountiful fruits of God's earth."

Shortly afterwards, the Constitution fell as an obstacle across the path of the economic planners. One can't attack the Constitution successfully in this country. But an attempt was made to do so by holding up the Supreme Court to ridicule— by calling the members "the nine old men," and hooting them. That maneuver was a rather conspicuous failure.

As time passed and our people were progressively more regimented, they grew restless and had to be quieted. For instance, if anyone said he wished we had the kind of government there was in his boyhood—a remark that was frequently made— it was fashionable for the propagandists to sigh, shrug their shoulders, and say, "Unfortunately we can't set back the hands of the clock." This silly answer—a form of wisecrack—was successfully used to silence people for a while. Of course it is utterly absurd. We can set back the hands of the clock and do, every time it gets running too fast. If we admitted such a doctrine in the metaphysical sense in which we were meant to take it, we would have admitted the doctrine of despair. It goes with the other much used New Deal slogan, "that we are in the grip of an inevitable trend." Both these shibboleths are utter nonsense, since they deny the functioning of free will and imply predestination. We are free agents still and can recover our rights as soon as we are ready to resume our responsibilities. We turned back the clock on Prohibition fast enough, once we appreciated what it was doing to us.

Again, we were constantly battered in those years by the statement that "the complexity of modern life requires a heavy government." It is worth considering that one, for it is often still accepted. The principal changes between life in the United States in 1800 and today appear to emanate from two causes: the growth of government, which we have seen has increased 1500 fold or 150,000%; and second, the growth of mechanical contrivances.

These latter have completely altered our life in four ways: first, they have vastly increased our comforts of living by improving our plumbing, central heating, preserved foods, etc.; second, they have given us almost instantaneous communication with any part of the earth by means of telegraph, telephone, and radio; third, they have furnished us with incredibly swift transportation by means of railways, automobiles and airplanes; fourth, they have supplied us with tremendous engines of power —mental and physical—engines to distribute our ideas, like typewriters, printing presses, movies, radios, etc.—power to move mountains or create needles, as we choose.

All these devices have not complicated life; they have simplified it. The complications of life tie a man up so that he cannot attain his desires and fulfill his purposes. But these contrivances have so simplified life that a man scarcely need take thought for his daily necessities and comforts, and have given him such power over nature that today he can accomplish a hundred or a thousandfold the work he could have 150 years ago. The control the gadgets have given man over nature have infinitely simplified life.

If any reader doubts this let him try for one day to accomplish his ordinary daily stint of work without making use of any device or convenience that did not exist in 1787. He will find he can accomplish little beyond continuing his existence, and have a poor and very expensive time doing that.

It is the weight of government that has complicated life and increased expenses: the privileges set up that must be enforced by officials; the sort of thing described in Chapter 7 where the many rules conferring privileges on middlemen have checked off all rational exchange of food and fuel from the country for textiles and hardware from the towns. The privileges given corporations, unions, farmers, storekeepers, etc., etc., are

what have complicated life, made it so expensive, and made
a horde of officials necessary to enforce them. This increase of
expense results in no higher pay for the producer. It is drawn
out of the economy and absorbed by the bureaucracy. The producer gets the same as before but everybody else has to pay
more for the same thing.

The individual solution of the specific problem is, of
course, up to the people themselves for solution according to
their own and not the bureaucracy's wisdom.

It is true that some of the inventions have so altered conditions that (the way we are running things) more government
is necessary in a few cases. For instance, automobiles require
good roads, traffic lights and enforced traffic regulations. The
broadcasting stations have to have their various wave-lengths
established by government. But if government were not so
eager to establish them, could not the companies do it by agreement equally well?

As the months of the bureaucracy's triumph passed, it was
manifest that almost all the actions of the New Deal failed
to conform with the ideas of democracy that most Americans
held. A great many thoughtful private citizens commented
adversely on this in letters to newspapers, at public meetings, etc.
These attacks, made in the old-fashioned manner, were singularly
futile in the face of our fast descent to totalitarian methods.
The government propaganda machine met them in a peculiarly
subtle and surprisingly effective way.

We were informed that the education of most of our well-
to-do citizens had been of a narrow order which had taught
them, without their being conscious of it, a selfish, old-fashioned
social philosophy, and that it was the duty of these people to
become broadminded and to adopt the more liberal, philanthropic point of view of the government. So conscientious were
many good people, that they determined to be broadminded.
Now the breadth of a person's mind is partly the result of his
experience and education, but mostly of his capacity to observe,
think, judge and evaluate. The moment one becomes determined
to be broadminded, one's mind ceases to function altogether, and
merely becomes set or determined. Once that condition was
reached by these good people, they had either to adopt what

the government said was "liberal" and cheer for it, though not understanding it, or admit that they didn't understand it and stand mute. So sensitive to government criticism had most of our educated citizens become, that they accepted all the changes in silence, overawed by this silly argument, and a great mass of opposition was withdrawn.

It would be unprofitable to go into all the distortions of truth. Some were outright lies, some merely false education (as in the above instance); some were designed, in accordance with revolutionary practice, to distract the public mind with controversial matters of no great importance. Perhaps one of the quaintest was brought out when it became the administration's policy to involve us in the Second World War, in spite of the country's desire. In 1940 the British Army, a mere handful compared to the Germans, had retired from Dunkirk, abandoning all their guns and equipment except the sidearms that many of them did not discard. This disarmed and draggled force, the somewhat mauled navy, the tiny but magnificent air force, and twenty-five miles of Channel were all that stood between England and destruction by Hitler. But it was a sufficient bulwark. Yet at that hour our government was pouring out the propaganda that Hitler, who couldn't cross twenty-five miles of water to tramp out the wreckage of England's might, was planning to cross half of Europe, three thousand miles of Atlantic, and conquer us, the untouched giant! This was done at the moment that the administration was without authority giving away fifty of our cruisers and re-equipping the British army out of our surplus. It was done to deceive us and frighten us, and the dreadful thing is that, in spite of its being a childish Hallowe'en Bogey, it did frighten us.

Perhaps the high spot of all the New Deal's propaganda was "The Four Freedoms" which President Roosevelt announced to Congress on January 6, 1941 (eleven months before Pearl Harbor), as a sort of objective for getting into the Second World War. These Four Freedoms were touted all over the country as something the nation greatly desired. In the summer of 1946, a Republican aspirant for nomination to the Presidency in 1948 actually quoted them to a Republican State Convention, expecting and getting cheers. They are: freedom of speech, freedom of religion, freedom from want and freedom from fear.

A moment's consideration shows that those four freedoms, as stated, are among the very few enjoyed by every life-term convict in Sing Sing Prison. If we, as a people, undertook a war that has cost us 308,978 human casualties and $223,689,000,-000, and that jeopardized our very existence, for these four freedoms, we have either been very ill advised or grossly misled. The objective does not appear commensurate with the cost. Yet, for the past fifteen years it has been fashionable in the United States to laugh at the Germans for the gullibility with which they accept propaganda!

Today in the summer of 1950, the propaganda departments —the most dangerous of all the governmental departments that are destroying our liberty, reducing our incomes and regimenting our lives—are said to cost $75,000,000 a year, which happens to be just the sum necessary to rebuild the vast Metropolitan Museum of Art in New York City. A huge annual expenditure surely, to put across the point of view of the bureaucrats.

All the uproar for socialized medicine emanates from the Public Health Bureau—a bureau that has no proper business in the Federal Government at all. Most of the demand for special privileges for the farmers does not come from the farmers themselves, but is whipped up for "their benefit" by the propaganda bureau of the Department of Agriculture. The same seems to be true of the Federal Public Housing authority. One at least of these bureaus of propaganda seems to be openly cooperating with similar bureaus in foreign countries for the general benefit of the foreign brethren in their lodge.

All the propaganda is put out in order to increase the bureaucracy and thus further to impoverish us, regiment us, and so decrease our liberty. Why should we pay $75,000,000 a year to be told what the bureaucrats want, as if it were what we want? We know what we want all right. It is less Government interference and the enjoyment of more of our own income. The propaganda bureaus have got even Congress—their creator—buffaloed. Congressmen hate them and fear them because of the pressure they bring to bear. Certain it is, that if we are ever going to get free from the totalitarian paralysis that is creeping over us and regain our liberty and our free enterprise, these government propaganda bureaus are one of the first things that must be destroyed.

CHAPTER 11

DEMOCRACY HAS ITS FACE LIFTED

"The voice is Jacob's voice but the hands are the hands of Esau"
GEN., 27, 22

THE SPRING OF 1932 found the business morale of the United States in the dust. Three years of steadily declining prices, three years of stagnant production, three years of constant fear that the banks would close, three years of the hidden expectation of personal bankruptcy were giving numbers of our business leaders stomach ulcers and nervous breakdowns. Nevertheless, groups of them began to organize to try to correct the country's troubles, which they instinctively felt were political and arose from misuse of government.

Many groups were organized. The Economy League, the Crusaders, the Liberty League, the Spirit of '76, were typical. The trouble with these groups lay in the fact that they did not clearly see what they were combating. Most of them merely had a vague idea that "government was too expensive." None had thought the matter through to its fundamentals. Unfortunately all of them failed. It is true the National Economy League did temporarily cut down the then scandalous diversion of the national income into the pockets of unworthy veterans, but they attacked a single symptom and not the whole disease. In fact, the leaders did not then recognize what the disease was. It is probable that the Liberty League came nearest to striking at the true root of the evil, for they evoked the first great blast of ridicule and vituperation from the newly organizing propaganda groups—a blast that was utterly undeserved, but so powerful and venomous as to put them entirely out of business.

168

It was perhaps the first example of a propaganda blast in the United States from those who believed in the German philosophy of managed economy. There have been many since.

These leagues were symptomatic of the political unrest in the summer of 1932. A nation traveling the road of managed economy, from free enterprise to an authoritarian state, is not unlike a drug addict moving from health to death by use of a drug. Such addicts often instinctively try to reform and break the habits which are killing them. It appears that the United States may have instinctively made such an effort that summer of 1932.

The leaders of the Democratic Party sensed the popular feeling and drew up a platform that showed real genius. They had, of course, been out of office for all but sixteen of the past seventy-two years; therefore, and probably therefore alone, most of the harmful measures had been passed by Republican administrations. As a matter of fact, up to 1932 the statutes leading toward a managed economy were merely the result of the hog instincts of the various businesses and industries, each trying to grab for itself by law more than its fair share of the national production or income.

The 1932 Democratic Platform read in part:

"We advocate:

"(1) An immediate and drastic reduction of governmental expenses by abolishing useless commissions and offices, consolidating departments and bureaus, and eliminating extravagance, to accomplish a saving of not less than 25% in the cost of Federal Government.

"(2) Maintenance of the national credit by a Federal budget annually balanced.

"(3) A sound currency to be maintained at all hazards."

This splendid platform, which promised almost everything that was needed to start back toward a free economy was adopted. Franklin Delano Roosevelt was nominated to carry it out. He was elected by 472 electoral votes to 59. He was a man of infinite charm, as silver-tongued an orator as ever spoke. So persuasive were his words, so pleasant his manner, that he often convinced his adversaries and brought them round to his

views. On his father's side he came of what is probably one of the
most remarkable families in the United States. He was brought
up as heir to a magnificent estate on the Hudson. At Groton
School and Harvard he received the best education that money
could buy. His manners were perfect. His appearance was attractive. He had inordinate charm.

After graduating from law school he went to work, although
there was no need for it since he had been blessed with ample
family wealth. His work was politics. He was ridden by an
insatiable ambition that was ruthless. When he was out of office
(he never was out of politics) he played at being a lawyer. He
was not a good one, but his charm and the great wealth of his
family easily got him a partnership in a respectable firm. He
apparently never had any financial sense at all, but with great
wealth behind him this made little difference. Once, in the early
1920's, he started a business that was so foolishly conceived and
so wastefully carried out that it passed in a few months into
insolvency and closed up. The incident was for a short time the
laughing-stock of his social acquaintances. The memory of it
was shortlived, for it was obliterated by his great tragedy—an
attack of infantile paralysis.

He met his illness with magnificent fortitude. He almost
conquered it by his will. At any rate he reduced it to insignificance. Through all that happened he never lost his touch with
politics. He knew everyone who was important, everything that
was going on. He studied politics, statesmanship, and political
economy as an art.

Finally, in 1928, he was persuaded, in spite of the effects of
his illness, to run for Governor of New York State to help his
friend Al Smith to the Presidency. He was elected. He was not
a particularly conspicuous governor. He was wasteful—but New
York was inured to that. In his second term he was very prodigal
with relief and even tried, by proclamation, to persuade people to
accept it. It was said of him sometimes that he was trying to
buy votes with public funds. But people paid little attention to
his administration of office. In most of his first term they were
drunk with the last glories of the boom. The rest of the time
they were sunk in their personal woes from the depression.

Everything considered, he appeared in 1932 to be an ideal
candidate for the Presidency. He was of old American stock, of

conservative background and stately presence. He had studied statesmanship intensely. He had shown personal courage and will-power. He knew all the important Democratic politicos. He had administrative experience. He was well-known throughout the country. His people were so rich that he appeared above financial corruptibility. What more could be desired in a Presidential candidate?

It is true that some of his personal acquaintances said that he was insanely ambitious, had no money sense, was untrustworthy, did not keep his word, was extremely vindictive, ruthless, and that he craved power as a drunkard craves drink. But these acquaintances were few and were in his social, not his political, world. Their words got no publicity and were of no importance.

What no one then seemed to know about him was that he was a convinced disciple of the German school of political economy, of the social planners, "the discipline under leadership" fanatics, and that he was intimately associated with its professors and other disciples of that creed. Yet he rode into the Presidency on the most American, free-enterprise platform that was ever written!

By 1932, there were a number of Americans who believed in the philosophy of the German political economists, and so in national economic planning. They were men—for the most part college professors—well dressed, well behaved, well spoken. They were not at all the type that the public looked on as revolutionaries, yet all these men believed in a strong authoritarian government and a managed economy, and were opposed to free enterprise, capitalism and individual liberty. They appear to have been gluttons for power, perhaps because few of them had ever wielded any. It is certain many of these gentlemen had studied the books on revolutionary technique and propaganda, a quantity of which had been published in the previous score of years. They had discussed them together and made plans; plans that were grounded on the moral tone and the general principles of those already in use in the totalitarian regimes of Europe. The plans were now however elaborate, carefully thought out, and subtle.

Oddly enough, in the spring of 1933 American business men apparently did not consider this group of intellectuals or

their beliefs as of any importance. Certainly some of the younger
business men must have studied under them; but it would seem
that those who did, dismissed the professors and their theories
as part of the philosophical nonsense so common in colleges,
and, if they considered them at all, dismissed them as too highly
theoretical for any practical purpose. Consequently, when these
intellectuals appeared clothed with power, the businessmen
were flabbergasted. They had no more plans to resist them than
they had to resist the Martians.

These intellectuals were very few in number, compared
with the whole population. They probably had had little hope
of ever getting into power in this country; their numbers were
too small, their philosophy was too unpopular. In fact, the popularity of their philosophy in this country could be then measured by the numerical strength of the Socialist and Communist
Parties, which was negligible. Nevertheless, in conversation they
made plans for what they would do, if——

In November, 1932, one of their number was elected President of the United States, on a platform that made the people
think they were headed back for the light form of government characteristic of the early days in the United States. In
February, 1933, the final phase of the depression-panic at last
approached. All the banks got wobbly. (The closing of the banks
is the normal end of every depression, as we have seen. In this
case it had been very much delayed by the governmental
efforts of the Hoover administration.) The country was wild
with fear of the loss of their possessions, and looking for anything—a Messiah even—to save them. In March, 1933, Roosevelt
was inaugurated. He made a glorious, confident speech in which
he said that "the only thing to fear was fear" and promised the
people a New Deal.

The people thought, from the Democratic platform, and
because of their desires, that what the New Deal promised was
relief from governmental interference with business and from
heavy taxation. The President kept to himself that what the
New Deal promised was the complete domination of business
by government. What the President thought proved more important than what the people thought.

Accompanying the new President to Washington came
great hordes of the disciples of planned economy, eager for the

offices they received. It was a heaven-sent opportunity for them. Perhaps it was a just punishment on the people of the United States for their long neglect of their government and of the true principles of government. The people laughed heartily at the hordes of impractical professors scrambling into political office and running things. They did not realize that these men were ardent believers in an authoritarian state; well-prepared by their studies and determined to take over the control of the country. From constant classroom speaking professors learn a good deal about handling mob psychology.

These planners came into power at a very fortunate time for themselves, since our people were distraught with their financial losses, and unable to think clearly because of their fears and worries. The economic planners preached true democracy and were prepared to seize power as fast and ruthlessly as possible. They appeared to believe sincerely that their proposed objective would benefit the people at large. Thus was the United States and the Democratic Party betrayed by the first political use in America on the national scale of the principle that the end justifies the means. Franklin Roosevelt was admirably qualified by nature for the part he had chosen to play. He had strong will, energy, intelligence, and charm. It was very appropriate that those who worked intimately with him in the White House should affectionately and reverently address him as "Caesar."

Even with control of the executive branch of the government, any attempt by a group to turn the United States into a managed economy state involved enormous difficulties. The people had a deep affection and respect for their Constitution and for that system of capitalistic free enterprise which they believed they still enjoyed. To succeed, the New Dealers would have to control the money power completely, and so the business of the United States; they would have to use this power to build a huge bureaucracy to perpetuate the totalitarian party in office, and use it also to reduce the country to real poverty. A poor commonwealth is more amenable to absolute authority than is a rich one, and a huge bureaucracy is necessary to inaugurate and maintain totalitarian control.

Because of the popular sentiment none of this could be

done openly and directly. It had to be managed by guile, deceit and indirection. Therefore to accomplish it, all the means of publicity available were devoted to discussion of the best way to restore prosperity. Arguments for and against various proposed steps quickly divided the people into groups, contending over matters of no great importance. Meanwhile the executive set to work to seize power as fast and ruthlessly as possible under the guise of helping restore prosperity.

The Constitution soon became a serious obstacle in the path of the New Dealers. They could not change it. Therefore they evidently decided to retain its form, since they had to; but by conspiracy among themselves and by bamboozling the confused Congress round to their will, they worked to distort its objects and its spirit so as to make of it a shell only, behind which to carry out their grab for power. This seems an impossible thing to do. It is not. It is only difficult. It had been done before in Germany and Italy.

Under the guise of restoring prosperity, the disciples of managed economy sought to control the banking power of the United States, because the banks, by controlling the savings of the people, control the business of the country. We have seen that in an economy of free enterprise the banking power is pulling in so many directions that it can never be very dangerous, but in a managed economy, where its whole force is controlled by one hand, its power verges on the absolute, since it is capable of ruling production and distribution with a rod of iron. This power appeared desirable to the New Dealers.

Immediately on his inauguration the President closed all the banks by executive decree, and forbade all dealing in foreign exchange or transfer of credit from the United States under penalty of fine and imprisonment. This was a wholly illegal act, but as most of the banks were going to have to close in a short time anyway, they closed without fuss.

Three days later, when Congress convened, the President had it pass an act legalizing all the decrees the President had issued in the past three days. In justice to the Congressmen it must be said that they were then a brand new Congress and in the panic state of mind of the rest of the country.

On April 15th a second decree was issued (not a law, mind you!) calling on everybody to turn in to the government-controlled banks all the gold he had, under penalty of a fine of double the gold held out, and of imprisonment. This was understood to be a temporary measure to bolster the national credit in the emergency. It was not in the least necessary for any credit or banking purpose. The credit of the United States was then perfect, and besides, in Uncle Sam's pocket alone was 40 percent of the entire gold supply of the whole world. It was a long step, however, in the direction of placing the power to issue fiat money in the hands of the state without its being noticed by the people. For with gold out of the way, no one would notice the depreciation of the currency which would have been obvious had gold been in circulation, because then the fiat currency would soon have been selling at a discount. The decree was obeyed with great patriotic fervor, whipped up by speeches. Thus were the citizens divested of their property through misuse of their impulses of patriotism.

The President's point of view has been well stated by Garet Garrett in a pamphlet entitled *The Revolution Was*:

> In his inaugural address, March 4, 1933, the President declared that the people had asked for discipline and direction under leadership, that he would seek to bring speedy action "within my constitutional authority"; and that he hoped the "normal balance of executive and legislative authority" could be maintained, and then said: "but in the event that Congress shall fail . . . But in the event that the national emergency is still critical . . . I shall ask Congress for the one remaining instrument to meet the crisis—broad executive power to make war against the emergency, as great as the power that would be given me if we were, in fact, invaded by a foreign foe."
>
> It is true that the people wanted action. It is true that they were in a mood to accept any pain killer, and damn the normal balance of authority between the executive and the legislative authority. That was a normal state of mind perfectly suited to a revolutionary purpose, and the President took advantage of it to make the first startling exposition of New Deal philosophy. Note his assertion of the leadership principle over any other. Discipline under leadership. Note the threat to Congress—"in the event that the Congress shall fail." But who was to say if the Congress had failed? The leader,

of course. If in his judgment the Congress failed, then, with the people behind him, he would demand war powers to deal with an economic emergency.

The word emergency was then understood to mean what the dictionaries said it meant—namely a sudden juncture of events demanding immediate action. It was supposed to refer only to the panic and the banking crisis, both temporary. But what it meant to the President, as nobody then knew, was a very different thing. Writing a year later, in his book *On Our Way*, he said: "Strictly speaking, the banking crisis lasted only one week . . . But the full meaning of that word emergency related to far more than banks; it covered the whole economic and therefore the social structure of the country. It was an emergency that went to the roots of our agriculture, our commerce, our industry; it was an emergency that has existed for a whole generation, in its underlying causes and for three and a half years in its visible effects. It could be cured only by a complete reorganization and measured control of the economic structure. . . . It called for a long series of new laws, new administrative agencies. It required separate measures affecting different subjects; but all of them component parts of a fairly definite broad plan."

That, apparently, shows what was in the President's mind, and shows it pretty definitely too, though at the time few people saw it. At any rate, he got by his decree of April 15th absolute control of all the gold in the United States, got the gold out of circulation, and was well started on his way to a managed fiat currency.

At about that time the United States Treasury was found to be practically empty. Business had been stagnant for the last three-and-a-half years and taxes are only a government levy on business. Government had been expending huge sums on relief and there was not enough business to bear a further levy. Besides, in spite of the Democratic Party's pledge to reduce government costs by 25 percent, those costs had been increasing in an unprecedented manner. The New Deal could certainly use fiat money, and presto, in spite of the platform, it came to hand. An amendment was tacked on to the Farm Relief bill compelling the Federal Reserve Bank System to take $3,000,000,000 worth of Treasury notes and authorizing them to print $3,000,000,000 worth of fiat money at the President's discretion. The majority of the people were not yet willing to allow fiat money to be printed, so the affair was camouflaged. The banks were required to take government bonds and the bonds were held to be such good security that it was all right to print money against them. So the money was there, the printing presses had been run twice—once to make the bonds, once to make the money—and everyone was happy!

By the same amendment the Congress further gave the President the power to devalue the dollar by one-half in his own discretion!

It is hard to see now why Congress did such a thing. By doing so they gave up their power over the purse to the Executive, when their duty was to protect it against him. This had been the duty of legislatures since Magna Charta. There was absolutely no need of their devaluating. The government was not only solvent; it had the best credit in the world. To be sure, like the rest of the country, Congress was under the spell of the President's charming personality. He had been built up by propaganda into a Messiah. He had asked for this power. Economic affairs had been made to look so complex that few might understand them. Besides, the President had not yet made the normal political appointments the Congressmen had requested. It began to look as if those who failed to follow his suggestions would not get their appointments and so could not reward those who had worked to elect them. Perhaps it would be wiser to follow the Messiah. The President was authorized to devalue the dollar at his discretion.

Next, at his request Congress repudiated the "gold clause" in all government and corporate bonds. This clause, which was contained in many bond indentures, guaranteed that the creditor should have his loan and interest paid "in gold coin of the United States of the present standard of weight and fineness." This clause had been commonly inserted in bonds since the time the "greenbacks" were used after the Civil War, in order to induce people to lend their money on the assurance that the debt would be paid back in money of like value. The Supreme Court held this act constitutional but immoral. So a further step toward a managed fiat currency was made.

The next step was to control the lending of the banks. Heretofore the whole credit of the country had been pooled in the Federal Reserve Banks, and any member bank desiring money and having proper security had the right to borrow there. A new law reduced this right to a mere privilege. The Federal Reserve Banks, controlled by Presidential appointees, might now refuse to discount loans for those bankers who failed to toe the mark, even if they had sufficient security. This effectually brought all recalcitrants to heel.

These five acts—(1) the act confirming the edict that closed the banks and preventing transfers of foreign exchange (2) the decree calling in all the gold (3) the act permitting fiat money and permitting the President to devalue the dollar (4) the act repudiating the gold clause in the bonds, and (5) the act giving the Federal Government, through the Federal Reserve Banks, the power to say how all the banks should lend their money— put the entire money power of the United States into the hands of the President. Furthermore, they were passed in such a way that they were discussed only as steps leading toward prosperity, which they were not, and never considered as instruments to impose a managed economy on the country, which they were.

But from the planners' point of view there was still danger that, through force of habit, so much money would seep back into the banks that they would not have to discount their loans with the Federal Reserve System and so might become again almost independent of government and its planners.

Up till 1933, almost everybody and every business that wanted to borrow money did so from banks, and so put themselves to an extent in the power of the banks. The planners wished to break this habit. They were averse to any power but their own, and thought it preferable that borrowers should put themselves in the government's hands—that is, the bureaucrats' hands.

The President said: "I am authorizing the Reconstruction Finance Corporation to buy newly-mined gold in the United States at prices to be determined from time to time after consultation with the Secretary of the Treasury and the President. Whenever necessary to the end in view we shall also buy or sell gold in the world market. My aim in taking this step is to establish and maintain continuous control. This is a policy and not an expedient."

There followed a deliberate monetary confusion that would have appeared insane even in *Alice in Wonderland*. Every morning the price of gold for the day was announced in Washington like a lottery number in the policy game. Always this price fluctuated. And this juggling was done with the relative prices of the dollar and gold when everyone supposed that the value of the dollar was a *certain* weight in gold. One ounce of gold had been worth $20.67.

No one outside of the charmed circle of planners yet conceived that a scheme was already far on its way to execution to change the free United States into an authoritarian state with a planned economy, and still retain the form of its venerated Constitution, by the use of methods that would have been inconceivable to the framers of that Constitution. No one, that is, save one poor devil named William Wirt who exposed their plan and was lied of, and ridiculed by propaganda, till he died of a broken heart.

Dr. Wirt's statement did have some repercussions before he was ridiculed to death. Among them the following New York *Times* editorial of March 30, 1934, deserved more attention than it got:

The Real "Revolution"

The efforts to "smear" Dr. Wirt and to whitewash the "brain trust" should not be permitted to distract attention from the basic charges in Dr. Wirt's letter. These have little to do with "Kerenskys" and "Stalins" but much to do with fundamental changes in our social, economic and political structure involved in measures already passed by or introduced into Congress. These measures, giving life to the New Deal, have made it possible for the government in Washington to:

1. Tell the American farmer how much he may grow and punish him with a fine if he grows more.

2. Tell American storekeepers what prices they must charge for articles they sell. (Already a man in Rochester has been arraigned for the crime of giving away a loaf of bread with a bottle of milk that he sold.)

3. Fix prices for services such as tailoring. (Already men have been punished in California, Michigan, Illinois and Alabama for charging a few cents less for pressing a dress than the price fixed in Washington.)

4. License industries, limiting their hours of work, their output, the prices of their products and even their right to modernize their plants.

5. Exercise powers of life or death over business operations through the arbitrary use of the tariff-making powers by the President rather than by Congress.

6. Attempt to control sources of credit through the securities bill and the stock exchange regulations and the new banking bills.

7. Confiscate personal property through the forced surrender of gold and the subsequent devaluation of the dollar.

8. Cripple an entire industry like aviation by preferring unspecified and as yet unproved charges of corruption and collusion in obtaining contracts and by summarily cancelling these contracts without a hearing or a fair trial.

These—to mention but a few of the departures from the old American system—do not signify "revolution." But through most of them runs the desire to consolidate arbitrary and almost dictatorial powers in the hands of the Federal government, and to set as a goal a sort of "planned economy" in which the Federal government is to determine the entire productive activities of the country. A planned economy implies not only a surrender of individual rights to the national government but the creation by the national government of a large bureau of "compliance" (to use the New Deal terminology for what used to be called "enforcement"). We shall have to have an industrial and agricultural "Cheka."

These changes lead, unless checked, to the establishment of a sort of economic despotism in place of democracy. This is the goal of much of the New Deal. And this, unless we misread the sound sense that is sandwiched in with the gossip and chaff in Dr. Wirt's letter, is what he warns against. Certainly most of his fellow-countrymen have so far failed to perceive that such a danger lies ahead.

It is not too late to call a halt. The President is still in "midstream" and the course that some of his advisers have been urging on him has not yet been run. There can be no possible doubt as to the nation's reaction once it knows the whole truth. Only if those who are seeking thus to effect unperceived changes in our system succeed in stifling discussion is there any fear of the outcome.

The fullest possible discussion of the New Deal is therefore imperative—including the ideals as well as the acts to date of the so-called "brain trust." The service of Dr. Wirt's letter has been to facilitate such an airing. It may be that the country wishes to submit to a regimented "planned economy." But before submitting it should at least have a chance to know that such a planned economy is another name for paternalism or benevolent autocracy, and that as such it is the negation of the American system under which this nation grew great and powerful.

Vitally important as the proposed discussion would have been to the United States, the bureaucratic propaganda of the New Deal was able to choke it off in a few brief days, to the lasting injury of the people of the United States.

So many crazy and fantastic things had been going on in the world of political economy that even the constant alteration of the price of gold aroused no marked comment among the people at large. But it did produce a great effect on the bankers.

Bankers are proverbially conservative. They have to be, to be successful, and they are trained in the history of the banking experience of the past. They knew that what established the value of money was the weight of the certain amount of gold it contained. They were thoroughly frightened and confused when they saw the weight of gold represented by the unit of money juggled about from day to day. It did not make sense. Looking at the past, they had recently seen the currencies of Europe inflated in many instances till they had become of no value. They confusedly decided that they were not going to lend good money, worth an ounce of gold for every $20-67/100, and get back six months later money of the same face value but worth only half as much in gold. They had seen what had happened in Germany. They got scared and would not lend readily. In fact they would hardly lend at all. This was exactly what the planners in Washington wanted—probably what they expected. Almost certainly "they had planned it that way."

Immediately on the failure of the banks to lend normally, the government set up a horde of Federal loaning agencies. The planners made great clamor about the suffering of humanity and how they would relieve it. They would loan money to practically anybody or any corporation. Home owners, farmers, veterans, corporations, small businesses, cities, towns—almost any group of the population could borrow from them. In fact, they were practically implored to come and borrow, for according to the planners the government was not only relieving the suffering of the borrower, but the money so loaned would create employment and hasten recovery.

The planners had everything to gain by this and nothing to lose. If the loans were bad, the loss would fall on the taxpayers. The borrowers were naturally grateful to the government for the loans. The planners were rightly beginning to think of themselves as the government. Soon it became obvious that the government was doing most of the banking business of the country. Washington became in fact the banking center. The bankers, that is business, that is free enterprise, had lost its power over its own money. The Federal Government had taken over that power and held its terrific concentrated force in one hand.

Now that the New Dealers had gained this, for them, so desirable power, they felt they might as well use it. There was no sense in juggling the currency further, for it had become their currency. They concluded their planned financial program with a double-barreled act that was perhaps natural but certainly not very ethical. At the request of the President on January 30, 1934, Congress passed an act confiscating or appropriating for the government's own use all the gold in its treasury, which according to the proclamation of the Secretary of the Treasury issued some nine months before, had been called in as a sort of patriotic deposit, allegedly to bolster the national credit in an emergency that never really existed. The next day the President fixed the dollar's new value at 59 percent of its former one.

Thus the government confiscated for its own use 41 percent of the value of the outstanding currency. Two billion dollars of this confiscated loot was turned over to the President as a "stabilization fund" to do almost anything he liked with. Thus was the money power taken out of the hands of business, which had earned it, and whose vital principal it was, for the benefit of government. The planned state, conceived in Germany, had captured the U.S.A.

Nothing in the Constitution specifically forbade any of the moves described, though they would have been inconceivable to the patriotic fathers of our country. They were all passed ostensibly to bring about recovery. It is certain that recovery after the 1929-1933 panic-depression was slower than recovery had ever been before, and might be said never to have occurred till the second war. It is certain also that these moves gave the government, now in the hands of the social planners, more power than had ever been dreamed of.

Besides, these moves had resulted in Congress' turning over much of its legislative power to the Executive. It had given up the power of the purse with which, from time immemorial, it was supposed to control him. It had delegated also much of its power to make laws by authorizing the executive agencies to make regulations which had the force of laws. Congress had been induced to thus abrogate much of its power because of propaganda designed to confuse it, because of the belief, also built by propaganda, that the President was a sort of Messiah, and because of fear that they could not get political appointments for their henchmen.

Thus the executive and legislative authority was pretty well concentrated in one hand, contrary to the fundamental intention of the Constitution. But by virtue of that same Constitution, which could not be wholly cast aside, it was not there indefinitely. The voters had to be cajoled into continuing it every two years, or the social planners might lose their grip. The accomplishment of this became the chief objective of the New Deal planners.

The two largest occupational groups in the United States are the farmers and organized labor. Each has a great many votes. Each buys the other's produce. Therefore any attempt to increase by statute the share of the national income that either group enjoyed was necessarily at the expense of the other group. The New Dealers could not afford to buy the vote of either at the cost of the other's vote. Therefore they had to resort to flimflam so that each group would see the benefits it was getting and neither would notice how it was paying for the other's benefit. This was done under the usual disguise of bringing back prosperity. It had the usual effect, of course, of artificially raising the prices of labor and agricultural products against the general public. The following methods were used.

To help the farmers, they were paid, as we have seen, for their pigs, cotton, and so on, which the government destroyed to the general impoverishment of the country. This created an artificial scarcity and raised the price of what remained. To continue this scarcity and keep up the prices against the public, the government began to pay farmers with money collected in taxes, for *not* raising crops. All the farmer had to do was to plant what government told him, gather what grew and be paid for what he might have raised if he had tried. This relieved him of a lot of work and worry but did not impair his income. It was soon noticed, and in fact became rather a rural scandal, that the loudest rooters for the New Deal got the fattest cheques.

When the war started, a food shortage became acute and the above method was changed. Farmers were not permitted to raise prices, but a bonus was given them to "offset the increased cost of production." All this required an increase in the bureaucracy to raise and distribute the subsidies. The cost to the country in taxes for the farmers' bonus was fantastic, but it kept the farmer satisfied. As Al Smith said: "No one ever shoots Santa Claus."

Of course the wage earners had also to be cajoled into voting for the New Deal. Garet Garrett's extraordinary pamphlet, *The Revolution Was,* puts it neatly:

> What the New Deal did for labor was to pass a series of laws the purpose of which was to give organized labor the advantage in its bargaining with the employer. As these laws were construed and enforced they did principally three things: They delivered to organized labor a legal monopoly of the labor supply; they caused unionism to become in fact compulsory, and then made it possible for unions to practice intimidation, coercion, and violence with complete immunity provided only it was all in the way of anything that might be called a labor dispute. The underlying idea was that with this

power added to it, together with a minimum wage and hour act, that made overtime a way of fattening the pay envelope, organized labor could very well, by its own exertions, increase its share of the national income enough to equal or overcome the farmers' new advantage. And this organized labor proceeded forthwith to do.

But there was at the same time an indirect subsidy to labor much greater than the direct subsidy paid to the farmer. Federal expenditures for work relief, amounting in the average to more than two billion a year, must be regarded as a subsidy to organized labor. The effect was to keep eight or ten million men off the labor market, where their competition for jobs would have been bound to break the wage structure. Thus union labor's monopoly of the labor supply was protected.

Thus by the statutory privileges conferred on organized labor, the labor leaders were largely able to decide the cost of all the manufactured products of the country. Those laborers so unfortunate as to be unable to get into unions were condemned to either the lowest forms of work or to perpetual "relief". The public was subjected to the inconvenience of constant strikes, and many private individuals were grievously injured while trying to get work.

There has been a corollary effect to giving by statute such tremendous privileges to trade unions, which has not been altered by the Taft Hartley Act (an act that has done something to mitigate the more outrageous privileges given to labor by the New Deal's labor policy), but which has had a very serious effect on the production, and therefore the income and wealth, of the nation. Today it is all but impossible for an employer to fire an unsatisfactory union employee, despite the fact that, if an employer is to manage a business, he must have disciplinary powers over those to whom he pays his money in wages. In a totalitarian state the manager has practically the power of life and death over the workers, which is a condition too hideous to contemplate. In a free economy the only power a manager had was to fire the unsatisfactory and put them to the inconvenience and expense of getting another job. This power was at times unjustly used; that is too bad. Nevertheless, without it there cannot possibly be any effective management. That power has been almost removed now (if one doubts it ask any manager in charge of union labor), and its lack has necessarily had a great effect in reducing the production, that is the income, of the country. Furthermore, the unions discourage individual efforts toward maximum production, and this also has its effect on the national income. But perhaps the worst effect of all is a tendency to kill all initiative and ambition in the workmen, holding them at the minimum standard of "getting by" with their work, and discouraging them from bettering themselves, and thereby the income of us all. If union labor was not protected by legislation giving it special privilege, natural competition would shortly break all this nonsense down and our production would be largely increased thereby to the general betterment.

The unions have gradually been able to reduce the working hours of their members from 72 hours a week to 40. They are now beginning to talk of reducing hours to 30. Even at 40 hours they have greatly reduced the potential individual production of the workmen available, and therefore of the country at large, which has cut the income of the country generally by a great deal. There are 168 hours in a week. Eight hours a day's sleep is generally considered sufficient. So 56 hours a week go in sleep. That leaves 112 waking hours; so if a union man works 40 hours a week he will work a litttle less than 36 percent of his waking time, on the production that makes his own and his family's living. Compared with the hours per week farmers and other people work, especially those self-employed, it seems a reprehensibly low percentage. It has certainly been found so by the authorities in the totalitarian countries. It has already reduced our national income and wealth materially, and now the unions threaten to reduce it by 25 percent more.

Besides all this, unions have done various things to slow up production, such as dividing up a simple job between several unions, thus making it very expensive and giving the unions opportunities to squabble among themselves over "jurisdiction" and have unnecessary strikes. They have fought against piecework, discouraged rapid production by insisting on promotion by seniority and not for merit, on equal pay irrespective of production, and even on dismissing fast workers, whom they have been known to beat up. They have forced employers to adopt "make work" rules and often to hire totally useless and unnecessary employees. All this on the theory that there is just so much work to be done, and that they ought to spread it over as many workers as possible. They don't seem to realize that there would be a demand for an infinity of their work if it were available at a fair price, and that all their efforts accomplish is to raise the cost of their product beyond what the public will pay. It is true that if they get work under their system they receive an exorbitant wage for it. Yet the system reduces the amount of their potential work because the public can't pay their prices; and since all unions are doing the same thing, all together they are thus constantly reducing the demand for their own products by raising the prices against themselves and the members of other unions as well as the general public. The ultimate result is less wealth for the country and less real wages for the members of the unions themselves.

Let us get back to the story of labor in the early days of the New Deal. Those eight or ten million potential producers who had been taken out of production to help organized labor had to be looked after by the economic planners and kept happy, for their vote was necessary. They were put to unproductive work, that is to destroying wealth, on the WPA and other projects, at high pay from the government, which collected it from the producers. The country was soon treated to the spectacle of its new paupers motoring in their own cars to play at work while on relief. Thus were their votes acquired, but so also were they brought under government control by economic pressure.

Almost anybody who wished to borrow from the government could do so in one of the many lending agencies. So the many borrowers were induced to surrender much of their freedom to their willing creditor. The forced savings of social security and old age insurance removed from the people the control of their own savings and the freedom of action and spirit such control gives. Under the guise of giving bank depositors security for their deposits, the controls over the banks were tightened. Thus power was grabbed as fast and ruthlessly as possible while only the truest democracy was preached.

In these ways the executive branch of the Federal government got control of finance and industry, of a large part of the votes of the farmers, of organized labor, of the reliefers, and of the borrowers who had taken out loans for their homes, their businesses and their emergencies. But there were still agencies in the country which had power of their own and were not controlled by the Executive. This, of course, was contrary to the plans of those who follow the German political-economic philosophy, and hold that all power should be under the executive branch of government in order that the leader may control it, the planners and the people, for the general good.

There were still in the United States, free and independent from the executive authority, the Federal courts, the Congress and the state and local governments. These might still give the planners trouble, and would have to be brought into line. Plans to this end had some success, but in the main they failed. The people of the United States woke up, dimly feeling that something was wrong. Though they did not clearly perceive what it was, nevertheless they thwarted the planners' intentions, but not before much harm was done to these governmental units.

The Supreme Court held the National Recovery Act unconstitutional. This outraged the New Dealers who did not want their plans interfered with. They tried to pack the Court with extra new justices, whose views favored a planned and managed national economy. The reaction of the public to this was so spontaneous and violent that even the dispirited Congress picked up courage and refused to obey. This was the first strong rebuff the New Deal got. Its practical effect was negligible, however, for death and resignations soon opened up a majority of the positions on the Supreme bench. The new appointees were good New Dealers, but for the most part had not previously been very distinguished jurists. This was not important. The Executive is the important part of government in a planned economy. In fact the propaganda had recently been holding the Supreme Court up to ridicule as "the nine old men."

The first Congress under the New Deal had been as subservient as a rubber stamp and had simply passed the bills the Executive sent to it with little or no debate. It yielded most of its power of the purse and much of its law-making power by giving the regulations of the executive agencies the force of law. The subsequent Congresses, however, contained many courageous men who were independent and critical. The plans were debated before they were passed, often attacked, sometimes defeated. This was very troublesome.

The New Deal, still operating under the form of the Constitution, could not very well attack the legislative branch of its own government, particularly when it was controlled by the Democratic Party to which the New Deal owed allegiance and pretended to belong. It therefore attacked the members of Congress who were pecking at it. It tried to "purge" these men and get rid of them at the elections. To the honor of our voters it seldom succeeded.

The New Dealers went further than this. A report of a Special Committee appointed by the Lower House of Congress to investigate un-American activities stated:

> The effort to obliterate the Congress of the United States as a coequal and independent branch of our government does not as a rule take the form of a bold and direct assault. We seldom hear a demand that the powers with which Congress is vested by the Constitution be transferred in toto to the executive branch of our government, and that Congress be adjourned in perpetuity . . . The creeping totalitarianism by which we are menaced proceeds with subtler methods. The senior United States Senator from Wyoming has called attention to the work of men "who in the guise of criticizing individual members of Congress are actually engaged in the effort to undermine the institution itself." Many of the efforts to purge individual members of Congress are based upon an assumption which reflects discredit upon the entire legislative branch of government. That assumption consists of the view that the sole remaining function of Congress is to ratify by unanimous vote whatever wish is born anywhere at any time in the whole vast structure of the executive branch of the government down to the last whim of any and every administrative official . . . Over a large part of the world today democracy has been long dead. Political processes which once assured the common man some degree of genuine participation in the decisions of his government have been superseded by a

form of rule which we know as the totalitarian state. The essence of totalitarianism is the destruction of the parliamentary or legislative branch of government. The issue simply stated is, whether the Congress of the United States shall be the reality or the relic of American democracy.

Here is perhaps the best place to state, and to state emphatically, that the New Deal Party and the Democratic Party are not synonymous terms. Most Democrats are sincere American patriots, believing from their hearts in the Constitution of the United States, believing in the rule of law, and in complete liberty of the individual under the rule of law, believing in free enterprise and the old American principles. Most Democrats yield no whit to the Republican Party on these principles. But unfortunately the form of the Democratic Party was captured by the disciples of a totalitarian state and a managed economy, just as the form of the constitutional government of the United States was so captured. In each case the New Dealers, acting within the form, completely subverted the principles and objectives of the organization.

The disciples of totalitarianism are clever and dangerous. Their one desire is power. They allow no morals or scruples to stand in their way. For them, any move that fosters totalitarianism is moral. They have thought long and deeply on the methods that will reduce us all to their power, whilst we have been mistakenly ascribing our own decent political morality to them. Furthermore, they surround themselves with a horde of sincere, well-intentioned bumblepuppies whom their clever arguments have subverted to belief in some of their immediate, tangible objectives. These bumblepuppies lend a most valuable and respectable aura of virtuous humanitarianism to their group. One of the saddest sights in the world is the terrible harm done by stupid but well-intentioned people, who often create the exact opposite of what they intend, because they do not think through clearly to the probable result of their actions. Perhaps it is on account of this that Gautama Buddha listed "discrimination" as the greatest essential human virtue.

Besides the Supreme Court and Congress, the units of state and local government presented possible centers of rival power to the New Deal executive power, which could not eliminate them and therefore sought to weaken them by several methods.

The new government money power was brought into play. Federal loans or grants were used to induce states, counties, cities, towns and villages to go in for great extravagances that they would never have indulged in if they had expected to finance them locally. It seemed unreasonable to refuse the Federal offers. Of course the United States Government kept some "say" in the way the money was spent and the improvements used. This method got them power in almost every locality. The people, of course, did not realize they were taxed twice for these extravagances; once openly by the locality, once clandestinely by the Federal government.

The clause in the Constitution which gives Congress power "to regulate commerce with foreign nations, among the several states, and with the Indian tribes," was used to seize local power in an extraordinary way. Its meaning was stretched out of all sense and reason, and interpreted to allow the Federal authorities to regulate and inspect every business and occupation connected, however remotely, with interstate commerce. For instance, chicken farmers were controlled because the chicken feed or the eggs might get into interstate commerce; elevator men were also taken over because some of the tenants in the buildings they worked in might be engaged in it. As all business is, or may be, connected with interstate commerce, everything today is Federally regulated and Federal inspectors are everywhere, to the great increase of government power.

All sorts of local agencies are duplicated by Federal ones; relief, agriculture, etc., etc. The Federal agents sit beside the local ones and, under the guise of helping, control and reduce their power. Probably today in every county seat there are nearly as many Federal agents as local ones. The latter are now undermined and impotent. Yet for 150 years the local government was satisfactory and an object of pride to the citizens. Certainly the nearer the control of a government agency is to the people it serves, the more satisfactory it is to those people.

All in all the New Deal was enormously successful in gathering power for the executive branch of the Federal government. It had multiplied the bureaucracy many times. It was quite as successful in impoverishing the nation, as study of our national income during the 1930's will show. These, of course, were necessary preliminaries toward bringing any people to select perforce the authoritarian form of government.

After the New Deal had been in the saddle for two or three years it had amassed sufficient power to take over control of all business, did it so choose, and run it exactly like bureaus of the government, making its executives, clerks and workmen government employees. There is some evidence the New Deal toyed with this idea—the logical conclusion of the German philosophy. But this scheme had been tried out in Russia and had failed miserably, causing a collapse of all industry and a long prostration that was very painful. Besides, it involved the danger of government, in its capacity of management, antagonizing all its workers, as management sometimes does; and in this country workers are still voters.

In both Germany and Italy an alternative method of business control had been evolved that had worked considerably less badly than had the Russian method. Business was allowed to continue to operate and to make some profit, but every detail of its activity was subject to minute government regulation and control. This method was planned for us here. It was carried out as a patriotic war measure. Everything a business got—raw material, machinery, labor—was allotted by government. The prices of all these were prescribed by government. What it was to do was assigned by government, which also established its executives' and clerks' salaries and the price at which it could sell its goods. All distribution of goods to localities was likewise regulated. All this was done with the constant threat that, if the business, or any component part thereof, did not function as directed, the government would take the business over. Several businesses were so taken over by government after the war, in the early winter of 1946, because labor did not behave as government thought it should. Then arose the embarrassing question of whether labor could strike against government, and the whole matter had to be hastily patched up with much oratory; for this was political dynamite.

Until 1941, the New Dealers had ostensibly done everything either to promote "recovery" or to establish "security." Yet recovery had delayed far longer than it ever had after any previous panic-depression. Dissatisfaction was in the air. Promises were unfulfilled. The people were galled by their loss of liberty and by the petty tyranny suffered at the hands of the hordes of bureaucrats. The New Dealers had done their political work —their real, not their ostensible work—far better. They had consolidated most of the country's power in the hands of their leader. They had multiplied the size of the bureaucracy many times. They had secured millions of votes by cash, favors and pressure. But, somehow, all this was also slipping. Even Mr. Willkie, with his "me, too" attitude, had gotten more than ten times the electoral vote Mr. Landon had received. The bankers had been beaten into such insignificance that they could scarcely be used any longer as whipping boys for the New Deal failures.

It was time to get the public's mind off these failures for a while.

In 1939, the old bureaucratic trick of starting a foreign war to take peoples' minds off their troubles at home was resorted to in Europe.

It does not seem possible that it could have been done. The horrible First World War was only twenty-one years old. Almost every voter remembered it. Almost every man and woman in every nation constantly prayed, "Give peace in our time, Oh Lord," and fervently longed for peace. At first it seems that war could not possibly have happened. But we must remember the worldwide political setup.

In 1939, Germany, Italy, Japan and Russia had huge bureaucracies each controlled by a dictator. England and the United States each had a huge bureaucracy; each was also virtually controlled by one man. A man who was democratically elected to be sure, but who while in office practically controlled the bureaucracy. Each bureaucracy governed its country, made its policy and by propaganda machines largely shaped its thoughts. Thus six men controlled the six countries of the world with military strength. Each of them had regimented economies; each was following the practice of trying to improve the economies by bureaucratic management and further regimentation. Therefore they were growing progressively poorer. Three of them were controlling countries whose population was too big for their territory. All of them were frantic, trying to divide an insufficient general income so everybody would have a sufficiency.

Anyone of them, through the control of his bureaucracy and his propaganda department, could involve his country in war and start the general conflagration. One, or more, of them did it to get the peoples' minds off their troubles at home and retain his own power.

Philosophically it makes little difference which was responsible. Whoever it was merely succumbed to the temptation the Devil laid before Christ on the mountain. We, the people, are really responsible, for by giving the rulers these huge bureaucracies we gave them this dreadful power. Without their control of the bureaucracies they would have been impotent to start a war in defiance of the tremendous popular sentiment for peace. For this reason alone, bureaucracies should be stripped to the bone and kept that way.

CHAPTER 12

OUR FOREIGN RELATIONS

"Cast out first the beam out of thine own eye"
LUKE, 6, 42

HOWEVER WE GOT INTO the Second World War, we have come out of it as victors, and the world, with the exception of the Communists, looks to us for leadership. Are we worthy and capable of such leadership?

If there was any national idealism behind our national acts, unfriendly to the Axis Powers, which precipitated Pearl Harbor, it was a national belief that freedom and free enterprise were essential, not only to ourselves but to mankind in general; that totalitarianism was a curse and that bullying small nations was a crime. This was the ideal of the people of the United States. It was also the ideal of the peoples of all our allies except the Russian Communists. It is an ideal for which hundreds of thousands of lives and untold billions of dollars worth of wealth have been sacrificed. Are we ourselves on the right track to accomplish this ideal for which we have already made such hideous sacrifices? Are we leading the civilized world, which is looking to us for leadership in this direction, along the right track?

It is axiomatic that no one can lead successfully unless he knows clearly where he is headed; that no one can manage the affairs of others while his own are in disorder and constantly disturbing him.

Therefore, as we assume the leadership of the world toward true freedom and free enterprise, it is fitting that, humbly and with reverence to God, we examine our hearts, our purposes, our national sins and errors, our dealings with other nations and the obstacles opposed to us, so that we may purify ourselves and proceed to our task with a clean conscience and a clear objective, united together in the true courage that comes only in the faith that our actions are blessed by God to set a worthy example.

It is an undoubted fact that we have no business and no right to interfere with the government, business or policy of another nation any more than they have a right to interfere with ours. Our duty is to see that we are strong enough to protect ourselves and our citizens against any one or combination of them that should become hostile. We cannot help influencing them by our example for weal or woe. Beyond that we should not go.

It is true no nation can be isolationist and ignore other nations. The Incas tried that and perished. But this does not mean that we have either the right, duty or business to force our views and policies on other countries by threats or by bribery, motivated either by dislike or by a desire to help them, or by forcing on them our "lights" and views. Their lights and views may reasonably differ from ours. That is their business. It would seem that we have enough and more than enough to do if we can adjust our own lights and manage our own government to serve our own people to their satisfaction!

Our newspapers and periodicals are constantly filled with discussions of the countless idiocies we euphemistically dub our "foreign policy." Perhaps this is another attempt to divide the people over controversial matters of no great importance while reducing them to poverty. Certain it is, that almost every such article deals with a controversy arising from our government's attempts to bully or bribe some other nation into acquiescence with its momentary view.

There are three possible choices for our national policy. We might become isolationists. We might continue as an international busybody, citizen-fix-it and general do-gooder. Or we might look well to our armaments and mind our own business. Perhaps the latter is the wisest course.

Up to this point this book has been devoted to exposing the economic errors we have committed as a people; those acts which have hurt our own prosperity (both as a nation and as individuals), by misusing a government which was designed to create liberty, and turning it into a vehicle to put unearned money into our individual pockets. It is not a pretty picture and we must never forget that it has been brought about by almost every one of us, either as individuals or in pressure groups, trying to get more than we have fairly earned, by government legislation "for nothing"—that is, from someone else. This chapter will deal with our recent national conduct toward other lands. It will divide itself into four natural parts: The United Nations; our relations with most countries whose economies are war-disrupted; and our special relations with England and with Russia. The last is the most important of all, as Russia has come to typify the totalitarian influence.

Many people believe that the one good thing which the second terrible World War has brought into existence is the United Nations Organization, created to insure lasting peace. Its charter's preamble opens with the phrase, "We the peoples of the United Nations." It might have been more accurate had it begun, "We the bureaucrats of the United Nations," for it was drawn by bureaucrats, in most cases appointed by other bureaucrats. It probably would have been a better document if it had been drawn by delegates elected by the people after a thorough discussion of the views they represented. As it is, it is doubtful whether one person in a thousand has read the Charter or has any idea of the organization's set-up. Nevertheless, it is a conscientiously drawn document and may be useful, though it is full of what Lincoln called "pernicious generalities." It is not, however, a sacrosanct document, and doubtless would be the better for thorough public discussion and criticism.

This is not the view of the propaganda mongers, apparently. It is now the custom for those who use slogans in place of thought to say, when the United Nations Organization is criticized: "You must not criticize it; it is the only hope of peace we have;" and roll their eyes and look sanctimoniously reproving in order to silence criticism. It would appear odd if a man argued that an egg must be good because it was the only one he had. Very often a bad egg is rather worse than none.

At any rate, it is possible that the constant argument

between the representatives of the various nations over their differences keeps their peoples (who otherwise might be thinking of pleasanter things) stirred up over those differences, and so engenders international dislikes and hatreds in the consciousness of the nations. This is not necessarily helpful to the spirit of brotherly love which is necessary for permanent peace.

Another objection to it may be that it provides another government echelon higher up, onto which lazy bureaucracies can unload the problems they do not want to solve, thus creating more bureaucracies. Already the not yet fully organized United Nations is confronted with a host of such problems—sociological, educational, scientific, cultural, eleemosynary and heaven knows what else. It was said in 1946 that a hundred and fifty such problems, ranging from providing movie projectors for devastated areas, to eliminating illiteracy throughout the world, (both privileges by force of law), were already before the UN Economic and Social Council which had not then even been organized.

As a further example of the sort of thing that the totalitarian-minded bureaucrats of the United Nations may charge themselves with—and get away with—we may remember that in the fall of 1948, Polish delegates called on the United Nations to help them make the United States stop feeding cereals to pigs and cattle while human beings in Europe and Asia were still hungry. Now considering that American farmers produced the cereal, it would seem just that they should decide how it should be used. It would also seem advisable, since if they are not allowed to do what they want with it after producing it by their sweat and toil, they are not likely to produce it another year. Again we may ask what possible right have even United States bureaucrats, let alone the bureaucrats of bolshevik, totalitarian Poland, to tell an American farmer what he shall do with the fruits of his productive effort?

When considering all this, it is essential to remember that the real object for which the organization of the United Nations was established was to prevent aggressive war. In furtherance of this object there has been a great deal of talk about the evils of aggression; a number of statesmen and generals of the Axis countries have been executed, not for war atrocities, but because they did acts which might perhaps be considered afterward by their enemies as acts of aggressive war, but which at the time appeared to them and everyone else as their duty to their own governments. This kind of execution revives a practice which most people thought had been abandoned by civilized countries after the death of Vercingetorix.

There has been long and enthusiastic condemnation of a new crime for which the extraordinary word "genocide" has been coined. Nevertheless, the United Nations has sat in almost complete silence and in utter inactivity while Russia has grabbed off by completely aggressive methods part of Finland, all of Esthonia, Latvia, Lithuania, Poland, Czecho-Slovakia, Rumania, Bulgaria, Jugo-Slavia (which later revolted from her), Hungary, Manchuria, Northern Korea and a large part of China. At this writing, Russia is behind armed aggression in Southern Korea. This is a record of aggression unparalleled in history. Furthermore, it has eliminated all the material gains that England, France and the United States made by their victory, for the original cause of the war was to preserve the territorial integrity of Poland and China.

It might be well for the people of the United States to reappraise the usefulness of the United Nations and query whether it is justifying its cost.

Quite aside from all this, which appears to be the intended essential function of the United Nations, consideration of our history has, or should have taught us that the closer a governmental unit is to the people, the more satisfactorily for the people it handles their problems; and that piling all problems into a great heap to be solved at a central point, infinitely complicates each problem and renders its solution less satisfactory. The essence and the strength of Anglo-Saxon government lay in its decentralization, which permits each local unit to solve its own problems on the spot and before they can become so large that they get complicated. Furthermore, many of the problems now being piled on the UN are not truly government problems at all, but concern such matters as regulating the general economy and distributing privileges to certain groups. If the UN is going to be a super-bureaucracy charged with regulating everything and everybody, it will not be a blessing but rather an intolerable burden.

The Charter of the United Nations set up merely the skeleton of an organization. From reading it, no one can tell

with what flesh and muscle it will be clothed or how it is going
to be made to work. Yet if it is vitalized by the old American-
British theory, with strictly limited powers and functions, adapted
to perform certain definite tasks only, it may be a great blessing. If, on the other hand, it develops along the lines of the
German-Russian philosophy of government as a super-state, su-
perintending and charged with running everything, everybody
and all business according to the wisdom of exalted bureaucrats,
it may prove a curse. As the Charter is drawn, the United
Nations Organization may develop in either direction.

Now let us turn our attention to our relations with most of
the countries of the world. These consist principally in trying
to rehabilitate those countries' economies after the strain of war,
by making them "loans." It must be always remembered that to
call these transactions "loans" is a conscious misuse of the word
by propagandists, of much the same sort as calling one who
believes in an authoritarian government, a "Liberal." They are
not loans. A loan is a voluntary assignment of one's own property
to another for a limited period of time only, and generally for
interest or some other advantage. These transactions are, in fact,
the removal by force of law of a portion of the assets of our
taxpayers by members of our government, and the giving of
those same assets by our bureaucrats to the bureaucrats of other
nations. A loan must be voluntarily made by the owner of the
property. These are forced levies of property extracted by force
of law from its owners—we ourselves—as taxpayers, and we
have no option to refuse to pay them. The "loaners" of the
property "lent" are not its owners. Furthermore, they are not
loans because they will never be paid back to the owners. No
one in his right senses ever expects them to be. They are not
even "forced loans." They are forced gifts of the sort Robin Hood
made the abbot give. Our bureaucrats pay for them out of the
taxes they get Congress to levy on us, or, in the event that these
are not sufficient—which they frequently are not—by inflating our
currency; that is by printing money against the security of government bonds.

In either event they cause a great rise in all our prices,
e.g., the present inflation; for if the government pays the producers for the goods to be given away in taxes collected from

us all as taxpayers, the amount of our present money outstanding remains the same, and our other forms of wealth, which are reduced by the gifts, automatically rise in price with reference to the money, because of scarcity. If they are paid for by printing money, the amount of our money is increased and of our other forms of wealth decreased, and the rise is correspondingly sharper.

It is silly to accept the slogan, fostered by the present-day government propaganda, to the effect that as long as production keeps up there can be no price inflation. It simply is not so, though it is true that production and the amount of currency in use are both factors in the ratio that determines prices. If the currency remains fixed and the other wealth of the country greatly increases, prices will fall automatically. If the currency is increased faster than the wealth, prices will rise no matter how great the wealth and the production of the country. If the currency outstanding is fixed and the wealth and/or production of the country diminishes, prices again rise automatically. It is just the question of supply and demand. The goods used in these transactions—loans to Europe—are made and given away, and so are, as far as we are concerned, destroyed, and have no effect in increasing the general wealth of the country in relation to the amount of currency outstanding. As far as their influence on our prices is concerned, it would be better for our wealth as a nation had they never been created. Our present inflation is partly the result of these gifts from our bureaucracy to bureaucracies of other countries.

In spite of all this there is no serious complaint from our people. These forced gifts are merely accepted as something that cannot be altered. In fact, in 1948 it was said quite casually in a public discussion of the "Marshall Plan" that: "Europe can get along quite well on a subsidy of $5,000,000,000 or $6,000,000,-000 a year." This means that it can get along quite well if every man, woman and child of our 140,000,000 people makes a forced gift every year to the Europeans of between $35.72 and $42.86 out of their annual average income, plus a large percentage more for the bureaucrats who collect and distribute the gifts.

Many intelligent people admit all the above facts are true but believe, nevertheless, that we should continue these "loans" to check the general spread of Communism. Let us examine this argument. It is indeed true that acute want and poverty is usually the spark which detonates a revolution to Communism. Acute want and poverty is not a natural thing. It is natural for men to create wealth fast and freely when left to themselves, as a glance at all the economies of history that were largely free will show. It is only when the selfish desires of groups and individuals to get something for nothing, that is from someone else, by force of law, has built up a great regulatory bureaucracy, and when that bureaucracy has strangled the whole economy by a myriad petty regulations, that an economy can break down and dire want occur. The remedy is not to build up the bureaucracies and selfish regulations further, till they result in a totalitarian state where only the most efficient and ruthless hogs get anything, but to break down both selfish restrictions and the bureaucracies that enforce them, and to let men's natural instincts lead them back to abundance.

The sorest spot in Europe outside the iron curtain is Germany. She suffered more physical damage than any other country, and for a long time had been suffering from Hitler's economic regulations. The end of the war found Germany's wealth dangerously reduced by this and by battle.

Immediately after she was occupied, the allies tore what remained of her economy to shreds. Partly for vengeance, partly because of desire for loot, they removed or destroyed a great number of her factories, on the plea that they might be used for war purposes (as what factory cannot?). Every form of economic regulation and restriction was applied, imports and exports regulated, every form of production licensed or rationed, prices and wages fixed at the same level Hitler had fixed them in 1936, in spite of the fact that the currency outstanding had been increased by means of the printing press from six billion marks to 70 billion marks, while the real wealth of the country had been reduced certainly by more than half!

The idea of the regulations was to produce a "new level of industry," and prices, wages, etc., were arbitrarily shifted around to bring about this desideratum. What they did produce was, of course, as always, a fearful series of bottlenecks and a complete prostration of industry and trade.

The only real market in Germany became "the black

market," a very wasteful one because, first, its very illegality raised its prices to cover the legal risk, and second, the dangers of participating in it made it enormously complicated in operation. As a simple example: German farmers were producing a good deal of food for which there was an enormous demand at very high prices. They had no idea of selling it at the legal prices which were ruinously low. They simply hid it to keep for their own use, or to sell or exchange on the black market. The half-starved city people went out to the farms at every opportunity to swap it for goods or pay exorbitant currency prices for it at black market rates. Thus myriads of city people were spending many laborious hours each week going out to the farms on foot or on bicycles to bring in their family food, and so wasted millions of man hours of labor, ran much risk and paid exorbitantly. Most of these evils and losses to the general economy could have been avoided had the normal methods of distribution been permitted.

This sort of thing went on in a different form in nearly every kind of human activity. The economy came to an almost complete standstill. Steel production in the American and British zones dropped from 17,800,000 tons in 1938 to 2,800,000 in 1947; coal production which the planners had made a special effort to build up, dropped from 206 million tons in 1938 to 133 million in 1947. So little was produced that general starvation became imminent in Germany, and we, the producers of the United States, were obliged to pay "reverse reparations" by our government's giving them our food. That much of this trouble and expense was caused by the regulations of our bureaucrats, civil and military, can be readily seen, or perhaps inferred, from the fact that when early in 1948 a number of these regulations were inexplicably removed, the production of Germany gained very satisfactorily.

So much for the effect of our economic regulations in Germany, on Germany. Let us look at their effect on another country. Take Holland, for example, though Belgium, Switzerland, France, Denmark and Sweden were very similarly affected. It must be remembered that Germany has, because of her resources and the character of her people, and in spite of her government and its frequent wars, been for a long time the productive heart of Europe, particularly mechanically. Many of the machines used in Holland were made in Germany. Under our regulations, Germany could not export to her. Thus, if Holland needed a new machine she could not get it. Even if a part broke it could not be had, and the whole machine became idle. Holland's production and employment were slowed down greatly if immeasurably. Again, the two great Dutch ports of Amsterdam and Rotterdam were designed to supply Germany with imports from across the seas; since she could no longer import because of our regulations, they became largely idle. A large part of Dutch agriculture was growing vegetables for Germany; since their import was forbidden this Dutch industry is mortally sick.

It must be borne in mind that many of these Dutch troubles are the result of the attempts of the bureaucrats of England, France and ourselves to regulate the German economy. In the part of Germany occupied by Russia, where everything is regulated, the conditions are said to be deplorably bad.

Now let us look at the countries of Europe that were our allies, or at least Hitler's victims. It is often said it is our duty to feed them. That is impossible, as a glance at the following figures will show. In 1939 we imported $280,965,000 worth more foodstuffs—crude and manufactured—than we exported. By 1946, by a Homeric agricultural effort, we managed to export $854,-817,000 worth more foodstuffs than we imported. (This is not a true comparison as to the amount of change in the direction of the flow of food, because its price had materially increased; but let us pass that.) The total dollar value production of farms in 1946 was $25,322,896,000. A little figuring will show that in 1946 with our Homeric effort we were able to export 3 1/3 per-cent of the food which our farms produced. The other 96 2/3 percent we consumed ourselves, and even so this 3 1/3 export caused a shortage here that, aided by our currency inflation, sent our food prices sky-rocketing. But then we have to remember that there are nearly three times as many people in Europe as in the United States, so our total help to them in this way can hardly be more than one and one-half percent of their requirements—a trivial amount surely.

On the other hand, we have seen that the number of people in our bureaucracy and the cost of our government had reduced our own potential income by 37 percent, not counting the great but immeasurable loss it had caused by stifling free enterprise with its licenses, regulations, etc. We know that the European countries are far more heavily burdened than ourselves by bureaucracies. Because of that, their potential production must be down more than 50 percent. Could we not, perhaps, furnish them with the greatest help by aiding them by our example to remove from themselves this crushing incubus? Our war victories, plus the world leadership we still have in production, give us a tremendous influence. Yet far from doing this, we are permitting our bureaucracy to encourage and expand itself and theirs; for all our loans require supervision, regulations, special privileges, etc., to apply them, and this work builds, rather than diminishes, the foreign bureaucracies. Bureaucracies and their regulations are what most hamper production.

True Americans hate these bureaucracies and their interference with freedom. They, and our own selfishness, are preventing that free interchange of goods in trade which would shortly reestablish us all as it did after the devastation of our Revolution and the terrible Napoleonic wars, and would now do were it allowed to get into operation. Yet, our bureaucracy is building up itself and all the foreign bureaucracies it can, for the benefit of the brotherhood.

It is also said by the propagandists that our bureaucracies make these loans to the bureaucracies of foreign nations to restore the purchasing powers of these countries so that in future they can buy goods from us. This brings us to the question: would a sane village storekeeper loan money to the village bum, knowing he would never be repaid, in order that the bum might buy goods from him? Obviously he would not, since he would see that he was giving him either his money or his goods, according to the way you look at it. No storekeeper would be such a fool. A village bum is created by his own bad economic habits, which have forged a chain of circumstances that holds him down. Any man might suffer a financial catastrophe, but one who had sound economic habits could get himself started up again in a week, and would really need little or nothing to live on, in the way of a loan, though his financial status might be greatly changed. A bum suffering from such an event would be tied down by his bad habits and would be unlikely ever to recover till he changed them. Any loan made to him would not only be a total loss, but would postpone the day when stern necessity—the natural law—the law of God—would compel him to change those habits and start on the upward road.

Let us apply the same principles that are so clear in a village to the larger international field. All the nations of Europe are suffering from the same evils that we have unwisely bound on ourselves by the chains of circumstance—the bad national habits of generations—but they are all suffering from a much stronger dose of them than we. All have the huge unproductive bureaucracies, the vast mesh of regulations checking production and keeping the latter occupied, the same mania for redistributing the earnings of the producers by privileges, taking them from those who fairly earned them and giving them to those who can muster pressure groups. All have, of course, made painful mistakes, since one cannot do wrong rightly. All have tried to mitigate the effects of their mistakes by further regulations and privileges of the same kind, thus confounding confusion. All are further on the road to ruin than ourselves. And more than ourselves, also, are they permeated by the virus of Communism, that cleverly devised and magnificently propagandized plot to put the whole control of the world in the hands of a few super-intelligent and ambitious men, insanely avid for power, and disguised so cleverly that many of the toiling masses who are designed to become its abject slaves are beguiled into longing and striving for it as their promised millennium.

It is sometimes argued that creating these goods to give Europe also gives employment here to those that make them. This is true, but it would be equally true if the goods were made here and given away locally or destroyed, which would not be seriously argued by anyone. By giving them away, our capital and effort in making them is destroyed and our wealth diminished, not increased.

Let us consider how these countries are running now. In most of the countries we are aiding, budgets are unbalanced. Great sums collected in taxes are used for armaments, subsidies for national industries running at a loss, food subsidies, increased pensions and family allowances, and "social security"—all requiring a host of bureaucrats taken out of production to administer them. Income taxes are so high no money can be saved for new machinery, or even to replace the old. Production, bound down by a myriad regulations, is slowed to a trifle of its potential. Our loans encourage this nonsense to continue, so general poverty results. To offset this, their governments print and distribute paper money in quantity, with no regard to the bullion behind it. This momentarily makes things look brighter, but the only real effect is raising prices of goods materially in terms of the diminishing value of money. This has to be offset by establishing ceiling prices on all necessities. This is not done on luxuries which are "not necessary," as the illusion must be preserved that a "free economy" is still in operation. The immediate result of this is to turn workers away from the production of necessities, for they can make more for themselves by making the unceilinged luxuries. Then more regulations have to be made to increase the necessities, and the producers of them are encouraged to increase their output by the loan of vast sums at low interest. The only way this can be done is by printing more money! All the rise in prices is the result, in the final analysis, of the printing of the paper money, but the government propaganda bureaus put the blame on "hoarders," "speculators," "the rich," etc., and few people trouble to think any further.

The governments issue the new paper money as payments of bureaucrats' salaries, as relief and other subsidies, as loans at low interest. When the prices rise, "ceilings" are put on the price of necessities. As there is too much money for the goods in existence and its value in goods shrinks, there is no profit margin in the goods that must be sold at a fixed price. These quietly disappear from the market as our own red meat did in 1946. General shortages develop. Priorities have to be "set up" to make the economy function, and ceiling prices "adjusted" to get the scarce goods into the market again. As the whole of any economy is interrelated, all this regulation slows the whole economy down to the necessary part of it, on which the lowest margin of profit has been set by law, and the whole economy, therefore, barely moves. All price ceilings naturally have the effect of increasing the demand because the price is cheap, and also of reducing the production of the supply because there is no profit in producing it.

With the great amount of money issued and the small amounts of necessary goods created because "the price of necessities must be held down," there is a lot of loose currency round.

This either goes into the black market at an enormous waste of time, cost and effort, or into useless "unceilinged" luxuries which, being unceilinged, it pays to make and sell. This surplus money would gladly go into imports from abroad if it were permitted to (as it recently did in Sweden when the barriers were removed). The bureaucracies do not permit this, because it would rapidly break the price of their own currencies in the international market if more goods were imported than exported and the balance paid out in currency. Each bureaucracy wants to keep the nominal value of its currency as high as possible in terms of other currencies, so as to be able to import as cheaply as possible and to sell at as high a price as possible.

Let us examine how the bureaucratic mind works on this problem.

The bureaucracies of all countries have by agreement set up arbitrary rates of exchange fixing the relative values of the currencies of their countries at a legal rate, a fixed percentage of the value of the dollar. The currencies were pegged to the dollar because, though its value is obviously constantly diminishing as more and more paper money is printed here, it has more real value in gold than almost any other unit of currency existent except, perhaps, the Swiss. The assigned value of the other currencies is almost purely arbitrary and they have apparently a far smaller real value than the one they are pegged at, (as is seen in the black markets). By this device they hope to get cheap imports but a high price for their exports.

Here is the way the system works. Say the legal rate of exchange for France is 119 francs to the dollar, the black market rate might be 280 francs to the dollar and probably the real rate would be 240. In France a bottle of brandy costs 1200 francs, which is about $10 at the legal rate of exchange but only about $5 at the black market or real rate. So a merchant, if he exported it legally to the U.S.A., would pay at the legal rate $10 for it. But as few Americans are willing to pay for a bottle of brandy a basic price of $10 plus the tariff imposed by our government, plus transportation charges and profits, the French manufacturer exports very little. He does not care much, for he can sell it at home easily because there is so much surplus paper money round for luxuries and a franc is a franc to him wherever it comes from. He is further discouraged from exporting it abroad because of the law by which the government of France takes over 90 percent of whatever dollar exchange he gets, at 119 francs to the dollar, for the stabilization fund, and he gets only about half the purchasing power in francs that the dollars would be worth locally.

On the other hand, an American typewriter manufacturer could legally sell a $100 typewriter in France for only 11,900 francs, which would pay him in French goods less than half of what he could get for $100 if he bought francs in the black market and bought goods to bring home, or half what he could get at the real purchasing power of $100 in France.

It is true that if the exporter of the brandy got $10 a bottle for it he would have gotten much more for it than a fair price, and that if the French importer paid only 11,900 francs for the typewriter he would have paid far less—both to the theoretical benefit of France. The trouble is that men being what they are, neither transaction is very likely to occur, and foreign trade has almost ceased. There is a great howl from Europe about "a dollar shortage." There is also a very considerable dollar shortage over here among people who will not give a fair return for a dollar!

The real truth of the "dollar shortage" is that the high arbitrary rate established for the franc in relation to the dollar has almost stopped our imports from France, and would also have stopped our exports to her had not our bureaucrats given their bureaucrats dollars, taken from our citizens, to buy American goods with. As soon as the gift dollars are spent there is a "dollar shortage," for at the legal rate France cannot import.

The truth is that "control" of prices, wages and exchange does not stop inflation. It just stops production.

This sort of thing is going on with every European country. In 1947, the goods we gave to other countries in excess of what we got back amounted to $12,700,000,000. Even that did little good. For example, in 1946 we let Great Britain have $2,450,000,000 of our taxpayers' money. This amounted to only 8 percent of what the British produced for themselves. If they had eliminated their huge and wasteful bureaucracy, with its regulations strangling every sort of production, they could not have failed to increase their production far more than 10 percent; the very man power released from the bureaucracy would have done that, let alone the tremendous stimulus provided by the removal of the restrictions.

Yet instead of using our example to bring about this great possible benefit by emphasizing the American ideal of free enterprise, we have permitted our bureaucracy to build up itself and the bureaucracy of England, according to the totalitarian ideal and to the grave injury of our own and the British economy. For it must never be forgotten that the administration of these loans requires many more bureaucrats, many more regulations, and much more supervision, to the far greater injury of both economies. All to the benefit of Communism in both countries.

Furthermore it is giving birth to all sorts of economic nonsense, as for example the purchase by Britain, Belgium and Holland of Canadian aluminum with funds provided by our taxpayers, at 16 cents a pound, and the selling of this aluminum back to our producers at 26 cents a pound, and impounding the difference in their own stabilization fund, as reported in the New York *Times*, December 15, 1948. Or that reported in the same paper of May 5, 1948, describing how Holland is facing a "serious overproduction of foodstuffs" that will have to be destroyed because there is no possibility of selling, because of exchange control; and that for the same reason Belgium and Luxemburg were prevented from exporting glass, textiles and machine tools for which there was a great demand elsewhere.

It must always be borne in mind in contemplating these affairs that Communist policy is seldom to be learned from its official statements, which are uttered for their propaganda effect. Communist policy must be deduced from actions. Those actions tend to prove that their foreign policy is to subjugate the whole world under the domination of their commissars, and that the best method of attaining this is to produce general destitution by checking production as much as possible. This can best be accomplished by the introduction of all sorts of governmental prohibitions, regulations and restraints. The famous Chambers-Hiss controversy tends to indicate that Communist influence has been and perhaps still is strong in the higher echelons of our own bureaucracy.

It may be well to give a little more attention to our foreign policy toward England, for in dealing with her we must realize that she may be more dangerous to our economy than the other countries of Western Europe and capable of doing us far more harm.

England has long been an exponent of the theory of managing her economy by granting privileges. As the inevitable result she has saddled herself with an immense bureaucracy, and between the wars had great unemployment.

Her performance in the Second World War was pitiable. The disasters of Dunkirk and Singapore were glossed over by the news and turned into heroic episodes. The loss of two major battleships to the aviators of Japan was conveniently and quickly forgotten. The victory of Montgomery at Alamein was in large part due to the timely arrival of American supplies and clinched by the advent of the United States armies. The British contribution to the Battle of Europe was not of first-rate importance.

In fact Britain's sole great victory was winning what Mr. Churchill so jubilantly called "The Battle of America." The diplomatic victory of getting us into the war preserved the British tradition of losing every battle and winning every war. It appears that it is in diplomacy alone that the power of the British Empire—once great in every field—remains unimpaired. England is a past master in coloring facts subtly for her own interest. Her diplomatic representatives are so utterly charming and attractive in person and so well trained in arguments, so apparently frank and sincere in their delivery of them, that it is next to impossible to resist their persuasiveness. In fact, in the past four decades it has been most noticeable that just before Great Britain wants some enormous favor of us, this country is flooded with personable Britishers of charming manners and address, who quickly penetrate every social gathering of influential men and women. There, they harp constantly on the facts that we are in reality one race, derive our culture from the same sources, and that therefore (God save the mark!) our interests have always been, and always will be, the same. So charming are they that they create sympathy and an atmosphere favorable to themselves wherever they go. So subtle and attractive are they, that we gladly forget that they waged a most atrocious war against us in the Revolution, massacring the garrison in Groton,

Connecticut, stirring up the Indians to every form of savagery, even by paying bounties for women's scalps; that in the Civil War they did everything short of actual hostilities to encourage the rebellion; that in the 1920's, when we asked them to repay the great sums loaned them *after* the hostilities had ceased in 1918, they refused to pay and called us "Uncle Shylock," to boot. It appears that with the single exception of the incident of the British Fleet at the Battle of Manila Bay in 1898, they have never done us a national favor.

Yet the record proves that, so charming and clever are their diplomats, whenever they choose to turn on their charm for us we appear willing to become their stooges, to accomplish their most unpleasant tasks for them, and whenever they pass their tin cup our government gladly fills it to the brim with the income of our producers.

The two World Wars have impoverished England. The long continued attempt to manage her economy by granting legally enforced privilege has very greatly reduced her production. The concomitant huge bureaucracy has taken hordes of people out of production. Her taxes are such, there is no saving for capital goods to increase the production. There is not enough income to go round, no matter how distributed. Her artificially pegged currency, held far above its true value, discourages exports and encourages imports whenever she can borrow from us. Winston Churchill is quoted in the New York *Times* of November 17, 1948, as saying: "We are living on subsidies provided by taxes on the heavily burdened people of the United States." This help, he said, springs from the desire of the people of the United States to aid Britain, "despite the Socialistic Government, whose ideology is the exact opposite of their own."

In England, individual opportunity has practically ceased. Taxes and privileges for others have taken so much of the fruits of production from the producers that myriads of people are simply finding it more convenient not to work, for government relief avails to keep them in idleness from actual want. The inevitable consequence is occurring—a completely managed economy and many kinds of property put under government ownership. The economy of a most civilized, orderly and highly organized industrial nation is indeed in a parlous state when a series of severe snowstorms can reduce it almost to chaos, as happened in 1946.

Today, Englishmen can't change their jobs without government permission; they can't buy or sell the necessities for carrying on their business without obtaining government permission by lengthy correspondence and the filling of many forms. They can't appeal to the courts from a decree of the executive. They are not allowed to buy what they want to eat, or drink— or grow it for themselves in many cases. They are virtually slaves. They think they are free because they can vote. The vote does not give freedom *per se,* though it may be a means to recapture it.

The "plan" for the "rehabilitation" of Britain has long been thought out; a great deal of it has already been put into execution. As a result the fortunes of those formerly rich in Britain, and there used to be a great number of them, have largely disappeared; the competencies of the former middle class are gone too, and all are reduced to the same drab level of poverty. They are not quite starving, but they are under-nourished, cold and short of everything. At the date of writing the great organizer —the leader, "the man on horseback"—has not yet appeared amongst them to "save" them.

When all this is considered, together with the characters of the men now controlling the British government and economy, and together with the vast skill that Britain has shown for nigh onto a century in shamefully exploiting her colonies by law, and other nations by diplomatic persuasiveness to their injury and her own advantage, it may be well if we look very skeptically on the blandishments and logical-sounding requests of her government to "save" her, and beware of her charming envoys, diplomatic and social, who may be sent among us to effect it.

Our relationship with Russia is the most important question in the international picture today. Let us look at her.

Russia has an area of 8,275,613 square miles, about one-sixth of the world's land surface. Her population is said to number 180,338,122 people. This gives it the density of 21.8 persons per square mile, which compares to a density of 44.2

persons per square mile in the United States today. That is, it
is about equal to the density of population in Kansas at the
present time, or to that of the whole United States in 1890, when
we had 62,947,714 people. Surely the Russians are not overcrowded. A glance at the map shows that Canada and the
United States lie roughly between the 32nd and 65th parallels
of latitude and that Russia and Siberia lie roughly between the
40th and 70th parallels. Therefore the great mass of these two
vast areas lie within the same parallels and little real difference
exists in that respect. Furthermore, from all that can be found
out, the natural resources of Russia and Siberia are proportionally
quite as great if not greater than those of the United States and
Canada.

The Communist planners had complete control over Russia from 1919-1939, without any war to trouble them. During
this twenty years of Bolshevik management, fifteen million people are said to have starved to death, several million to have
been executed, and according to reports, between fourteen and
twenty million are in the prison labor camps, being slowly
worked and starved to death as political prisoners. It is common
knowledge that prior to the second war the condition in which
the Russian workers subsisted was almost sub-human. The fact
that the chief complaint of the Germans who are under the
Russian occupation is that the Russians are not house-broken but
defile their own quarters as a matter of habit, shows that the
conditions in which they were brought up were below that of
many animals. The pay that the mass of people received for
their long hours' work rarely brought them the simplest necessities of life. From all this it would at first appear that the planners failed rather signally in their first field of experiment—
Russia.

But did they fail? The Communist leaders themselves are
doing pretty well, thank you. The leading Communists, officially
over here, have acquired the finest residences of our New York
millionaires for their homes—the J. P. Morgan, the Ogden Mills,
the Herbert Pratt, the Percy R. Pyne, (the latter acquired by
subterfuge) houses, are or have been their dwellings. Could it be
possible that the objective of the Communist leaders was not to
raise the living standard of the Russian worker, any more than
it is the object of the bureaucrat to do the work with the max-

imum efficiency, or that of the early New Dealer to cure the depression? Could it be possible that the object they had in mind was to raise themselves to wealth and power, honor and influence?

It is obvious the Communist leaders are immensely able and ambitious men, or they would never have been able to get so much of the world under their domination. It is equally obvious that they are utterly wicked and unscrupulous men, totally devoid of any religion, or they never would have occasioned the mass executions, imprisonments, starvation and suffering that mark their careers. They are past masters of the art of propaganda, since they have made many laborers believe that Russia, which almost every first hand report states, and every side-light shows to be a perfect hell for the masses, appears to be an Elysium for the working man. Furthermore, they have converted to their views large groups of those sophomoric men and women who dub themselves "the intelligentzia" because they have discovered within themselves an ability to theorize. These are the people who contemptuously refer to the producers and business men—the true backbone of the country—as "economic royalists" or "tired business men."

Let us examine how the Communist leaders have used their propaganda to extend their control over the world. The only areas they have ever conquered in the old-fashioned way, by armed invasion, are Poland and the Baltic States. Every other country that has become their victim has been conquered by infiltration. They train their disciples to insinuate themselves as much as possible into key positions of the government, press, movies, unions, universities and women's organizations of the country to be conquered, and through them work unremittingly to bring about their end. They can only work effectively in a highly organized state, one with a huge bureaucracy. They can bring their work to fruition only in a serious economic crisis, and that can occur only where an economy is tied up with thousands of regulations and much wasteful government spending. On June 6, 1950, Commander W. T. Greenhalgh, USN, stressed in a speech before the Industrial College of the Armed Forces the declared policy of Lenin, repeated by Stalin: "We shall force the United States to spend itself into destruction."

Communist leaders gain their ascendency over their own

members, their fellow travelers, and their future victims, by an alleged ideology. They advocate some privilege that by itself looks as if it might be a good thing and that brings the promise of something "for nothing," that is from somebody else to some large group, and hence is popular. That tends to make them and their ideology popular too. Most of those who help them work for these privileges see no further than the openly-stated immediate end. But the Communist leaders know that every privilege granted ties up the economy further, disciplines the people to further economic control and brings nearer the complete economic collapse which, under Communist leadership, will result in their complete economic control. Those who seek privileges for themselves do not see that they are furnishing the stones for our totalitarian prison house, but the Communist leaders do, and use the cupidity of individuals, who want something for nothing, to eventually imprison them.

The Communist conception is obviously rather old. It got its first field for practical application in Russia after the First World War. Russia was then largely conditioned for it. It had an enormous bureaucracy. The economic police-state of the Czars had very greatly tied up production and the war had caused great want. Even so, it required a long, bloody civil war to clamp it on there. That war showed that all the Russians did not want Bolshevism. The huge armies in concentration camps, the many desertions to the Americans, French and British, show that many do not want it now. Bolshevik and Russian should not be synonymous terms; all Russians are not Communists, and there are Communists everywhere who are not Russians.

In 1918, Russia was the only country conditioned to accept totalitarianism. Shortly, other nations bound down by economic restrictions went over; Germany and Italy notably, for their governments were totalitarian and differed from Russian Bolshevism chiefly in the fact that, like Tito's Jugo-slavia, they did not take their orders from Moscow.

In 1916, the United States was not conditioned at all for totalitarianism. Since then we largely have been. We accept meekly all economic regulation. We have developed a huge bureaucracy. We vote gladly for special privileges in the form of "social benefits." We have been shown that many powerful positions in our bureaucracy, our press, our movie industry and our colleges have been infiltrated by Communists, and we do little about it. We are often glad to receive our political information as "packaged thought" from sources often largely run by those who believe in socialistic and totalitarian ideas. We have permitted many branches of our Federal bureaucracy to set up "public relations bureaus" which disseminate their own views under the authenticating seal of "Government" to get us to form pressure groups to force our elected Congressmen to follow the lead of the appointed bureaucracy that it is designed to control. The propaganda from these bureaus never advocates our changing to an authoritarian state. It advocates a vast number of individual acts, "each for the benefit" of some great group, but the composite effect of all these acts ties up our economy, builds our bureaucracy, slows our production, conditions us to docile obedience and leads us steadily into the position where a totalitarian form of government is inevitable.

There is a danger that the leaders of Communist Russia will force us into a shooting war with them. We should prepare for such an eventuality most thoroughly in a military way. But if it comes, it will be merely the Russians, not the Communist leaders, who will suffer, and we will probably win it in the field.

Our greatest danger lies in the totalitarian state that we are permitting to be built up within our own borders by managed economy fanatics, who plan eventually to take us over as they have the Balkan States, Czecho-Slovakia, China, Northern Korea, yes Russia herself. They are getting us, as they are more rapidly getting England, and will accomplish our utter subjugation if we remain in our present confused lethargy. Then for a few centuries freedom and free enterprise will vanish from the earth and the want and the tyranny of managed economy will succeed, to the great material benefit of leaders whose most effective weapon is the selfish, but suicidal, mania of our own citizens to tie up and strangle our economy in order to get special privileges for themselves. Our financial ruin is their surest road to power.

Let us look at what our foreign policy of being an international busybody, citizen-fix-it and general do-gooder has cost us in dollars over the last decade. Here is a summary of foreign trade balances over the past decade.

	Trade with Foreign Countries	
	Exports*	Imports*
Year	(in 1000's)	(in 1000's)
1939	$ 3,073,619	$ 2,211,884
1940	3,925,653	2,521,685
1941	5,025,691	3,227,623
1942	8,076,572	2,723,403
1943	12,947,842	3,334,925
1944	14,256,319	3,890,570
1945	9,756,278	4,084,651
1946	9,431,428	4,835,603
1947	13,825,707	5,328,859
TOTAL	$80,319,109	$32,159,203

$80,319,109,000   Exports of wealth in trade.
32,159,203,000   Imports of wealth in trade.

$48,159,906,000   Loss of wealth in trade.

During these years the amount of gold imported was $5,110,000,000 †; also, during this time, Americans abroad spent about five billion dollars—a form of invisible import. This must be deducted from the loss in trade, leaving a net loss of $38,049,906,000.

A study of this table shows that between 1939-1947 our Congress and our bureaucracy gave to Europe by means of "lend lease," "the Marshall Plan," etc., over 38 billion dollars. This is approximately one-eighth of our entire gross national wealth which is estimated at 305 billion dollars. It is also nearly twice the cost of the First World War. It is more than half of our entire remaining net wealth.

This practice is being enthusiastically continued.

In view of the fact that it is the manifest policy of the

* World Almanac, 1949, page 249.
† Ibid, page 274.

directing minds of Communism to build big bureaucracies and bring about general extreme poverty in order to dominate the world, is it unfair to ask this question?

Does it seem probable that our foreign policy is the result of the considered opinion of the people of the United States; or is it rather in accordance with the deep-laid plans of some master minds of the Communist persuasion?

CHAPTER 13

WHERE WE ARE AT

"Let us humbly confess our sins before God"
THE BOOK OF COMMON PRAYER

THIS CHAPTER IS A summary of our present position. We have come out of the war in a serious financial predicament. According to reliable estimates our national debt is about $216,-500,000,000, our state and local debts $16,200,000,000—approximate total public debt, $232,700,000,000. The citizens of the United States are said to hold assets of $305,000,000,000. Assuming these figures to be a reasonably close approximation of the facts, that leaves the net wealth of the United States, after deducting the public debt, at only about $72,300,000,000. At present then the national ratio of public debt to the private assets from which it must be paid, is about 76%. That is an alarming figure certainly, and not one that any private banker would be willing to increase, but still it is not yet as bad as it was at the time of the adoption of the Federal Constitution, and we got clear then in thirteen years.

Again the condition of our currency is badly confused, not as badly as it was in 1787 but sufficiently to induce thought. When our First Congress met, we had just indulged in an orgy of attempting to make ourselves rich by printing money in enormous quantity. We were thoroughly sick of our debauch and doing our utmost to achieve a stable currency and return to the system of getting rich by producing wealth—the only way it can be done. We accomplished this in less than a decade, under the able guidance of Alexander Hamilton.

Today we have forgotten the terrible suffering produced by a great currency inflation. We are not exactly indulging in a new orgy of it, but we have discovered again that a little inflation produces a slight and pleasant economic stimulant, much like that of a cocktail when one is tired. We have been taking a good many such economic cocktails lately; not enough to produce disaster, but only just a little hangover in the shape of the rise in the cost of living that has overtaken us. The bureaucratic propaganda departments have given a dozen complicated and untrue reasons for the rise in prices. But it is very simple. Whenever any form of wealth, including money, becomes over plentiful, its price drops in relation to the other forms. In the case of money, a drop in its price is called a rise in all prices.

Let us just look at what we, or rather our bureaucracy, has been doing to ourselves lately along this line.

In 1915 the First War boom was on. The amount of money in circulation was $33.01 *per capita*. The cost of living index was 72.5. Since much money was brought into circulation as a result of the war, in 1920 there was in circulation $51.36 *per capita* and the cost of living index was 143.3. By 1933 the money in circulation was back to about $36.79 *per capita* and the cost of living index at 100.2. From then on the amount of our currency outstanding *per capita* has increased almost steadily till 1949 when it was at 184.41 *per capita,* and the cost of living index was at 168.+. Is it any wonder that the cost of living as measured in dollars has increased?

The preceding two paragraphs give the essential cause of the trouble, but give it in an absurdly simplified form. In the first place, in 1914 we had $1,604,000,000 gold in the country and only $1,533,000,000 of dollars currency outstanding. In January 1949 we had $24,466,324,100 of gold and $27,492,909,902 of currency outstanding. This vast increase of gold in the country is, of course, due to our extremely high protective tariffs, each giving special privileges to one group or another, which have prevented other nations from paying for our exports to them economically by any exchange of goods, and so forced them to pay in gold. In this way we have accumulated about four-fifths of the world's gold supply.

This is doing us no good. In fact, since we have printed

more than 100% of currency against it, it is raising our prices and is a strong factor in the present "inflation." Its effect on other nations is very severe, for it reduces the amount of their currency that can be anchored "to gold," or backed with gold, to an amount far smaller than they need for their trade. This results in their paper currency being wildly inflated, largely worthless and constantly fluctuating. Furthermore, the presence of such a large percentage of the world supply of gold is a constant threat to us of the very danger that destroyed the economies of Spain and Portugal in the sixteenth century.

Aside from its decorative value the only use of gold in a free world-economy is to adjust quickly any discrepancies in the balance of international trade. With 80 percent of it in the hands of one nation, and that one the greatest exporter and producer of all, its usefulness is greatly impaired. If all the gold of the world were buried in the vaults of Fort Knox, it would have no value at all in the world economy. We have already approached too closely this monopoly of gold.

The second over-simplification of the rise in prices, being the result of the *per capita* increase of currency outstanding, is the omission of the very great effect of the expansion of credit by the banks. In our previous discussions of panics, we have seen that in periods of booms banks have greatly expanded their credit, or bank deposits, and so, in effect, the currency outstanding in the country, and thus increased the price of everything; and that in the panics they have so curtailed this credit currency because of their own fear, that prices have tumbled to absurdly low levels. Of late this credit currency has been very cautiously used by the banks and has acted as a brake on the government's policy of expanding enormously the amount of actual currency in circulation. The generally accepted theory nowadays is that the cost of living varies directly with the amount of currency outstanding and the amount of credit currency in existence, times the velocity with which it turns over, or is spent. In 1947 the amount of bank credit currency outstanding was the same in percentage of actual currency as it was in 1933, and the velocity only about four-fifths as much, but the currency outstanding rose in that time from $36.74 to $196.41 *per capita*, and the cost of living from 92.4 to 153. 1933 was the depth of a depression. 1947 was extraordinarily prosperous.

After these somewhat complicated explanations of unessential points, let us get back to the over-simplified paragraph, which said, in substance, that the government, by increasing the amount of currency outstanding has invited a catastrophic inflation. This inflation has occurred in only a moderate degree, because the bankers have not increased deposits, that is issued credit currency, in anything like the proportion they used to, and because the people are not spending money as fast as they did. Both these are psychological factors and could change in an instant. The former might be controlled by government, but is not likely to be for political reasons; the second could not be controlled. The only factor of the three which the government could control directly is the amount of currency outstanding. Yet in the face of the danger of a runaway inflation, the government is frequently increasing it in two ways. First, whenever an exporter, because of the tariff, has to take a gold payment, he must sell the gold to the government for paper money, which thus increases the amount in circulation. Second, whenever the government overspends, as it has done often of late, it "borrows" what it needs from the banks by forcing them to buy its bonds. This does not disturb the banks much, because when they want their money back they can sell their bonds to the Federal Reserve Bank (now practically a government agency), which prints new money to pay for them, thus again increasing the currency outstanding.

Our monetary condition is not as bad as it was after the Revolution, but it is not good.

The outward and visible form of our government has not changed much since the founding of the Republic, when we made our extraordinary recovery. But we saw in considering the New Deal how the outward form had been twisted by the New Dealers so as to give an almost preponderant power to the executive branch; and the executive branch is in the complete control of the President. This gives him inordinate power. Such power that, should we elect a clever, ambitious man of the wrong type—the dictator type—he could readily impose an authoritarian state on us and cinch it on. He has the power, through the propaganda bureaus, to beguile our attention from what is being done to us. We have seen this happen.

Great power is an amazingly corrupting possession. The emperors of Rome had great power. The office of emperor was the summit of human ambition. It was not an hereditary office. The emperors were chosen by the Senate, or the legions, or by force. Since it was the summit of human ambition, there must have been an enormous number of men who wanted it. Therefore it took a man of extraordinary ability and energy to get it. Yet of all the brilliant, able and forceful men who attained the purple, all but a handful went insane or became degenerate while wearing it. For modern examples, take Hitler and Mussolini. Such a strong medicine is great power.

Are we wise in entrusting such power over ourselves to any man? All men are fallible. That is a fact and can never be corrected. Unless a man is given great power by statute, his failures make little difference and injure him and his disciples alone. Once he is given great power by law, his failures affect the whole country and become great national tragedies. The danger to ordinary people, thus made evident, can be readily avoided, not by searching for the non-existent infallible man to clothe with power, but rather by not giving any man great power by force of law. It was to avoid the danger of having the power of one man built up by law to a point where he could greatly injure others, that the framers of the Constitution devised the safeguard of dividing the great power of government between the executive, legislative and judicial branches of the governmental framework, so that no one man could have too much. Today the executive branch has managed to break down this balance of power by its ability to control all patronage and by the custom that has been forced on Congress of delegating legislative power to executive commissions. Since no legislature can regulate economics, it must perforce turn such regulations over to commissions if it wants to indulge in this foolish practice at all.

It is true we elect our President. That is, we can vote for one of two candidates selected by the conventions of the two great parties. The delegates to these conventions are exclusively politicians, and generally bureaucrats. There is an unwieldy mass of them at each convention, who are controlled by "party leaders" —most able men who are generally sincerely patriotic. These leaders decide on the successful candidate by discussion and by "deals"; the rest of the delegates follow them. Even the leaders rarely know the true character of the candidate. They are, of course, influenced by the favors they expect to receive from him. Much less do they know the character of the Vice President who may inherit the power, and who is almost always selected by a political deal which gives little or no consideration to the true character of the man selected.

It is not safe to entrust such power over ourselves to a man so selected. It is not the method of selection that is wrong. It has worked reasonably well in the past. The danger lies in the extraordinary power the recent Congresses have placed in the one man's hands. The last Republican Congress did nothing to resume the vast power the preceding Democratic ones had ceded to the President. This is regrettable and it is hard to see a worthy motive for their inaction. The legislative branch of our government still could recapture its full powers as granted by the Constitution.

So great is the President's power today that he must decide almost every conflict of views that arises in the vast multitude of the bureaucracy, as if he were a European dictator. No single man could possibly do this. Therefore he has had to surround himself with a small army of assistants, who perforce make most of the decisions. The President is so surrounded that he is ceasing to be the man we elected and is becoming a group—in other words, "The Presidency" just as the King of England has ceased to be the man and become "The Crown." Of course the President, the only man elected in "the Presidency group," has the legal power to control them all. But still he is only human, and when he finds himself constantly, almost exclusively, surrounded by several hundred intelligent, non-elected bureaucrats who make most of the decisions, and who can, to a large extent, control the information he receives, he would have to be more than human not to be most heavily influenced by the bureaucratic point of view.

How far our situation has advanced along totalitarian lines may be seen in the guides to economic policy so clearly set forth in Mr. Truman's message to Congress on the status of the country's economy, delivered January 7, 1949:

As we turn from consideration of the facts of our economic situation to a program of action, there are several broad principles which I believe should guide us. These principles should help us to keep clearly in mind where we want to go and how certain roads rather than others are the surest and quickest way of getting there.

First, we should remember that the goal we seek is the greatest prosperity for the whole country and not the special gain of any particular group. That is why the Employment Act of 1946 calls upon the President to present an economic program aimed at continuous "maximum employment, production and purchasing power." I firmly believe that this goal is attainable.

Maximum employment for 1949 means that nearly one million additional job opportunities should be provided for the labor force. Maximum production means that our increased labor force and modernized plant should strive for a 3 to 4 percent increase in total output. Maximum purchasing power means that the sum total of market demand by Government, business, and consumers, domestic and foreign, should be proportionate to our productive capacity. It must not be more or we shall suffer inflation. It must not be less or we shall suffer unemployment and under-utilization of our resources.

Second. We should think and work with a reasonably long look ahead, not keeping our eyes just on the problems of the moment. Our immediate tasks must be placed in the perspective of our long-range national objectives. While we must deal promptly with the problem of inflation, we must not unduly hold back undertakings that are needed to preserve and develop our employment opportunities and our productivity in later years. Policies needed to develop our resources and to prevent depression in the long run must be reconciled with policies needed to curb inflation in the short run.

We must pursue affirmative programs for housing and health, for education and resource development. Yet the fight against inflation prevents us from undertaking these long-range programs with the speed and on a scale that would otherwise be desirable. In the recommendations made in this economic report and in the budget which will be transmitted to the Congress in a few days, I have sought to reconcile these objectives in a way that strikes the safest balance.

Third. In order to have a yardstick for appraising strength and weaknesses in our economy and the adequacy of Government programs, we need concrete objectives for economic growth, and particularly standards for a better balance between production and consumption, income and investment, and prices, profits, and wages which will be conducive to sustained economic progress.

In the annual economic review of the Council of Economic Advisers, transmitted herewith, there is a detailed treatment of our growth possibilities over the next few years. This shows how our employment, our output, and our standards of living can rise if we encourage and place major reliance upon our free enterprise system, conserve and develop our natural and human resources, retain our faith in responsible Government, and do not relax our efforts.

This study by the Council of Economic Advisers shows that action is now needed on the long-range programs which I set forth in the concluding section of this economic report.

Fourth. We are dedicated to the principle that economic stability and economic justice are compatible ends. The fact that our total purchasing power is now at record levels cannot blind us to the equally important fact that the incomes of many people have not risen apace with the cost of living and that they have become the victims of inflation. A prosperity that is too uneven in the distribution of its fruits cannot last.

Fifth. We must fulfill the requirements of our essential programs—national defense, international reconstruction and domestic improvements and welfare—even if doing so may require the temporary exercise of selective controls in our economy. We want the greatest amount of economic freedom that is consistent with the security and welfare of the people, but we do not want to sacrifice that security and welfare because of narrow and selfish concepts as to the acceptable limits of Government action.

If we could have the amount of national defense that we need, make the contribution to international reconstruction to which we are committed, and at the same time maintain and expand our standards of living, now and in the future without any kind of selective controls over the economy, that would be most highly desirable. And it is possible that we may not, in fact, be forced to use such controls. But we would rather have these relatively unpleasant restrictions on our freedom of action for a while than imperil our security or allow our human and material resources to deteriorate.

Sixth. The vigorous commitment by the Government to an anti-inflation policy should not obscure the fact that the Government is equally committed to an anti-depression policy. In fact, curbing inflation is the first step toward preventing depression. And in times like the present, when the economic situation has mixed elements, the Government needs both anti-inflationary weapons and anti-deflationary weapons so that it will be ready for either contingency. It may even be necessary to employ both types of measures concurrently in some combinations, for some prices or incomes could rise too rapidly while others could be falling dangerously. The same dictates of prudent policy which call for higher taxes in a period of inflation would call for tax adjustments designed to counteract any serious recessionary movement.

Note well that the whole tone of this quotation assumes the complete authority, as well as the complete duty, of our government to regulate entirely our economy. Neither such authority nor such duty was considered a prerogative of American government before the advent of Franklin Roosevelt. Neither of them is at all compatible with an economy of free enterprise.

Of course the execution of such a plan as Mr. Truman proposed will require a vast increase in the numbers of the bureaucracy, who must be taken out of productive work to assist in making the regulations and enforcing them. But the essential question is: Who makes the delicate adjustments in this taking and giving process, which will result in the maximum benefit to all?

It cannot be Congress for we have seen that legislative bodies are too large and have too universal interests to be able to decide effectively which particular Peter to rob, for what benefit to which particular Paul.

The judicial branch of our government seems to have decided to acquiesce in matters of government regulation and not to interfere.

That leaves it up to the executive branch of the government to adjust this delicate balance which will justly divide the fruits of the production of the country. Of course, under those brief intervals when the people of this earth have temporarily seen an economy of free enterprise working, the good Lord attended to all this by his natural economic laws which rewarded the intelligent and industrious, and penalized the slothful and foolish. But many people were dissatisfied with their desserts under the natural economic laws, and so management of the matter has been turned over, by statute at least, to the executive branch of government. So the delicate adjustment of our national economy for the greatest and fairest distribution of its income is in the hands of Mr. Truman and his executive department of our government.

Mr. Truman is a good, conscientious, hard-working man, apparently without a shade of the dictator complex. But no man could do such a job, and furthermore Mr. Truman's successful endeavors and his training have not been along economic lines. The work, then, will have to be done by the bureaucracy. Of course the bureaucracy *might* accomplish it, but history is replete with instances of bureaucracies attempting to manage economies "for the greatest benefit of all." There is no single example of success. Most attempts seem to have produced the greatest detriment for all.

The main visible difference between our present government and our early one is in the size of our bureaucracy, which, as we have seen, had increased by the beginning of World War II from one bureaucrat to every 42,130 of the population to one bureaucrat to every 28 of the population, and had by removal into its ranks of potential producers, and by taxation, reduced the income our producers might have had to 63% of its potential; not counting the tremendous but immeasurable effects it has surely produced by tieing up the sources of production with its regulations. Its average cost during the years 1929-1941 before the war, was 28% of the total income of the country—an insupportable amount, since no one saves so great a percent of his income.

Our bureaucracy is strangling our economy to death. It is the primary source of all the economic discontent in the country which surely rises from the people's lack of sufficient individual income to meet their needs. Yet it has skillfully taught us as a nation that it, and it alone, can provide us as individuals with a sufficient income, in spite of the fact that it produces nothing itself and lives by consuming the income of all.

The worst and most dangerous part of the bureaucracy is its various and numerous, so called, "Publicity Departments." These are nothing but propaganda factories. One evil effect of these propaganda bureaus is the burden they put on Congressmen. Directly or indirectly these publicity departments organize pressure groups through agricultural associations, labor unions, women's clubs, etc., who have vast membership and whose key positions are often said to have been infiltrated by Communist sympathizers. Many of these groups have been organized by sincere American patriots, to help along the United States. They naturally attribute to their associations' paid employees the same high motives they themselves feel. They therefore tend to have complete faith in the pronouncements of "their" associations, and accept their "packaged thoughts" as Gospel, passing them along in the form of "pressure" letters to their Representatives in Congress.

The Congressmen are swamped under these "packaged thought" letters. They are pretty worldly wise. It is not hard for them to trace the "packages" back to the propaganda departments. Nevertheless, they have to be polite and consider their constituents' views, or they will not be re-elected. If the Congressmen have clear views on the issues in question, they will follow them. But these politico-economic questions of granting privileges are often made to appear pretty complicated, and are slow and difficult to think out. The Congressmen are often too busy and resort to "Public Opinion Polls" to find the true sentiment of their district.

These polls showed their value in assessing public opinion in the election of 1948.

One set of laws that seems as well designed as any to injure and reduce the production of the country and thus the real income of everyone in it, are those connected with "unemployment insurance." From the cleverly selected name of these laws, "unemployment insurance," and of the agency that administers it, "United States Employment Service," or "U.S.E.S.," many people would naturally assume it was a good thing. Let us look at it, as it really is, under the camouflage of its lovely names.

It started under a Federal law passed in 1935 and the operation of it was passed over to the various state governments as they acceded to its principles, the control of the whole being carefully retained in Washington by an ingenious device. It is in no sense "relief." Relief is the result of quite another set of laws. It makes no difference whether those who draw the benefits of unemployment insurance are destitute or wealthy.

Under Federal leadership each state passed a supplementary law to cooperate with the Federal scheme. These laws naturally differ in detail, but conform to the general plan, which, as advertised, is that anyone who loses his job (provided that job is one of 45,000 kinds of a job, all carefully defined in the U.S.E.S. bible) may draw unemployment insurance benefits for from 20 to 26 weeks at the rate of from $20 to $25 a week until the U.S.E.S. can get him a job exactly similar to the one he lost, at the same rate of pay and in a convenient locality. To do this the applicant must first register at the office of U.S.E.S. (the Federal agency) and have his application approved. The money for all this does not come from the Federal government, it does not come from the general funds of the states, it does not (contrary to general belief) come from those insured, except in Alabama and New Jersey where the insured nominally pay one-third of the premium. The money is collected from all employers at the rate of 3% of their pay rolls. Thus it is a direct tax on production, increasing the cost of it, and this increase must be passed on in higher prices to the consumers. It must be remembered that this cost is not only the initial one of the producer, but is added also by the manufacturers, the processors, the wholesalers, jobbers and retailers, along the whole line. Ten percent of the money so collected by the states is paid over to the Federal government, that they may by their suggestions bring "conformity" to the whole plan.

What the Federal authority thus collects it can return to the states in its discretion, not necessarily to those states from which it is collected. It generally uses its discretion by passing it out to those states that follow its suggestions most closely. In the autumn of 1948 the Federal government part of U.S.E.S. had collected, and not yet distributed, some $831,000,000 of these funds. One is apt to accept the "suggestions" of anyone who has the power to distribute so much to one's own outfit. The money power, coupled with the fact that all applicants for benefits must apply first to U.S.E.S. (the local Federal offices) and be approved by it before they draw their benefits from the state collected funds, gives the Federal Government pretty nearly complete control.

Unfortunately the whole thing is not run as an employment agency but as a super-boondoggle. For instance, two-thirds of the operating funds of the agencies, both state and Federal, are devoted to the salaries and costs of those paying the approved applicants. (This, of course, does not include the amounts paid out.) The other third goes to those charged with seeking employment for them. In doing this no attention appears to be paid to the "help wanted" ads in the papers. Each applicant must fit himself into one of the 45,000 classified jobs in the U.S.E.S. bible, and have a similar job presented him. He need not look for one himself.

This bible is worth study. It describes minutely each job that may be lost. The descriptions are interesting. Examples follow:

"A pretzel salter; a laborer process. Salts pretzels by hand, preparatory to baking, fills a perforated salt can with coarse salt from a supply can or barrel; stands near an oven and sprinkles salt on pretzels, moving on conveyor after they have been dipped in glazing solution."

"Almshouse keeper: A manager who manages an institution supported by public charity or taxes for the benefit of the poor."

"Beach comber: a term applied to any person who obtains his living by gathering the products or refuse from the beach."

Anyone who loses such a job is entitled to the benefits of unemployment insurance for the full time, unless U.S.E.S. gets him another precisely like it, convenient to his home and at wages that he and the U.S.E.S. office regard as suitable. It must be exactly the same kind of a job. A doughnut sugarer's job would be no substitute for a pretzel salter's, nor a clam digger's for a beach comber's.

The attitude of the head office has been to treat the whole scheme of Unemployment Insurance as a potlatch, or general gift-giving, service. The official order to the staff workers is to "pay liberally and with enthusiasm." The names of those drawing benefits are "confidential information," so no one can know who the recipients are and they may enjoy anonymity in their community. The amount of wages that the applicant should receive in his new job is liberally set by the U.S.E.S. office. It makes no great difference whether the applicant lost his job by coming to it drunk, or by spitting in his boss's eye, or whether he refuses to take a precisely similar job to the old one at the same or better pay. That is, it does not in thirty-six states, although if he does one of those things he is likely not to be permitted to draw the benefits until two, four, or six weeks have elapsed; then he can come back and draw it for the full period. In twelve states such conduct does disqualify him from the benefits.

In most states, strikers are not eligible for unemployment benefits; but those who are "locked out" are. Labor unions can successfully get round this by having a few key workers strike and so force the closing of the plant. The rest are then considered to be locked out, and draw the unemployment benefits, and the cost of the strike to the unions is very low indeed.

The law in itself, as drawn, is sufficiently injurious to the country, as it increases the cost of all goods and removes all incentive to get work for half a year at a time, but the way it is administered makes it a serious curse to the country. Many people, who have no idea of working at all permanently, such as housewives, get a job for just long enough to qualify under the unemployment insurance, and then draw the benefits for half a year and repeat. Sometimes two people will live together, and work and loaf on unemployment insurance alternately, every six months. As the benefits of the unemployment insurance are free of all taxes and incumbrances, and as salaries are now all subject to deductions for income tax, old age pensions, etc., many of these people quite logically take all the deductions from any salary they may work for, then deduct what they would get as the unemployment benefits, and figure that the remainder is what they are really working for and that it is not enough to compensate them for their effort. Therefore they decide to quit and loaf. So we have today's amazing picture: Industry screaming for workers, and at the same time the productive employers of California alone paying out three-quarters of a million dollars a day to the beneficiaries of unemployment insurance.

The whole picture is so harmful, so insane, that one wonders how it could occur at all, even in the present age of economic insanity. Perhaps there is a key to it in the charge that the person who was in charge of the training of personnel, all down the line on the employment side of the program, was a woman—employed at $8,000 a year, who had the responsibility of going from state to state, interviewing and instructing and supervising the personnel of the employment service, and who on November 17, 1948 was suspended from her job in the government service by the Regional Loyalty Board in Washington. The Loyalty Board said that, "on all the evidence, the Board finds reasonable grounds for belief that the individual is disloyal to the Government of the United States—the evidence showed that Miss —— among other things has been very active in the Communist-dominated C.I.O. Public Workers of America, and was a local union president and member of the national executive committee."

This is all aggravated by the minimum wage law, for a person who cannot produce enough to justify the minimum wage will not be employed. So he will produce nothing and live on relief.

On December 8, 1948, the New York *Journal* reported that the National Industrial Conference Board had found "the Federal, state and local governments distributed $9,000,000,000 in welfare payments to individuals last year under the social security, public assistance and veterans' program." The average cost of these gifts is $150 a year for each of the 60 million people gainfully employed!

The New York *Times*, January 23, 1949, reported that on the week ending January 7, the unemployment insurance and the veterans' readjustment rolls showed 467,880 people locally drawing insurance benefits. The same day the paper carried about twelve full pages of "help wanted" advertisements.

As was the case in 1787, the whole rest of the world is bound in economic chains. At the start of the Republic, we managed to break these down by our own example and by the incredible success with which our untrammeled economy functioned. Today we cannot furnish this example; our economy is largely chained and only slightly free. It is a pity this is so; our prestige of today would give our good example far more weight than it had then.

As in 1787 we are nervous about being attacked by an outside power. Then we did little except talk about our danger. The result was the nearly complete disaster of the War of 1812. Today we are making tangible efforts toward war readiness and we should do so. But even our War Department is attacked by the plague of bureaucracy.

This looks pretty serious and should be studied and corrected. We need a good and a large armed force now, if we ever did, as a defense against Russian attack. But we must always remember that we won the last two wars because our partially free economy could outstrip the production of all the economies of other nations who were more tied up by regulation. We are in the way of losing that tremendous advantage today.

We need more than an army to resist the Russian attack, for we have seen in a dozen instances in other nations that the most effective Russian attack comes from within—through their trained workers, planted in their victims' bureaucracy, the labor unions under Communist leadership and all their organizations built up under the protection of economic statutes. Today, June, 1950, one can scarcely pick up a newspaper without reading of this type of infiltration into our own organizations, and little is done about it. This internal attack inflames by propaganda certain groups, generally the economically lowest and mentally stupidest; and forces through legislation giving them an unfairly large percentage of the national income, thus further injuring the productive economy which is the chief factor in our military success. Remember that in order to get control of a country the Communist leaders must first have economic misery in that country, and then a well integrated bureaucracy. Their objective is, therefore, to create that misery and multiply that bureaucracy.

After all, the fundamental American concept is that on earth the all-important unit is the individual—the child of God. Jointly he created the state to be his servant, in order to protect him from undue interference from others and from the state itself, so that without interference he could create the kind of life he wanted, make what he wished, keep what he wished, dispose of what he wished, under the natural economic laws— the laws of God, so long as he did not injure, rob or unduly interfere with others. The sooner we reaffirm our faith in that concept, the better for us as a nation and the worse for Russia and all totalitarian nations or nations with managed economies. For all these latter seem to hold the state to be an instrument through which one man, or group of men, may rob others of the fruits of their toil without punishment, by decreeing that economic immorality is legal.

Probably the greatest difference of all between our country today, and our country in the days of its great prosperity when the Republic had just been founded, lies in the mental attitude of our people. Then everybody realized that what he produced was his, that what was used in the cost of government was paid for by him and by everybody else, that the government was his servant and that it was not designed either to push him round or to enrich him, beyond giving him opportunity to enrich himself. Then almost everybody understood economics, for economics is merely common sense. It was manifest that if A made a superlatively good bargain with B, B must have made a superlatively bad one. If credit was increased so was debt. If a subsidy was given to one group it was taken from others. It is all as simple as that. Economy is common sense, and common sense is simple. The trouble is that today everybody is mixed up about economy. For years every group with a personal economic axe to grind has tried to confuse the subject by proving that the grinding of their axe would help everybody. To do this, they built up complex castles and cities of words, using abstruse terms, unfamiliar expressions, specious arguments, etc., deliberately to confuse the public into believing that their axe should be ground for the public weal. Much of the public believes that this deliberately designed confusion is economics. They can't understand it, of course, as most of it is deliberately incomprehensible nonsense. Therefore they come to believe that economics is a very complicated subject. It is not, fundamentally.

All sorts of groups are mixing it up. Trade associations, manufacturers, farm leaders, unions, the unemployed—all for the advantage of their own pockets. College professors do it to increase their prestige by solving mysteries. Union leaders do it to befuddle the people into according their workmen more than they deserve and so gain the plaudits of their henchmen. The bureaucrats do it to increase their numbers and power.

The odd thing is that the general public submissively swallows all this propagandized economic twaddle almost without a murmur. Most people say quite frankly they don't understand it, and don't try to. Many partially see through it and then start pressure groups to grab off some extra special privileges for themselves. The vast majority of the intelligent, energetic and efficient part of the community, whose qualities have naturally and inevitably given them a better position on the economic ladder than the stupid, lazy and ineffective, generously do not oppose "socialistic legislation for the benefit of those less fortunately placed." Meanwhile those imbued with the Communist virus, who control most of the vehicles of propaganda, see clearly that the hog instincts of those seeking privilege for themselves, and the generous impulses of those who approve of social legislation, are both leading to the universal yoke of totalitarianism. They encourage enthusiastically the selfish interests of the former and the generous attitude of the latter; for it is clear to them that both groups, whatever they think they are doing, are unconsciously but ably bringing about a totalitarian state, which both the former and latter group really abhor.

Truly, discrimination is one of the greatest and most useful of human virtues. One of the saddest sights in this country today is the vast number of good, kind men and women, who, with the best intentions possible, are working industriously, energetically and effectively to bring about a condition the exact reverse of what they intend to produce, simply because they have not taken the trouble to think out the ultimate result of their acts and see only the immediate ones. The Communists see quite clearly that the sum of all these immediate "beneficial" results lead directly to a totalitarian state.

Propaganda has built such an aura of virtue around everything labeled "social benefit" that those who can see beyond their own noses and can divine where we are all being led, are afraid to lift their voices. If they do they are overwhelmed with a torrent of abuse, denouncing them as anti-social, reactionary and obstructive. It has got so that political candidates for office rarely speak of anything except giving "benefits" to the "underprivileged," which is the modern propaganda term for ineffectives. They appear to forget the ineffectives are, thank God, a very small percent of our population. The vast majority of Americans today are efficient, up-and-coming citizens who are paying for all these "benefits" by the loss of their liberty as well as of their money. So strong has been the propaganda that the vast majority do not appear to see this, and silently acquiesce, or even applaud the mouthings of the equally blinded political candidates. Yet anyone who thinks of it for a moment can see that the nation depends for its success, its prosperity, its development, and the good it may do in its history, on its efficient citizens. Therefore it is apparent that it should be run primarily for their benefit. Even were the ineffectives a majority of the nation, instead of a tiny minority, no government could be run by, and for the benefit of, the inefficient. Such a government was tried once, very early in our history, by the "gentlemen adventurers" in Jamestown. The "starving time" followed very shortly and very severely, as it always will and inevitably must, whenever this experiment is tried.

It may be profitable to consider this situation from the historical point of view. At all times there are great numbers of people who prefer to loaf and who gladly sacrifice much of their comfort to enjoy this luxury. Whenever a nation is enjoying a period of vigor and growth, these loafers are quite properly abhorred, everything is done to discourage them, they are penalized by jail sentences. (See the laws of Elizabethan England against "stout vagabonds" and "sturdy beggars.") This is to the true benefit of the loafers and the people as a whole. Whenever a nation is decadent and degenerating, the loafers undergo a sort of apotheosis. Everybody worries about them and tries to help them in their idleness, thus greatly accelerating the general disintegration of the whole people. Examples are Imperial Rome with its "bread and circuses," present day England with its "dole."

The odd thing is, that this disease of a worn-out and decadent nation should have gotten a hold on the virile, energetic and vigorous United States. It was imported here by the New Deal from Europe to replace the American system of the "work house," where those who would not work for themselves were taught better by being made to work for the county. It has greatly increased the bureaucracy. It has been encouraged by our Anglophiles, those silly people who think we should copy anything British. Far more sensibly it is encouraged by the Communists who see exactly where it is leading us. It is not, and never has been, needed in these United States. Though we have tied up our economy by our foolish habit of trying to enrich ourselves by giving one another statutory privileges, we have not tied it up to such a point as to make this affliction necessary. Here it has become simply a legalized racket. It is odd that our people, who are almost universally still energetic, virile and self-reliant, have permitted the practice to go on as long as it has. The sooner we get rid of it the better for the freedom and for the pocketbooks of one and all of us.

Perhaps it is another effect of propaganda, and the *zeit geist* thereby developed, on the American people. Together they have induced an extreme submissiveness to any form of imposition or outrage perpetrated on them, provided it is done by a public official or in the name of government. In the summer of 1948, for example, a group of Oregon officials stopped all cars leaving the state on the public highway, and asked each car load how long they had been in the state and how much money they had spent. Presumably they were highway officials gathering statistics to impress the state legislature with the importance of the services of their department in order to press through a larger appropriation for it. This was no work for which the Oregonians should have been taxed. The questions were impertinent, prying and none of their business. There were so many cars that they were held up in a long queue and delayed half an hour—a species of arrest. Though everyone cursed, all answered the questions and submitted like sheep.

Yet not two hundred years ago it was not unusual for the American colonists to toss King George's officials into the horse pond, or clothe them in tar and feathers and ride them out of town on a rail. This unfortunate habit was again indulged in by the Pennsylvanians at the expense of George Washington's revenue officers, when they tried to collect a tax on whiskey. Regrettable as this practice undoubtedly was, it showed a laudable intention not to be imposed on by government. A spirit that is sadly lacking in the United States today.

Now the combination of the national habit of looking to government for pecuniary favors, the enormous bureaucracy this has built up, the lack of funds for productive and venture capital because of the cost of the bureaucracy, the propaganda departments and the submissiveness that they have produced in the people, coupled with the fact that the well-trained believers in the Russo-German political economic philosophy of the totalitarian state have insinuated themselves into key positions in the bureaucracies, the unions, the motion-picture industry, even apparently into some of the colleges, and other places of importance—all this has forged a chain of circumstances that logically must lead us to totalitarianism.

There is no other logical end. Our production, and therefore our income and prosperity, will decline. Many will turn to government for further relief, thus aggravating the situation till the producers get discouraged with the share of the national income they are allowed for their efforts. Then they will quit those efforts and turn in shoals to join either the bureaucracy itself or the unemployed reliefers, since those occupations are better paid, considering the effort expended, than others.

Then the government will be faced with the impossible task of dividing an insufficient total income so it will give everyone a sufficiency. The standard of living will fall. There will not be nearly enough to go round, no matter how divided. Hunger, disorder, perhaps a war started by a desperate government, will follow. Then will come "The Leader," the dictator with his "plan," with shouts, paeans of praise, parades and youth movements. In our desperation we will put him over us. Then we will work when, where, at what, and as long as, he chooses, and for what he chooses to pay us. Then we can buy what he lets us, amuse ourselves as he wants, read and think what he directs, and be told that we are living the more abundant life that he planned and endowed us with.

CHAPTER 14

WHAT CAN WE DO ABOUT IT?

"Ye shall know the truth, and the truth shall make you free"
JOHN, 8:32

THE PROSPECT FOR THE future is dark indeed, but there are hopeful elements in the picture. Unnoticed factors have a way of overturning the most logically drawn conclusion.

In the first place, we still elect our President and Congress, our governors and legislatures. They could reverse the present trend permanently and drastically in two months, and would, if the people made it clear that they wanted them to, and wanted, instead of this three-quarter-managed hodgepodge, an economy of free enterprise with personal liberty and full opportunity for all.

We have some $24⅓ billion of the world's $30.5 billion gold supply, and about two billion of silver—enough hard money if properly used in an economy of free enterprise, to set the wheels of industry all over the world awhirring. If released, it could be sold to European nations in return for their honest produce. In their hands it would do more good by stabilizing their currencies and economies for nothing, than would a thousand expensive Marshall plans. Now it is almost as useless as if it still lay undisturbed in the mines.

There is a great demand and a great need for the production of goods. Large parts of Europe and Asia are in misery, reduced to a starvation level. They have no gold but they are willing to work, and many of their specialties and luxury articles, which they make so well and we scarcely bother to make at all, would find a welcoming market here in exchange for what

we could send them. If a free economy existed, such imports
would be pouring in now. Surely it is better for us to get something in return for our produce, instead of giving them the money
to pay for it, as we do now in the form of "loans." But our high
tariff and their currency control prevent our importing these
goods.

We are enjoying very good times now, due to the war
shortages, government spending and the inflation. It is a tremendously encouraging thing and a great tribute to the virility,
energy and ability of our people, that after having bound our
economy by a myriad hampering restrictions of privilege and
removing one-eighth of our potential producers by putting them
into the bureaucracy, we are still able to create great quantities
of wealth when there is, as at present, a great need. It is also
a very lucky thing, for with the true national *per capita* income
as high or higher than it has been for decades, and no legitimate
excuse for unemployment, it gives us an opportunity to appraise
the long-term condition of our political economy before it is
too late.

We may not have many, or perhaps any, more of these
opportunities. Once another wave of unemployment strikes us,
the howls of the unemployed plus the maneuvers of the managed
economy disciples will make it difficult indeed to straighten
things out. It is well to bear in mind constantly and vividly
that good times are followed by booms and booms by busts.
Under the political-economic rules we have set up, our next
bust is liable to be our last, or anyway our next to last.

Some thirteen millions of our young people are back from
having won the greatest war in history. They are justly proud
of their records, self-confident, tired of hardship, sick of discipline and being ordered around. They are willing, and eager
to enrich themselves. They are the men—young as they are—
who built healthy cities in steaming jungles and waterless deserts,
who put roads over the Himalayas and the Arctic wastes of
Canada, built harbors in atolls, laid airfields in tree-covered
swamps. They want to be ordered around no more, they want
freedom from regulation, a chance to get rich and enjoy the
luxuries so long denied them. They want to get busy, to make
their pile, to rise in the world, to prove themselves in peace
as they have in war. Their energy alone, if released from regu-

lation, would cause a burst of production and an increase of national income and wealth that would eclipse the one after the Revolution.

Then there are the older people of our country, brought up to admire independence, who want to stand on their own feet, who love liberty. It is true most of these people have never thought deeply about government, since for generations practical Americans have not had to, because the framers of the Constitution thought so splendidly. It is also true that for the past score of years they have been fed every sort of propaganda to the effect that they should lean on government for support, or at least for "security." They have not, however, often fallen for this. Nine-tenths of them are still "rugged individualists" who want to stand on their own feet and go ahead and make a pile of their own. They don't understand what has been done to them by their own and each other's greed. All of us hate regulation. All of us are taxed to death and are unhappy. What do we want?

Today almost all Americans would say they wanted less interference from government and more income.

This desire is almost universal in the United States today. It carries with it the implied question, "How can this be obtained?" The answer to it is, in its essence, the same as the answer to the request made by my guests on the farm so long ago, "draw the line between necessary and harmful laws and regulations in such a way that it could be used as a principle, or dividing line to which all could refer." The facts and theories explained in this book now make the answer plain.

Stated succinctly, the function of government is to insure its citizens the greatest possible freedom from interference by each other or by government. Therefore it should concern itself with the conduct of people, and of government, and with nothing else. The rules of conduct should leave it up to every citizen to make his living as his desires and abilities permit under a stable rule of law.

Beyond this, government should not go. It is not framed to create wealth and cannot do so. It should not try to help anyone economically, since helping one always hurts others, and each miracle it passes requires many more to catch up with it. This is the more true because every economic regulation requires enforcement, and every additional bureaucrat is a double drain on the income of the country since his own production or true income is stopped, and his maintenance must be paid for out of the income of others.

History shows that great general prosperity occurs only where something approaching a free economy has been reached, and that prosperity always diminishes as government economic regulation increases. A free economy alone offers unlimited opportunity to all. It produces the greatest general wealth. Furthermore it is the only system that gives the people complete freedom.

The above four paragraphs state the axioms on which true political economy should be based.

Now when the people of the United States say they want no interference from government and more income, they are consciously or unconsciously asking for a free economy.

We might plan for a free economy. We would never succeed in getting an absolutely free one, since there are no absolutes in human relations. Our people, having thought the matter over, might even decide that they wanted to bestow privileges on some members of society. But it is certain that if we deliberately planned to eliminate all laws conferring privileges, we might accomplish a tremendous amount to recover the conditions that made us such a miracle of prosperity in the youth of our nation, when we accidentally created a free economy that it took nearly a century to strangle.

How could such a change in our internal policy be brought about?

Montesquieu said: "The people, possessing the supreme power, should do for itself all it is able to do; what it cannot do well, it must do through its elected representatives." Governor Ellis Arnall of Georgia has said: "The way to get rights is to assume responsibilities." Perhaps those two quotations put us on the right track. In the early days of our Republic, Americans did not heap all their problems together and pile them on a vague "Government in Washington" for solution. They tried to grapple with each problem at home where it was small, and solve it there themselves. Is their example unworthy of following?

Our people are virile, energetic, self-reliant. Though muddled and befogged by the rivers of propaganda poured out by the bureaucracy and those who wish for totalitarianism, almost all of us long for a free economy. Almost all of us hate the very idea of a totalitarian state. Almost all of us despise the inefficient, the loafer, the cadger, the sturdy rogue who wants to live without work. All of us want a life enriched by material things, cheap and in plenty.

Yet, although vast hordes of Americans actively and vigorously believe in a free economy, talk for it and mildly work for it, and although almost all of them passively believe in it but have not thought much about it, it will be a difficult thing to get a bare majority of them, or even a big minority of them, aggressively insisting on it.

If one stops to think about it, one realizes that the American people have had only one opportunity to vote against a managed economy. That was in 1932, when the splendid platform of the Democratic Party pledged itself to establish free enterprise, the old American principles, and to knock 25 percent off the (then comparatively small) bureaucracy. It was opposed by the Republican Administration, which was decidedly paternalistic and trying to arrange everything in Washington by regulating all business. Our people voted on the policies as laid down in those platforms. The Democratic one received 472 electoral votes. The Republican 59. That no reform ensued was owing to the betrayal of the decision of the people by the New Deal.

Since 1932, the issue has never been allowed to come up. The Democratic Party backed the New Deal after it got going. It had to. There were so many good jobs involved, and the active members of a political party are primarily interested in jobs. The Republican Party, inspired perhaps by a jealous longing for those jobs, dropped all thought of trying for an economy of free enterprise, and began yelling "me too" about everything the Democrats had done, and at the same time advocating further benefits, privileges and regimentation on their own account.

Yet everyone who travels about the country and talks to those he meets, knows that the whole country loathes this tax-supported regimentation, and longs to achieve a government where a man can live his own life and make his own money without government interference and without crushing taxes. If given a chance, nine-tenths of them would vote for free enterprise and the destruction of the bureaucracy today, as they did in 1932.

Bureaucratic propaganda has put us all on the defensive, but the same type of propaganda seems also to come in a milder degree from our commercial advertising broadcasts, financed by our businessmen. This, at first, is very surprising. Let us consider it. First, it may be well to remember that our political news commentators are mostly chosen for their mellifluous voices and ability to make amusing quips, and not for their deep wisdom, knowledge and ability in statecraft. Second, it is much easier for these gentlemen to follow the beaten track marked out for them by the bureaucracy, and not to rush off on startling and controversial paths of their own. This is the more true since the government licensing of radios gives the bureaucracy a certain power over them. Therefore, whenever government is thinking of giving a special privilege, a grant in aid or a subsidy, the matter is usually discussed from the point of view of the rosy, eagerly expectant beneficiary, and not from that of those who are to be despoiled that government may make the gift. Furthermore, the idle, the worthless bums, the lusty rogues, are never so designated when some government grant, nominally for their benefit but actually designed to increase the bureaucracy, is discussed. Then they are always referred to as "the unfortunate," "the under-privileged," "the poor," or some other name to excite sympathy. The fact that the efficient, upstanding, useful producers of the country are compelled to pay for the grant, is never even hinted at. All this is perhaps because the sponsors who finance these broadcasts regard them purely as vehicles for advertising, judge them solely by their efficiency as advertisements, and rarely, if ever, listen themselves to the twaddle they are paying for. This is unfortunate, for though these broadcasts are momentarily building up their sales, they are not infrequently, simultaneously building up the chains of taxation and regulations that are already crushing their companies and themselves almost to death.

The queerest thing of all is, that there is no propaganda drive at all in the country for what everyone really wants, namely a free economy. No one ever says: "It is not government's function to rob Peter to pay Paul. It should keep out of economic matters. What we should have is a free economy!"

Once the businessmen of the country do say that, and say it loudly, the situation will change fast. These petty discussions, over which branch to cut off what bureaucratic tree, will stop the moment we see that it is the whole bureaucratic wood that must be cut down, and the free economy reestablished. The businessmen of the country, little and big, are getting wound up to do this now. They are driven to it. When they move they must rely on themselves, not on the political parties. For the political parties are largely dominated by bureaucrats or would-be bureaucrats, since few people work actively in party politics without expecting to get something for themselves. The aspirants for elective office have to stand in well with these bureaucratic gentry, for the way things are now, all candidates for office are dependent on them for both nomination and election. In fact, both our present political parties seem now to take seriously and literally the ironic gibe of Voltaire, who cried before the French Revolution, "The art of government consists in taking as much money as possible from one part of the citizens to give it to the other!" But all this would change quickly once the candidates for office realized that the people, who after all have the votes, were actively against the idea of a managed economy and paternalistic government, and wanted their freedom back, and a great cut in taxes.

How this will be accomplished no man can say, for no man can foresee the future, but let us suppose. Suppose, for instance, a group of big advertisers got together and began flooding the air with a demand for freedom and a free economy; held up to scorn the policy of legally robbing some groups for the benefit of others; attacked the big and little abuses of the vast bureaucracy that is ordering everybody about and siphoning off everybody's income; asked why the efficient should be penalized for the idle, lazy loafers, and why these latter should be paid for their own vices at the expense of their betters; in other words, made a strong attack on the entrenched greed of the bureaucracy and took a strong stand for that freedom which can be had only with a free economy. It would mean giving up only the pleas they are now making for additional privileges for themselves and concentrating on a unanimous demand for a free economy which would benefit them all, and everybody else besides. To do this nowadays, basic economic laws would have to be clearly stated and explained. This will not be difficult. Economic laws are such simple common sense that the mere statement of them will convince 95% of mankind of their truth. The hog wash poured over them by persons interested in distorting them have made them look infinitely complicated. This hog wash can easily be swept away and the people made fully conscious of what the real economic laws are, so that they can easily start their own reasoning from a sound basis.

Such an attack would be monstrously effective. All men desire freedom, all men hate taxes and bureaucrats. This is especially true of Americans. Ours would be the popular side, for everyone wants freedom, and many there are who can barely stomach the present trends in spite of the sugar-coatings of benefits and privileges which are supposed to make them palatable. Thousands of bureaucratic abuses could be, and should be, held up to ridicule and contempt. Furthermore, the tremendous advantage of truth would be on our side, which our opponents sadly lack. Justice would be on our side, for though it may now be legal, it is manifestly unjust to rob Peter to pay Paul. Most important, public opinion would be on our side, since above all things true Americans love liberty. Once let the American people see what they want clearly, and what has been done to them, and they will strike, and strike fast, to get their desire.

Once the flame of liberty is rekindled, it will flare far, for it is the very essence of the American spirit. Once blazing again, all will follow the beacon. The daily press, much of which has been fighting stoutly against the Communist menace, will lead in a crusade for liberty. Even the movies must follow, for to live they have to cater to the spirit of the times.

It may be argued that it would be impossible to get the big radio advertisers together on such a program, since their own privileges are too dear to them to risk sacrificing. That may be true. But it seems hardly possible that any business executive would not see now, that if all the restraints, taxes and regulations which are the necessary results of others' privileges were swept away, the benefits to him and his business would be so great that he would scarcely notice and never miss the loss of his own legal privileges and benefits, which in the present

tangled economy seem so valuable. The elimination of all government rules and regulations, except those based on the Ten
Commandments, would bring a greater benefit to any business
today than any special privilege government has granted or
could grant.

It may be that the great advertisers will never do this. If
not, some patriotic group will. It must be done. America is stirring uneasily today in the bonds of her government-trammeled
economy. Americans are too independent to submit to being
slaves of any totalitarian dictator. Some group is bound to take
the lead and destroy the present menace. It had better be done
soon. During the next few years we can do it quietly with the
ballot box. In a few decades, the growing totalitarian character
of government will make it impossible to do without bloodshed.

It may be argued that a return to an economy of free
enterprise would upset our present economy dreadfully. That is
true; it would. But our present economy had better be upset, and
upset soon, if it be rapidly leading us into the slavery of a totalitarian dictatorship. As a matter of fact, the upset would not be
nearly as sudden or disastrous as one might at first suppose.
Even with three-quarters of our people thoroughly aroused (as
they were for repeal of Prohibition) and fighting for a free
economy and personal liberty, and against the bureaucracy and
our present crushing taxes, the change would perforce be very
slow and gradual. Business and industry could adapt themselves
to meet it. Many a business man and industrialist may be so
short-sighted as to try to save his own particular special privilege from the general clean-up and fight for it, while welcoming
and urging the elimination of everyone else's privileges. Many
a subtle and specious argument will be advanced that such a
law of privilege is not one of privilege but a rule of conduct
which, if violated, will unduly injure others. It will be a long,
slow business, but as it progresses, business, production, income
and wealth will increase more and more rapidly; for the history
of the human race has shown that the less regulation of the
economy by government, the greater has been the national and
the individual prosperity.

It will be argued that a nation with a free economy cannot
exist in a world where all the other nations are so heavily regimented by government. At the start of our Republic, western

Europe was more heavily ruled and regimented by privilege than it is today; South America bowed beneath the heavy rule of Spain and Portugal; Japan was out of bounds; China groaned under the corrupt bureaucratic rule of the Manchus, and Russia had a government under the Czars almost as autocratic and almost as full of privilege and almost as bureaucratic as it is under Stalin today, though less cruel. We, a little, new, insignificant Republic, alone had free enterprise. We prospered unbelievably. So much so that not only did our wealth increase at an incredible rate, but our example was more or less followed by all other nations, to their great benefit. Is it not likely to be the same now, when we stand a king among nations? If today we were following the true American policy, instead of reluctantly dragging along after the example of the paternalistic states, the other nations would rush in to follow our example, the whole economy of the world would start leaping forward together. The totalitarian dictators might even find that, to save themselves, they would have somewhat to follow us too. That would tend to break their power. There is no question that if we decide to go into a free economy, we can do so alone. Nor that in doing so, we should immeasurably benefit ourselves and, by our example, greatly benefit all other nations.

It does not matter much what the particular means is, that will fan to flame the deep love of liberty that glows in the heart of every true American. For though history shows that mankind seldom recognizes its own foolishness while indulging in it, it also shows that when things get so bad that man has to think deeply, he eventually straightens himself out. Today, any one who talks to thoughtful people in any section of the country about our government, will realize from the indignation and bitterness expressed that we are just about at the turning point. The important thing is to raise our battleflag and get together.

We don't need any great national leader for this. What we need is to have groups of energetic citizens spring up in towns and villages all over the country and make an intensive drive to break down legal privilege and the excessive bureaucracy. The chances are they will find an Augean stable to clean up right at home. Soon they will get in touch with similar groups elsewhere; county groups will get busy, then state groups, eventually a national group. Perhaps the thing will work much as the League for Prohibition Reform did with its thousands of patriotic women workers. But there will be great differences. In the first place, each locality will have to decide for itself which local privileges and which local bureaucratic jobs and bureaucrats they want to get rid of, for that is a purely local question and they should not pass the buck back to a higher echelon, which cannot in the nature of things know as much about the local problem as they do. Then they will have to stage a political fight to enforce their decisions. Often they will find that local jobs and privileges are protected by State statute from elimination, since many a thoughtful bureaucrat has protected his job by statute against this very contingency and so have many other beneficiaries of privilege. This will require getting in touch with other groups with a view to eventually getting the statutes repealed.

Second, they will have an awful job learning just how their government functions and getting to understand it. For the bureaucrats with their overlapping echelons of government have prepared a maze more complicated than the one which Theseus threaded, into which to retire and escape from an outraged public.

Third, if they make any progress at all, they will be vituperated and held up to opprobrium in every possible way. They must expect that, for that is the chief bureaucratic and totalitarian weapon. They may even be persecuted by public officials. These three things will make the fight harder than the Prohibition one.

There are, however, two factors that will make it easier. First, the fight can be won without amending the Constitution. That is a great advantage since a two-thirds majority will not be needed. The second great advantage is that the ladies will in all probability have far more cooperation from highly efficient business men than they had in the former struggle that they won almost alone. For in the present instance the gentlemen are not only constantly hampered and irritated by the loss of the large part of their freedom that is already gone and that they know in their hearts they must recover sometime and

somehow in order to live happily, but also they are sorely hit
in their pocketbooks—a most sensitive portion of gentlemen's
anatomy.

No specific plan could or should be laid down. Once the
movement starts, local leaders will evolve and foregather with
others till State and National groups will coalesce. The individuals of ability who will be uncovered will each gather fol-
lowers in accordance with their wisdom and energy. Together
they will accomplish the job right. That is as it should be.

Few people seem to realize that the situation is so bad
today that were our producers each to devote a few hours a
week to breaking up the bureaucracies and the economic regulations, Federal, state and local, they would make more money
for themselves and their businesses than they could possibly do
by continuing at their routine jobs for those few hours. It is
obvious that the government is taking 30 percent of the profits
of every man and every business by taxation. It is equally obvious that a few hours weekly, sacrificed to a universally beneficial course, could not possibly, if devoted to routine business,
increase their profits by any similar percentage. When this *is*
fully realized by businessmen, the ladies will have plenty of
assistants. But there will be a tough fight.

Our national situation with regard to the bureaucracy is
not unlike that of a family which has long been living beyond its
means. Once such a family takes the plunge and drastically
cuts its expenses, it finds the "impossible" change to a simpler
life, pleasant. It is relieved of innumerable worries. It finds
itself going up in the world and getting richer, instead of
constantly sliding further down hill. It becomes cheerful and
looks forward, instead of sadly longing for the old days.

Once the spirit of liberty, that is smoldering among our
oppressed people today, bursts forth as a strong flame and the
people demand low taxes and economic freedom, the bureaucracy will go. No one can tell in detail how it will go, any more
than how a free economy will work in detail. Nevertheless,
certain things are obvious. The propaganda departments should,
and probably will, go first, because they are our greatest danger,
the strongest weapon of the bureaucracy, and because they are
already getting irksome to the Congressmen who have the power
to kill them. Then the useless, expensive and silly bureaus should

go, like those which print at great expense pamphlets telling women how to fold diapers, masons how to build chimneys and picnickers how to put out a fire. They would never be missed at all. Then the cancerous bureaucratic growths in the Federal government should go—those like Federal education, Federal health, etc., which have no business in the Federal government at all and are of no advantage to anyone except the bureaucrats. All this would decrease the cost of government and leave the people more money to spend on what they want. Those ventures the government has made into private business could be sold back to private enterprise—projects like the T.V.A., the Hoover Dam, and so forth. The various types of government insurance could be sold to private concerns, to the great benefit of the insured as well as to private business, for the insured might get some of their forced savings back by cancelling their policies. In the same way, government loans to private individuals and corporations could be sold to local banks. All this would cut the absurd cost of government administration and bring a lot of money in to pay off the national debt, so reducing taxes, benefiting everybody and hurting nobody but the dismissed bureaucrats and the totalitarians.

When it came to removing privileges, there undoubtedly would at first be screams of pain from the short-sighted members of the groups that lost them. But their removal in pairs, so to speak, would practically neutralize their effect. For instance, if the protective tariffs were removed from manufacturers, and simultaneously the government subsidies removed from farmers, their relative share of the national income would remain about the same, but the cost of the expenses of all the bureaucrats administrating these privileges would be removed from everybody. The former bureaucratic administrators would be forced into production, to the increase of the national production and the further benefit of everybody. Especially benefited would be the "deprived" manufacturers and farmers who would retain their same relative share of the increased national production, plus the saving in taxes which this reduction of the bureaucracy would effect.

When the flames of liberty begin to flare up, they may do so all over at once, or in a spotty way in different localities.

In either case they will have a lot to feed on. There is scarcely an incorporated village in the country whose inhabitants would not be greatly benefited in their pocketbooks and in their economic opportunities if its corporate existence were abolished. There is scarcely a city, town or county in the United States whose inhabitants would not be benefited by the elimination of from 75-95 percent of its public employees. As the flames of liberty flare, the public spirited citizens will examine these local bureaucracies, not as taxpayers' associations do now with a view to try to discover whether they are spending too much on what they are pretending to do, but with a view to discovering how much of the work they are "doing" should be done at all; of eliminating the unnecessary types of work having to do with economic regulations, and having what remained done cheaply. Such a task successfully accomplished would, in most cases, cut the taxes of any locality between 75 and 90%, would benefit everybody and hurt no one in the locality except the bureaucrats and the court-house gang.

Bad as the local governments are, the State ones are generally worse, some approaching the absurdity of the Federal government; for as a rule the further the government is from the direct observation of the people who control it, the more its abuses flourish. It must be remembered that the roots of the bureaucracy are in the localities, and a strong attack on the roots will destroy the evil tree.

It has taken a long while to build this monstrous bureaucracy. It will take time to destroy it, for the bureaucracy will fight hard with specious and emotional pleas for its life. This is not a bad thing. It will slow down the change so that the economy can adjust itself to it. The important thing is not where we are on the road to freedom, but in which direction we are going. No one can foresee how the thing will be worked out. No plan can be made. No dashing leader will be wanted. The native sense of the aroused people, at the time and on the spot, must be trusted to act for the best.

Several things are certain. Our three-quarter-managed economic system of today cannot remain stable. Hourly it is drifting to a fully managed one. A fully managed economy brings inevitably poverty, starvation and slavery. Americans will not stand for this. As soon as they see clearly where they are headed they will turn about and destroy privilege, the managed economy and the bureaucracy, and establish their freedom. If the people act soon they can cure the situation by the ballot box; if they delay long the bureaucracy may be so strong it will require bloodshed. Therefore it is the solemn duty of all who see the situation to arouse the American people to their task.